*Macmillan Literary Lives*
*General Editor:* Richard Dutton, Professor of English,
University of Lancaster

This series offers stimulating accounts of the literary careers of the
most widely read British and Irish authors. Volumes follow the
outline of writers' working lives, not in the spirit of traditional
biography, but aiming to trace the professional, publishing and social
contexts which shaped their writing. The role and status of 'the
author' as the creator of literary texts is a vexed issue in current
critical theory, where a variety of social, linguistic and psychological
approaches have challenged the old concentration on writers as
specially gifted individuals. Yet reports of 'the death of the author'
in literary studies are (as Mark Twain said of a premature obituary)
an exaggeration. This series aims to demonstrate how an
understanding of writers' careers can promote, for students and
general readers alike, a more informed historical reading of their
works.

**Published titles**

*Morris Beja*
JAMES JOYCE

*Richard Dutton*
WILLIAM SHAKESPEARE

*Jan Fergus*
JANE AUSTEN

*Paul Hammond*
JOHN DRYDEN

*Joseph McMinn*
JONATHAN SWIFT

*Kerry McSweeney*
GEORGE ELIOT (MARIAN EVANS)

*John Mepham*
VIRGINIA WOOLF

*Michael O'Neill*
PERCY BYSSHE SHELLEY

*Leonée Ormond*
ALFRED TENNYSON

*George Parfitt*
JOHN DONNE

*Gerald Roberts*
GERARD MANLEY HOPKINS

*Felicity Rosslyn*
ALEXANDER POPE

*Tony Sharpe*
T. S. ELIOT

*Cedric Watts*
JOSEPH CONRAD

*Tom Winnifrith and Edward Chitham*
CHARLOTTE AND EMILY BRONTË

*John Worthen*
D. H. LAWRENCE

**Forthcoming titles**

*Cedric Brown*
JOHN MILTON

*Deirdre Coleman*
SAMUEL TAYLOR COLERIDGE

*Peter Davison*
GEORGE ORWELL

*James Gibson*
THOMAS HARDY

*Kenneth Graham*
HENRY JAMES

*David Kay*
BEN JONSON

*Mary Lago*
E. M. FORSTER

*Alasdair MacRae*
W. B. YEATS

*Philip Mallett*
RUDYARD KIPLING

*Ira Nadel*
EZRA POUND

*Grahame Smith*
CHARLES DICKENS

*Gary Waller*
EDMUND SPENSER

*John Williams*
WILLIAM WORDSWORTH

*Barry Windeatt*
GEOFFREY CHAUCER

# Gerard Manley Hopkins

## A Literary Life

Gerald Roberts

MACMILLAN

First published 1994 by
THE MACMILLAN PRESS LTD
Houndmills, Basingstoke, Hampshire RG21 2XS
and London
Companies and representatives
throughout the world

ISBN 0–333–56820–6 hardcover
ISBN 0–333–56821–4 paperback

A catalogue record for this book is available
from the British Library

Printed in Hong Kong

# Contents

Contents

# Preface

*Sometimes we may pull out a play or a poem . . . and see whether it reads differently in the presence of the author. But this again rouses other questions. How far, we must ask ourselves, is a book influenced by its writer's life – how far is it safe to let the man interpret the writer? How far shall we resist or give way to the sympathies and antipathies that the man rouses in us?*

\* \* \*

*One way of approaching* Robinson Crusoe *. . . [is] through the life of the author. Here . . . in the heavenly pastures of biography we may spend more hours than are needed to read the book itself from cover to cover . . . Only now and then, as we turn from theory to biography and from biography to theory, a doubt insinuates itself – if we knew the very moment of Defoe's birth and whom he loved and why . . . should we suck an ounce of additional pleasure from* Robinson Crusoe *or read it one whit more intelligently? For the book itself remains.*

Virginia Woolf, *The Common Reader*[1]

The principal aim of this book is to set and evaluate Hopkins's poetry within the context of his own life, particularly that part of it which was spent as a Jesuit, when his major work was written.

As Virginia Woolf's words remind us, it is not always easy to achieve this without implying that biographical knowledge is the indispensable key to critical appreciation. 'Background' information might indeed enable us to understand what was not clear before and, by so doing, increase our ability to enjoy, but the poetry, in Hopkins's case, remains precisely what it was and our critical approach is, or should be, on radically different lines from the biographical.

The few facts provided by his great friend and first editor, Robert Bridges, a rather romantic and brief biography by a fellow Jesuit,[2] and a scattering of personal reminiscences of unreliable value, meant that, until 1935, Hopkins was a shadowy figure. Since that date, his letters, journals, many books and articles, popular and scholarly, have made him one of the most written about, not necessarily best documented, figures of his time. Part of his Jesuit career was minutely covered by Fr Alfred Thomas in a work published in 1969[3] but it was not Fr Thomas's purpose to make a personal assessment of the success of these years or of the poetry written during them.

Later biographical studies have attempted a more literary approach, without neglecting the all-importance of the Jesuit life in so doing.[4] Even in those periods when no or little poetry was being written – and Hopkins was abnormally sensitive to such times – his spiritual and practical life as a member of that order went on unabated and, no doubt, continued to influence the poetry he was still to write. In Mark Twain's image, a poet is like a reservoir, perpetually accumulating what will eventually result in (to use Wordsworth's phrase) the 'spontaneous overflow of powerful feelings'.

Writing in her *Four Metaphysical Poets* more than fifty years ago, Joan Bennett declared that a 'background of common experience' as a human being is the principal requirement in reading Hopkins, adding, however: 'Given two readers of equal sensibility the more widely read has always an advantage.'[5] Although I recognise the truth of this qualification, I would not seek to exaggerate it: the reader of Hopkins who knows 'everything' about the poet is in danger of not seeing the wood for the trees. In the end, as Virginia Woolf puts it, the poetry 'itself remains', and the appreciation and enjoyment of it is the ultimate purpose to which this study is directed.

### Notes

1. V. Woolf, *The Common Reader*, Second Series (London, 1965) pp. 263 and 51–2.
2. Fr G. F. Lahey, *Gerard Manley Hopkins* (London, 1930)
3. Fr A. Thomas, *Hopkins the Jesuit: The Years of Training* (London, 1969).
4. The most recent of these biographies, Norman White's *Hopkins: A Literary Biography* (London, 1992), came too late to make use of in this book.
5. Reprinted in *Hopkins: The Critical Heritage*, ed. G. Roberts (London, 1987) pp. 289–90.

# Acknowledgements

The author is grateful to Professor Dutton, General Editor of the series, for his help and encouragement in writing this book. He would also like to thank Fr Edwards and Fr Holt of the Society of Jesus for granting access to the Archives of the English Society at Farm Street, London. Fr Turner SJ, Archivist of Stonyhurst College, has kindly answered a number of queries. The author has made frequent use of the facilities of the University Libraries of Lancaster, Sussex, and Royal Holloway, as well as the British Library, where the staffs have been uniformly helpful.

G.R.

# 1
# The Road to Parnassus

*There is a unity in Hopkins's work which consists of a gradual refining and deepening of certain experiences present in the poet from the very beginning, rather than in the discovery of new experience.*

J. Russell (ed.), *Gerard Manley Hopkins: Poems*[1]

By the time of his death in 1889, when Queen Victoria (who had come to the throne seven years before his birth in 1844) still had fifteen years to reign, less than a dozen poems by Hopkins had appeared in print. None of these would be considered important by later readers, nor did they appear in contexts likely to attract serious critical attention – comic verses in the Stonyhurst Magazine, a piece from pre-Oxford days printed in *Once a Week*, other poems in religious monthlies – these gave no indication of the riches which were in store for posterity.

But there is no good reason for thinking his contemporaries would have liked his great poems, whose style and tone jarred so violently with the fashions Victorian readers were used to: Bridges, who became Poet Laureate after Hopkins's time, was sceptical; Coventry Patmore, the Catholic poet and a correspondent of the 1880s, confessed he was unable to cope with their originality; and the Jesuit editor Fr Henry Coleridge refused them for *the Month*. His preconversion poems, however, were in many respects what might have been expected from a precocious and cultured young Victorian with pretensions as a poet, exploiting a variety of forms, echoing Keats and Tennyson, and showing a strong inclination to the sensuous.

If Hopkins had been remembered by these poems, so much more to contemporary taste than the later ones, he would now be known, if known at all to the twentieth century, as a minor versifier with a certain metrical fluency and imitative talent. But the remarkable happened. Not only did he resume writing poetry after a seven-year break from 1868 to 1875 while training for the Society of Jesus, but

1

what he then produced and continued to write until the end of his life was a poetry transformed in form and style, new both for himself and his century. There is no simple explanation of how and why this took place. The first, perhaps crucial formative influence on him was a highly cultured family life, representing the best of Victorian middle-class values. Manley, his father, was the founder of a successful insurance company and an author: apart from technical and historical works, he wrote reviews for *The Times*, attempted a novel, and published a volume of poetry *Spicilegium Poeticum* (? 1892), which, despite occasional flashes of humour, is very conventional work, with no hint of his son's originality. He was also an active member of the Anglican Church: a church-warden at St John's, Hampstead; a teacher in the Sunday School; and was involved in establishing an Anglican Mission in Hawaii, for which country he was consul-general in London for many years. His *History of Hawaii* (2nd edition, London, 1866) does show a gift for vivid description of natural catastrophes and, coincidentally, notes how Catholic missionaries were more successful than Anglicans, a truth he was ironically to have some experience of in his son's conversion the same year.

So far as we can judge, he headed his large family of eight in the best Victorian *pater familias* style,[2] loving and loved, but more distant from his children than his wife Kate, whose accomplishments included a delightful private memoir of her own early life, *The Mirror*, a fondness for music, and a piety which made a deep impression on young Gerard.

Born in 1821 she, like him, had been the eldest of a family of eight, and was also sent away to school. Her marriage to Manley Hopkins in 1843 began an apparently stable and harmonious relationship that lasted until her husband's death in 1897. She survived until 1920, dying at the age of 99 but able, in spidery yet legible handwriting, to thank Robert Bridges for the first edition of her son's poetry (Gerard's early death was an exception in what was in general a long-lived family).

Gerard spoke more than once in his correspondence of his approval of the married state (see, for example, *Letters of Hopkins to Robert Bridges*, 3 April 1877) but that he felt more at ease with his mother than his father may be reflected by the much larger number of letters that he wrote to her in his life as a Jesuit. When he does write to Manley, the tone varies between the facetious and the semi-formal, and it is perhaps significant that in the Journal his mother is first mentioned on page 17, his father on page 59.[3]

Gerard's brothers and sisters showed a variety of talents. Arthur, born in 1847, became a successful professional illustrator of books and magazines, and his oils and water-colours were exhibited at the Royal Academy, a direction which Gerard's own career might have followed had he not felt that 'the higher and more attractive parts of the art put a strain upon the passions'.[4] Lionel, born in 1854, worked for the British Government in China for over thirty years and became an acknowledged scholar of the language. Grace, the youngest sister, was a composer, although she published little, while Milicent, the eldest sister, was received into an Anglican religious order.

To complete the picture, the large number of Hopkins relatives were often successful and accomplished figures, among them Uncle George Giberne, a very able amateur photographer, whose sister became a friend of Newman and a Catholic nun on the Continent. Family celebrations (including the acting of little plays), visiting and holidays played an important part in Gerard's childhood which, as far as one can tell, was lived in an atmosphere of stability, culture and prosperity. In England's economic life the so-called 'hungry forties' had given way to an upsurge in the trade cycle in the 1850s and 1860s, and the Hopkins's never seem to have wanted for money. The first time that Gerard signalled his awareness of Disraeli's 'two nations' was in 1871 when, as a Jesuit student, he lamented to Bridges that it was a 'dreadful thing for the greatest and most necessary part of a very rich nation to live a hard life without dignity, knowledge, comfort, delight, or hopes in the midst of plenty – which plenty they make'.[5]

Highgate School from 1854 to 1863 was an extension of the middle-class values of his home-life. Part boarding, part day, it had a growing roll of 130 pupils and a new Headmaster, Dr Dyne, who was set on raising its scholarly reputation. He was a harsh disciplinarian with whom Hopkins did not get on, although, in view of his achievements at the school, Newman might have been correct, a few years later, in guessing that formal discipline would bring out the best in him.

Not only did he win a closed exhibition to study Classics at Balliol but, in 1860, at the age of 16, he gained the Highgate Poetry Prize with 'The Escorial', a historical and highly atmospheric account of Philip II's great palace, written in Spenserian stanzas. One of its sources was Ford's famous *Handbook for Travellers in Spain*, whose anti-Catholicism is mirrored in Hopkins's emphasis on cold and gloom but it is also possible that in this concern with faded glories we are seeing early evidence of that melancholy which beset Hopkins more obviously in his later life: the impermanence of beauty and all human affairs is a theme that runs throughout his poetry.

In 'The Escorial' narrative is incidental to description and atmosphere, and Tennyson and Keats are often suggested. 'Mariana and the Moated Grange', for example, in:

> in the straying gleam
> The motes in ceaseless eddy shine and fall

or 'The Eve of St Agnes':

> The Altar-tapers flar'd in gusts.

Both verses from which these lines are taken demonstrate the ease with which Hopkins handles the pentameter:

> upon the wall
> Rich Titians faded; in the straying gleam
> The motes in ceaseless eddy shine and fall
> Into the cooling gloom.

His ear for sound, seen in the vowel music in these lines, is also apparent in the delightful Aeschylus translation of the same year with its assonance, alliteration and internal rhyme:

> Divinity of air, fleet-feather'd gales,
> Ye river-heads, thou billowy deep that laugh'st
> A countless laughter, Earth mother of all,
> Thou sun, all seeing eyeball of the day.[6]

The image of the sun as an eyeball has a touch of metaphysical shock (although it is almost spoiled by the repetition of the 'all' from the previous line).

Hopkins was first published in *Once a Week* (for which his father wrote poems and essays) in February 1863 and was sufficiently proud of the poem 'Winter with the Gulf Stream' to point it out to a correspondent in the following month. He told Bridges later that he enjoyed the challenge of terza rima: the development of the following image across the line and verse shows his confidence:

The bugle moon by daylight floats

So glassy white about the sky,
So like a berg of hyaline                   [*glass*
And pencilled blue so daintily,

I never saw her so divine.

He uses the couplet form in 'A Vision of the Mermaids' which he wrote (and illustrated) at Christmas 1862, choosing subject-matter that was popular with mid-Victorian poets but again shunning narrative for mood. It begins as if there is a story to unfold:

Rowing, I reach'd a rock – the sea was low –
Which the tides cover in their overflow

but no Forsaken Merman emerges; the poet remains an onlooker, describing the gambolling of the mermaids and the richness of the setting, until darkness falls.

The imagery is erotic, the key-colour red (in a variety of forms):

spikes of light
Spear'd open lustrous gashes

and

Now all things rosy turn'd: the west had grown
To an orb'd rose, which, by hot pantings blown
Apart, betwixt ten thousand petall'd lips . . .

The writing has the excess of a young man's poem (one thinks of the description 'bloody broth' that Hopkins later applied to Swinburne) and the colouring, scene-setting and imagery suggest the painter's imagination. Keats again influences the diction:

Others with fingers white would comb among
The drenchèd hair of slabby weeds that swung . . .

and, possibly, the melancholy, which is introduced late, and with little obvious reason, into the poem:

> a sweet sadness dwelt on everyone;
> I knew not why . . .

The onlooker finds the atmosphere all too familiar but (like classic depression) its causes cannot be easily understood: 'I know the sadness but the cause know not'. However, the mood has nothing of the bitter intensity of the 'terrible' sonnets that Hopkins was to write more than twenty years later in Dublin and, if it were not for our knowledge of that period of his life, we might merely assign its presence here to the adolescent imagination.

'Spring and Death' (which may, in fact, have been composed at Oxford) tells of the inevitability of death even at a time when the first impression is that of the growth of new life. Written as an allegory, with a characteristic Hopkins message of the mortality of human things, it finds an obvious companion-poem in the later and much better known 'Spring and Fall', where the cycle of Nature is again the standard by which mortality is judged. By comparison with the simplicity of the later piece, the allegory seems laboured and the style imitative – Tennyson and Coleridge are struggling together here:

> As I walk'd a stilly wood,
> Sudden, Death before me stood:
> In a hollow lush and damp,
> He seemed a dismal mirky stamp
> On the flowers that were seen
> His charnelhouse-grate ribs between,
> And with coffin-black he barr'd the green.

These pre-Oxford poems offer only a few clues of the poet Hopkins was to become. Form and metre are handled with at least technical competence but diction and imagery are full of echoes of nineteenth-century poetry. The stress on the sensuous, the themes of melancholy and mortality might be characteristic of any young poet of the time. An authentic voice, especially a spiritual one, is far from emerging at this point; Oxford, the next stage in his career, was to be crucial in developing it.

**Notes**

1. *Gerard Manley Hopkins: Poems*, ed. J. Russell (London, 1971) p. 7.
2. See David Roberts, 'The Paterfamilias of the Victorian Governing Classes', in *The Victorian Family*, ed. A. S. Wohl (London, 1978).
3. *Journals and Papers of Hopkins*, ed. H. House and G. Storey (London, 1966).
4. *Further Letters of Hopkins*, ed. C. Abbott, 2nd edn (London, 1970) p. 231.
5. *Letters of Hopkins to Bridges*, ed. C. Abbot (London, 1970) pp. 27–8.

# 2
# Choosing the Master

*The truth is that we do not enjoy masterless freedom; we are continually threatened by psychic factors which, in the guise of natural phenomena, may take possession of us at any moment. The withdrawal of metaphysical projections leaves us almost defenceless in the face of this happening, for we immediately identify with every impulse instead of giving it the name of the 'other', which would at least hold it at arm's length and prevent it from storming the citadel of the ego. . . . It is . . . incumbent on us to choose the master we wish to serve, so that his service shall be our safeguard against being mastered by the 'other' whom we have not chosen. We do not create 'God', we choose him.*

C. G. Jung, *Psychology and Religion*[1]

Having been awarded the closed exhibition from Highgate to Balliol, Hopkins went up to Oxford to study Classics in the spring of 1863. *Literae Humaniores* – Greek and Roman history and culture – dominated studies in mid-nineteenth century Oxford, just as Latin and Greek continued their hold over the curriculum of the public and grammar schools. At this period, Classical Studies at Balliol were 'at their highest point'[2] and the men to whom Hopkins read his essays were an awesome galaxy of talents. Benjamin Jowett reached the peak of his career slightly after Hopkins's time with his work on Plato and Thucydides and his Mastership of Balliol but his strong personality both impressed and amused his new student. Robert Scott, the current Master of the College, was an Anglican clergyman, whose great *Greek–English Lexicon*, compiled with his Oxford colleague Henry Liddell, was reprinted many times in the second half of the century. Thomas Green was a Fellow of Balliol who achieved particular distinction in the field of German philosophy. Although an agnostic, he and Hopkins shared a mutual respect for the other's character and intellect.

But the figure who was to become the most widely known of his tutors was Walter Pater, the polymathic scholar, appointed Fellow of Brasenose in 1864. His wide cultural interests found a natural response in Hopkins, and they continued to keep contact when the latter returned to the city as a parish priest in 1878. His best known work, *The Renaissance* (1873), with its appeal to 'the poetic passions, the desire of beauty, the love of art for art's sake' and to the need to maximise each moment of experience, reflects much of the outlook of the early Hopkins. Its claim that 'Failure is to form habits,' seems to hint at Hopkins's later concept of inscape, whereby a fleeting experience impresses itself on the consciousness with a new intensity and freshness; in Pater's words, sets 'the spirit free for a moment'.[3]

At Oxford, as in the public schools of the day, Greek was given more emphasis than Latin, a situation reflected in allusions and influences in Hopkins's own writing. As James Bowen has recently pointed out,[4] the study of Greek life and literature offered both a moral example for headmasters like Arnold and a social and political lesson for the Victorian ruling classes (the less appealing aspects were usually skated over). Writers about Ancient Greece looked for and found parallels with life in modern Europe and in Britain in particular. J. P. Mahaffy's *Greek Life and Thought* (the author was a celebrated don of Trinity College, Dublin) described the 'Hellenistic world' in its Golden Age as 'divided, as Europe now is, into a complex of first-class and second-class powers' and suggested that the Macedonian went through the Greek world 'as the Englishman has been accustomed to go through Europe – the acknowledged superior in physique, and the citizen of a nation which had dominated the world'.[5]

Admiration for Grecian values – perceived as beauty, imagination, clarity of thought and emphasis on the importance of the social bond – went hand in hand with a coolness towards Christian doctrine: most of Hopkins's tutors were Broad Church or even agnostic by inclination. He might easily have lapsed into the atheism of a celebrated Balliol predecessor, Arthur Clough, whose background had been just as privileged and early religious life full of scruple. They went through similar Victorian traumas of conscience: it might have been a remorseful Hopkins, not Clough, who wrote repentantly as a young man: 'Instead of turning to God last night I wrote a sonnet,'[6] or exclaimed in 'Dipsychus':

> Twenty-one past, twenty-five coming on;
> Half of life departed, nothing done.

Clough's eventual scepticism finished his Oxford career as a Fellow of Oriel, and there is more than a touch of the cynical in some of Hopkins's later poems and letters, but in his early years at Oxford it was the High Church party which won his support. The University was still influenced by the after-effects of the Tractarian controversy of the 1830s, although Newman, whose key role in the movement had been the final cause of its official disapproval in 1841, had long since become a Catholic and departed to found the Oratory School in Birmingham. His former followers, Pusey, Liddon, and Keble, who remained Anglican churchmen, continued to exercise a strong High Church influence in the University and on Hopkins himself, whose poetry began to take an increasingly religious turn.

Significantly for someone from his middle-of-the road Anglican background, it was the Old Testament which, to begin with, was most drawn upon, although had 'A Soliloquy of One of the Spies in the Wilderness' been written in a different verse form, a Browning monologue would have come to mind:

> Are you sandblind? Slabs of water many a mile
> Blaze for him all this while,

and colloquially eccentric too is the phrase the 'Nile/Unbakes my pores.' Elsewhere, George Herbert is suggested:

> Must you be gorged with proof? Did ever sand
> So trickle from your hand?

More individuality is shown in Hopkins's choice of one of the dissentients as the narrator, while the original verse-form with its emphasis on rhyme, including the occasional internal one,

> Sicken'd and thicken'd by the glare of sand,

the alliteration and assonance,

> Wasteful, wide huge-girthed Nile

anticipate the major role these features were to play in his mature verse.

The incomplete 'Pilate' is another monologue in which the self-accusing judge of Christ ponders on his own suicide by self-crucifixion. The concern for detail, rather than emotional exploitation of the subject-matter, anaesthetises the morbidity of the picture:

> Thus I shall make a cross, and in't
> Will add a footrest there to stand,
> And with sharp flint will part my feet and dint
> The point fast in, and my left hand
> Lock with my right; then knot a barken band.

According to tradition, George Herbert was a major reason for Hopkins's attachment to the Anglican Church, and 'Barnfloor and Winepress' (published in the ecumenical *Union Review*, September/October 1865) and 'New Readings' are characterised by the ultimately joyful sense of the redemption of the poet's sinfulness through Christ's sacrifice, symbolised in the bread and wine of the sacrament:

> Although the letter said
> On thistles that men look not grapes to gather,
> I read the story rather
> How soldiers platting thorns around CHRIST's Head
> Grapes grew and drops of wine were shed.

'Heaven-Haven', in some manuscripts under the title of 'Fair Haven – the Nunnery', is one of the best known of his early poems, yet nothing could be further from the fiery intensity of the 'Wreck of the Deutschland' or the agonised suffering of the Dublin sonnets than its escapist vision of the religious life. A highly romanticised picture of the pleasures and quiescence of conventual existence, the sea-imagery of its last verse uncomfortably recalls the weary mariners of Ulysses falling victim to the Lotos in Tennyson's poem:

> Surely, surely, slumber is more sweet than toil, the shore
> Than labour in the deep mid-ocean, wind and wave and oar.

In the same vein of somewhat sickly naivety is 'For a Picture of St Dorothea', inspired by the apocryphal story of a young woman whose simple faith led to the conversion of a Roman lawyer. Hopkins must have been particularly attracted to the idea of her devotion since, as Professor MacKenzie points out (*Collected Poems*, Oxford, 1991), he wrote four versions of the poem, at least one of which offers the first attempts at sprung rhythm:

| | |
|---|---|
| *The Pronotary Theophilus* | Bút they cáme fróm the south, Where winter's out and all forgot. |
| *The Angel* | The bell-drops in my mallow's mouth Hów are théy quenchèd not? |

In this dramatic version, partly scanned in Hopkins's own hand, the speaking voice naturally dictates the rhythm.

By contrast, his epigrams show his sense of humour had not deserted him; Bridges may not have liked this aspect of his friend's verse but less severe readers have enjoyed the good-humoured satire of examples like 'On a Poetess':

> Miss M's a nightingale. 'Tis well
> Your simile I keep.
> It is the way with Philomel
> To sing while others sleep.

With 'Easter Communion', dated Lent 1865, we come to the first of Hopkins's sonnets, the form which, in various modifications, he was to come to use most regularly as a poet. Here, four rhymes are used; the octet describes the penances practised by the faithful and the sestet the reward that awaits them. It is a distinctive poem, which both suggests and rises above the work of the contemporary Catholic priest-poet, Fr Frederick Faber, who had died in 1861 after a life which had some parallels with Hopkins.

Educated at Harrow and Balliol, ordained Anglican priest in 1839, he became a Catholic in 1845 and then a priest, founding the Birmingham Oratory within the next few years. He too felt God in Nature but had struggled like Hopkins to reconcile his poetry with his vocation as an Anglican priest, although as a Catholic these doubts seemed to vanish. In his poem 'Ash-Wednesday' he dealt with the subject of penance, addressing God:

> Strengthen my drooping heart:
> And let me stop each wayward sense
> In pure and secret abstinence,
> And from the world depart.[7]

This is the restrained, submissive tone of 'Heaven-Haven', but in 'Easter Communion' a sharper note had entered Hopkins's description of religious experience:

> Pure fasted faces draw unto this feast:
> God comes all sweetness to your Lenten lips.
> You striped in secret with breath-taking whips . . .

Language is chosen for its compactness of expression and quality of sound: alliteration and assonance are both important. There is even an element of wit which recalls a Donne poem: the stripes of the scourge are given religious significance in a metaphysical image:

> These crooked rough-scored chequers may be pieced
> To crosses meant for Jesu's.

The climax of the poem, a humorous play on the idea of bent knees, is again reminiscent of the seventeenth-century poetry of wit:

> Your scarce-sheathed bones are weary of being bent:
> Lo, God shall strengthen all the feeble knees.

Like so many of his contemporaries he fell a permanent victim to the charm of Oxford, its university life, architecture and the city's surroundings, and the two sonnets dated April 1865 reflect the feelings he later expressed in Liverpool that 'Not to love my University would be to undo the very buttons of my being'.[8] Composed with the conventional octet/sestet division, they show the young poet's increasing skill in conducting an argument in verse. The first repeats the theme of the poet's love for the city and incorporates something of his later Scotian vision[9] of an experience which has both general and individual impact:

> this to me
> As public is my greater privacy,
> All mine, yet common to my every peer.

The second sonnet is remarkable for the ingenuity of its precise detailing of the poet's response to the architecture of an Oxford college as he approaches yet nearer to the building:

> Thus, I come underneath this chapel-side,
> So that the mason's levels, courses, all
> The vigorous horizontals, each way fall
> In bows above my head, as falsified
> By visual compulsion, till I hide
> The steep-up roof at last behind the small
> Eclipsing parapet . . .

Characteristic of his new-found interest in the experience that is both available to all and to the individual in particular is the conclusion:

> [The scene] may be to many unknown men
> The one peculiar of their pleasured eye,
> And I have only set the same to pen.

The following sonnets are less unusual at first sight. Bridges noted that two of them must 'never' be printed and seems to have been offended by their romantic character as much as by artistic faults.[10]

Apart from the sonnets, one of the most interesting of the early poems is 'The Alchemist in the City', dated May 1865, a monologue by an alchemist disappointed of worldly fame who seeks isolation and death. He watches embarrassed the achievement of others in contrast to the unlikelihood of his own success and, as he views all round him, wishes for the 'houseless shore'

> Or ancient mounds that cover bones,
> Or rocks where rockdoves do repair
> And trees of terebinth and stones
> And silence and a gulf of air.

This desire for the 'wilderness' to some extent anticipates 'Inversnaid' but the melancholy described is morbidly enervating and has nothing in common with the energy of the later poem. The regular iambic metre suggests the resigned tone of the speaker, whom it is tempting to identify with Hopkins rather than a *dramatis persona*.

The next few poems, if we are to accept the arrangement of the 4th edition, continue the gloomy, introverted atmosphere. 'Myself unholy, from myself unholy', in the conventional sonnet-form which Hopkins had now adopted, describes the poet yielding to the 'sultry siege of melancholy' as he looks to his friends for moral perfection and cannot find it:

> This fault in one I found, that in another:
> And so, though each have one while I have all . . .

It is a scrupulosity which reflects the soul-searching that was probably true of Hopkins at this time; the climax of the poem offers the answer to his quest but does not tell us that peace has been achieved:

> No *better* serves me now, save *best*; no other
> Save Christ: to Christ I look, on Christ I call.

Uncertainty and dissatisfaction also appear in 'See how Spring opens with disabling cold' (echoing Milton's 'But my late spring no bud or blossom sheweth'), although the nature of the 'yield' hoped for, whether spiritual or material, is left uncertain. The frustration is a less intense version of the self-disgust of the 'terrible' sonnets and is also to be found in an incomplete poem of May 1865:

> Trees by their yield
> Are known,

but the poet's 'sap' is 'sealed' because he does not truly love God.

In 'My prayers must meet a brazen heaven' he is weighed down by such a sense of sin that contact with God seems impossible. Writing one might say in the spirit of the conscience-ridden Clough he feels 'unclean' and his prayers are without the feeling and sincerity that are necessary to reach God:

> My heaven is brass and iron my earth:
> Yea iron is mingled with my clay,
> So harden'd is it in this dearth
> Which praying fails to do away.

But the next two poems, dated October 1865, are in a more optimistic spirit. Love of God and a sense of the power of God's love has been achieved: peace has entered the soul of the poet. The first of these is a sonnet which begins with soothing 'ee' and 's' sounds:

> Let me be to Thee as the circling bird,
> Or bat with tender and air-crisping wings
> That shapes in half-light his departing rings . . .

Musical imagery dominates the poem: the poet has found his 'music in a common word' ('Love'), although 'The authentic cadence was discovered late':

> I have found the dominant of my range and state –
> Love, O my God, to call Thee Love and Love.

More religious reflection seems to be the motive of 'The Half-way House', a poem which presumably owes its title to the *Apologia pro Vita Sua*, where Newman calls Anglicanism and Liberalism half-way houses to Roman Catholicism and Atheism respectively: the line 'My national old Egyptian reed gave way' appears to express Hopkins's final rejection of his Church. 'Love' is again a key and much-repeated term which is personified in the style of a Herbert poem:

> Love I was shewn upon the mountain-side
> And bid to catch him ere the drop of day.

The quiet simplicity of the ending, in which the poet's quest is consummated, shows the same influence:

> You have your wish; enter these walls, one said:
> He is with you in the breaking of the bread.

Although his actual reception into the Catholic Church was not to be until a year later, it seems he may have found some sort of peace by the time of these two poems.

Dated January 1866 is the unfinished 'The earth and heaven, so little known', a series of delightful Nature pictures, in which the theme is the centrality and permanence of the human vision alongside the continual change of Nature:

> The earth and heaven so little known,
> Are measured outwards from my breast.
> I am the midst of every zone . . .

The perception of this truth becomes the occasion for a series of what the later Hopkins would have seen as inscapes of the natural world:

> The sky is blue, and the winds pull
> Their clouds with breathing edges white
> Beyond the world.

A later poem, 'That Nature is a Heraclitean Fire', again comes to mind:

> Cloud-puffball, torn tufts, tossed pillows flaunt forth,
>     then chevy on an air-
> built thoroughfare: heaven-roysterers, in gay-gangs
>     they throng . . .

Here too, if we judge the incomplete earlier poem correctly, the principal idea at issue is the primacy of man, created immortal by God amidst the ever-changing elements of Nature.

Hopkins was also under the influence of conventional literary models in 'The Nightingale' and 'The Queen's Crowning'. In the first, Frances recalls her lover Luke, unaware that he has already drowned at sea. Related almost entirely in the form of a monologue, its tragic-romantic theme set against land- and sea-scape is full of Pre-Raphaelite touches. The nightingale

>             might have strung
> A row of ripples in the brook,
>     So forcibly he sung,
> The mist upon the leaves have strewed,
> And danced the balls of dew that stood
> In acres all above the wood.

The last verse sets two contrasting pictures against each other, of life and comfort, and of pain and death:

> Thus Frances sighed at home, while Luke
> Made headway in the frothy deep.
> She listened how the sea-gust shook
> And then lay back to sleep.
> While he was washing from on deck

> She pillowing low her lily neck
> Timed her sad visions with his wreck.

It would not be difficult to imagine a painting ('The Lover's Dream'?) inspired by the narrative qualities and calculated restraint of feeling in these lines.

Of less importance is the conventional ballad-imitation, 'The Queen's Crowning', with all the usual elements of tragic love, murder and the supernatural, and a year or so later this interest in romantic subject-matter takes another fling in 'The Elopement', a poem written while Hopkins was at the Oratory. As in 'The Nightingale', he takes the woman's part:

> I saw the stars like flash of fire.
> My heart irregularly shook,
> I cried with my desire,

but parody rather than seriousness seems to inform the poem, which, in a somewhat metaphysical or perhaps farcical image, describes the sound of the woman's heart threatening to give the lovers' tryst away:

> O heart have done, you beat so high,
> You spoil the plot I find my true love by.

It was in a truer love than this that Hopkins's years at Oxford found their climax.

### Notes

1. *Jung: Selected Writings*, ed. A. Storr (London, 1989) p. 246.
2. Carl Schmidt, 'Classical Studies at Balliol in the 1860s', in *Balliol Studies*, ed. J. Prest (London, 1982).
3. Quotations are from the 'Conclusion' of *The Renaissance*.
4. 'Education, Ideology and the Ruling Class', in G. W. Clarke (ed.), *Rediscovering Hellenism* (Cambridge University Press, 1989).
5. J. P. Mahaffy, *Greek Life and Thought* (London, 1987) pp. 152 and 215.
6. Quoted in K. Chorley, *Arthur Hugh Clough* (Oxford 1962) p. 25.
7. F. W. Faber, *Poems*, 2nd edn (London, 1857) p. 135.
8. *Further Letters of Hopkins,* p. 244.
9. Duns Scotus was the Franciscan philosopher who lectured at Oxford and died in 1308. His metaphysics, which came to be seen as a deviation

from orthodox scholasticism, are explained with relevance to their influence on Hopkins in J. Pick, *Hopkins, Priest and Poet*, 2nd edn (Oxford, 1966). See also Christopher Devlin's discussion in his edition of the *Sermons of Hopkins* (London, 1959) and his essay in the *Hopkins Casebook*, ed. M. Bottrall, (London, 1975).

10. Quoted in *Hopkins: Poems*, ed. Gardner and MacKenzie (London, 1970) p. 250.

# 3
# The Convert

*A convert is undeniably in favour with no party; he is looked on with distrust, contempt, and aversion by all. His former friends think him a good riddance, and his new friends are cold and strange; and as to the impartial public, their very first impulse is to impute the change to some eccentricity of character, or fickleness of mind, or tender attachment, or private interest.*

Newman, 'Private Judgement'[1]

Hopkins's poems and Journal of 1866 show him coming closer and closer to joining the Catholic Church. His conversion was a gradual process, not an impulse, based on his increasing theological and emotional dissatisfaction with his life in one Church and need to find spiritual fulfilment in another.

That becoming a Catholic made some careers impossible and others more difficult seems to have been a consideration that played no part in his decision. Mid-Victorian England was becoming more tolerant, but public outbursts of anti-Catholicism, whether from Gladstone against the Vatican Decrees in 1874 or city mobs inspired by defrocked priests, continued into the 1870s and 1880s.

During the time he was making up his mind, Hopkins was careful to whom he revealed his feelings, avoiding as far as possible placing awkward moral responsibilities upon those nearest to him. His parents did not learn of his intentions until he wrote to them from Oxford after a decisive visit to Newman in September 1866. But he talked beforehand to some of his Oxford friends, to Edward Urquhart, already an ordained Anglican priest in Oxford, and to his great friend Addis who 'went over' with him (and much later, to Hopkins's distress, came back again).

Robert Bridges, who was to play such a large part in his life (and posterity), he told on the eve of his visit to Newman. When a pupil at Eton, Bridges had himself talked of becoming an Anglican priest, but at Oxford had emerged the sceptical believer that he remained the rest of his life. An undergraduate at Corpus, his first meeting with Hopkins had been some time in 1863 or 1864, and although his interests were as much sporting as academic, he had finished with a second in Classics in 1867. His father had died when he was ten, but the family was well off. There was no need for him to work for a living, yet he chose to become a doctor and laboured with a great deal of loyalty and devotion in St Bartholomew's and other London Hospitals until 1881, when he retired after a severe illness.

From then on, he devoted himself to his family, many friends and poetry, which he had already begun to publish (much to Hopkins's surprise) in 1873. Thereafter he published regularly and was appointed Poet Laureate in 1913. Throughout Hopkins's Jesuit life he functioned as surrogate father-figure and literary agent, a valued link with an extra-religious world that was sometimes tested by an over-zealous expression of opinion by Hopkins who was forced more than once into apology to reinstate the friendship.

Their religious difference partly explains why Hopkins only told him at the last minute the reason for his visit to Newman in September 1866 and illustrates the social and emotional pressures of that time. There was an anguished exchange of letters with his parents ('O Gerard my darling boy are you indeed gone from me'[2]), but intellectually he was unwavering. Psychologically, he appears to have been as balanced as anyone could be expected to be in his circumstances. His notebooks at Oxford, over-scrupulous as they sometimes reveal him, suggest nothing abnormal to the modern psychiatrist:

> No evidence of any clinically important mood disorder can be found. On the contrary, he does conform to the strong, resilient mental disposition of those who have a meticulous, scrupulous, and even obsessional tendency in youth and adult life. Those with such a disposition may show a proneness to depression in late middle and old age.[3]

Early in this crucial year, the 'Habit of Perfection' described the attractions of the religious life in the terms of one who sought it, perhaps, as a peaceful escape from the unbearable conflicts of conversion. The poem rejects noise in favour of the silence in which, it is presumed, God's voice alone can be heard; the eyes are closed against the confusing scene presented by the outside world; the mouth needs only the simplest food; the nose – with some relaxation of abstinence – enjoys the smell of the incense; the hands open the tabernacle and hold the chalice.

Yet the poem suggests the sensuous even while it rejects the notion, not only in such images as 'feel-of-primrose hands' and 'plushy sward', but in the richness of the 's' sounds in every verse of the poem, the half-rhymes and assonance:

> This ruck and reel which you remark
> Coils, keeps, and teases simple sight.

In contrast to the rich High Anglican suggestions of 'The Habit of Perfection' is the sombre 'Nondum', dated Lent 1866 and full, at times melodramatically, of the tones of Victorian doubt. Like Keble's 'Second Sunday after Easter', which asks 'And wilt Thou hear the fever'd heart / To Thee in silence cry?', Hopkins begs for a response from the 'unseen King', but still,

> Deep calls to deep, and blackest night
> Giddies the soul with blinding daze
> That dares to cast its searching sight
> On being's dread and vacant maze.

There is, however, too conscious a seeking after effect that results in laboured exaggeration:

> My hand upon my lips I lay;
> The breast's desponding sob I quell;
> I move along life's tomb-decked way
> And listen to the passing bell
> Summoning men from deathless day
> To death's more silent, darker spell.

The lack of vitality in the conventional language of these lines is a sign of Hopkins's failure to find an appropriate vehicle for his feelings, and only the plea for 'patience' in the following stanza provides a characteristic touch.

His reception into the Catholic Church in the autumn of 1866 saw the virtual cessation of his poetry for the next nine years. As early as November 1865, he had written: 'On this day by God's grace I resolved to give up all beauty until I had His leave for it.'[4] The impression must be that even at this time he had thoughts not just of becoming a Catholic, but of entering the Church as a priest or contemplative.

Hopkins's sense of the inappropriateness of the aesthetic impulse may be compared with Fr Faber, who while an Anglican priest from 1839–45 was deeply worried by what he felt to be conflicting responsibilities:

> I have felt, more strongly this Advent than ever, that I have very sinfully permitted the man of letters to overlay the priest. Now the necessity of parish duty comes like a divine interference with my wilfulness, and I do not think that I am so far [worldly] as that I should dare to neglect that duty.[5]

It has been too easily assumed that Hopkins decided, eventually, to give up poetry because he became a Jesuit, whereas distrust of material and sensuous values had become increasingly apparent in his verse. The process of moving from Anglicanism to Catholicism and then to the Jesuit priesthood simply reflected related aspects of a personality that yearned for the absolute and austere truth of total dedication.

After a not unexpected first in Classics in 1867, he began a short spell of teaching at Newman's Oratory School in Birmingham while he tried to resolve his future. He had attempted to come to a decision in the summer of 1867 but had had to record in his diary: 'Nothing is decided'.[6] By June the following year, however, under the encouragement of Newman, the uncertainty which had destroyed his power of 'applying to anything'[7] was over. He wrote: 'Since I have made up my mind to this [becoming a Jesuit] I have enjoyed the first complete peace of mind I ever have had,'[8] words that recall the Anglican convert-hero of Newman's *Loss and Gain*, who, kneeling before the altar on his reception, felt 'in the possession of a deep peace and serenity of mind, which he had not thought possible on earth'.[9]

Mere conversion had been *his* Half-way House. The tide of idealism that was carrying him along at that time is reflected in the remark he made at the beginning of 1868:

> Ruskin is full of follies but I get more and more sympathetic with 'the true men' as agst the Sophistik . . . Philistine, Doctrinaire,

Utilitarian, Positive, and on the whole negative (as Carlyle wd. put it) side, and prefer to err with Plato'.[10]

But if the priesthood and the Jesuits represented the fulfilment of his idealism, there was much that he still had to learn about them; the abandonment of poetry he made part of his commitment.

### Notes

1. Newman, *Essays Critical and Historical*, vol. ɪɪ (London, 1977) pp. 338–9.
2. The words are his father's. See *Further Letters of Hopkins*, p. 97.
3. Dr F. Letemendia in *Notebooks of Hopkins*, ed. N. MacKenzie (New York/London, 1989) p. 35.
4. *Journals of Hopkins*, p. 71.
5. Faber, *Poet and Priest: Selected Letters*, ed. R. Addington (Glamorgan, 1974) pp. 93–4.
6. *Journals of Hopkins*, p. 152.
7. *Letters of Hopkins to Bridges*, p. 22.
8. *Further Letters of Hopkins*, p. 51.
9. Newman, *Loss and Gain*, 6th edn (London, 1874) p. 430.
10. *Further Letters of Hopkins*, p. 231.

# 4
# Hopkins and the Jesuits

Despite his misgivings of 1866–7, Hopkins still composed the occasional lines and wrote regretfully to the Oratorian, Fr Ryder, in July 1868 that he would still like to 'sing [his] dying swansong'.[1] Perhaps Fr Ryder remembered him when he wrote many years later:

> Jesuits . . . are not often either reformers or poets, for the Jesuit not only lacks time for it, but commits himself to no course which he cannot pursue with a definite object. . . . Literature as such . . . has a tendency to irritate him as a possible derogation from the *usum necessarium*.[2]

Hopkins burnt his manuscripts in May 1868 in what was as much a symbolic as a literal act of renunciation, for it is clear from what he wrote to Bridges that he wanted preserved what he had written:

> I cannot send my *Summa* for it is burnt with my other verses: I saw they wd. interfere with my state and my vocation. I kept however corrected copies of some things which you have and will send them that what you have got you may have in its last edition.[3]

During the two years between conversion and entry into the Society he went through different states of mind on the question of his poetry, varying between a resolution not to write any more to a cautious hope that a little might yet be possible:

> I want to write still and as a priest I very likely can do that too, not so freely as I should have liked, eg nothing or little in the verse way, but no doubt what would best serve the cause of my religion. (February 1868)[4]

However, it was in July of that year that he spoke of his 'dying swansong' and this suggests that further acquaintance with his Order and its expectations had made the prospect of composition after his entry still less likely.

There is no explicit prohibition against verse as such in either the Jesuit *Constitutions* (compiled by St Ignatius and his companions between 1539–56) or the *Spiritual Exercises*, the progressive series of contemplations designed by St Ignatius for Jesuit and layman alike. Despite Fr Ryder's (not unjustified) scepticism of Jesuit attitudes towards imaginative literature, the Elizabethan Robert Southwell, as Hopkins knew, was at least one honourable exception and, in his own time, Clement Berraud, with whom he was to spend part of his training, published poetry and plays, even if entirely conventional in style and subject. In Hopkins's case it is difficult not to imagine that the question of his poetry was not raised in some form in the retreat he made before entering the Society and the interviews he had with the Provincial and his advisers. In view of the poetic silence that followed for seven years one can only draw the conclusion that, for whatever reasons, one or both sides determined that he should not spend time on his verse until further notice.

In the *Spiritual Exercises* at least they might have found messages which, judged with Victorian scruple, were not encouraging to the priest who wanted to express himself in verse. The injunction, 'Give glory to God,'[5] and the concept of 'conquest of self' could easily be negatively interpreted by an idealist like Hopkins who was suspicious of personal pleasure. 'The higher and more attractive parts of [painting]', he wrote in February 1868, 'put a strain upon the passions which I shd. think it unsafe to encounter'.[6] Self-indulgence, or the threat of it, was one of those failings he had joined the Society to escape.

It is interesting to compare the experience of Hopkins joining the Society with that of other nineteenth-century converts. One of the lesser temptations he rejected was worldly prospects, which his father seemed to have in mind for him,[7] and which were also suggested to Henry Kerr, one time captain of the famous 'Bellerophon' – the ship on which Napoleon had surrendered – who became a Jesuit in 1867 at the age of 29. A friend remonstrated that he had 'sacrificed a promising career' and chosen a 'martyr's crown'.[8]

Augustus Law, also an ex-seaman, was the son of an Anglican priest and entered the Jesuit novitiate in 1854. He too was the subject of persuasion from his powerful uncle, Lord Ellenborough, similarly without effect. No doubt, like Hopkins, his determination was only strengthened by appeals to his material well-being.

A decision to join the Jesuits that seems to resemble Hopkins's in very little is described by the ex-Ushaw student, Andrew Steinmetz, whose discernment of his vocation was entirely impulsive:

> I shall never forget the glow of enthusiasm that sent the blood rushing through my heart when I first conceived the idea of becoming a *Jesuit*.
>
> It was in London – in Fleet Street. I can point out the very stone of the pavement on which I stood at that eventful moment. Hardly an instant was given for consideration. The idea took complete possession of my mind, and I believed it to be an inspiration.[9]

He abandoned the Jesuits almost as soon as he joined them, and this account seems a parody of that religious experience – whether describing becoming a Catholic or a Jesuit – so feelingly recorded by Hopkins at the beginning of 'The Wreck of the Deutschland':

> I did say yes
> O at lightning and lashed rod;
> Thou heardst me truer than tongue confess
> Thy terror, O Christ, O God.

In fact we have no record of Hopkins's thoughts at the time when he decided to join the Society – the Journal confines itself to little but the barest information – but on 19 May he went to see the Jesuit Provincial, Fr Weld who, with the assistance of four assessors, judged his suitability as a Jesuit. The *Constitutions* list the necessary qualities, none of which offered any special difficulty for a man of Hopkins's character, but the so-called General Examen 'which should be proposed to all who request admission into the Society of Jesus' made more painful demands:

> Everyone who enters the Society, following the counsel of Christ our Lord that 'he who leaves father' and the rest, should judge that he should leave his father, mother, brothers, sisters, and whatever else he had in the world. . . . He should be as one who is dead to the world and to self-love and who lives only for Christ.[10]

This became part of that pain of exile, which he described in his

Dublin sonnets, a loneliness which played an important part in his melancholy.

Nevertheless, the Jesuit life seemed to Hopkins one in which he would find fulfilment and which would give his own life meaning. He told a friend: 'It is enough to say that the sanctity has not departed from the order to have a reason for joining it'.[11] Two important influences in that choice were Newman and the Jesuit Fr Henry Coleridge, the first a figure of almost God-like respect, the second probably the man most in contact with what Hopkins was thinking during the crucial few months. Both were literary men, both acknowledged, however, that first and foremost they were priests.

Newman had known Hopkins since the latter wrote to him in August 1866, begging to see him with a view to reception into the Church. This was a period of what may be called renewed fame for Newman, whose *Apologia pro Vita Sua* had been written as a result of his controversy with Kingsley while he was Headmaster at the Oratory. After receiving Hopkins into the Church, he welcomed him to his school in Edgbaston from September 1867 – April 1868, a particularly worrying time for Hopkins, as we have already suggested, while he was resolving his future.

Newman encouraged him towards becoming a Jesuit, just as he had done John Walford, the ex-Etonian master, who acted as a guide to Hopkins on an earlier visit to Birmingham and became a Jesuit at about the same time as him. Newman was often ready to direct likely converts to Farm Street for help,[12] although his view of the Society was tempered by caution. He was suspicious of Jesuit influence within the Church and wrote: 'From their wonderful system, and from their natural commendable *esprit de corps*, the Jesuits . . . tend to swamp the Church.'[13]

The same Fr Coleridge who had much to do with Hopkins becoming a Jesuit had at one time been invited by Newman to join the Oratorians, the religious Congregation to which he himself belonged: Newman told a correspondent in July 1869 that he had 'rightly or wrongly, long thought that Fr Coleridge's vocation lay in a different direction'. Coleridge was a person of all-round talents and it might be that Newman thought these unlikely to flourish given what he described as the Jesuit tendency to 'circumscribe the allowable liberty of the mind'.[14] Whatever the qualities Newman recognised in the typical Jesuit, it seems by his reply to Hopkins of 14 May 1868 ('Don't call "the Jesuit discipline hard", it will bring you to heaven'[15]), that he saw them, potentially, in Hopkins, and it was providential that while the latter was teaching at the Oratory, the priest who came to give the boys a four-day retreat was Coleridge himself.

For there would surely have been much about him which Hopkins would have admired. Then in his forties, and originally of a staunch Anglican family, Coleridge had gone to Eton, taken a first in Classics at Trinity, Oxford, become a Fellow of Oriel (like Newman) and then an Anglican curate on the family living in Devon. His admiration for Newman led to conversion in 1852, and he became a Jesuit five years later. Those years as a curate racked by doubt are well described by a writer in the Jesuit periodical *The Month* after his death: they suggest what any convert might have felt as he considered his future. Coleridge was linked to his childhood Church by

the halo of venerable names, and monuments, and institutions, which surrounded him at Oxford, and the tender memories of a home such as his sweet Devonshire, full of the gentle pieties of domestic life and of a rare culture.[16]

When he became a Catholic, he had to be received by the Redemptorists because of family opposition to the Jesuits, although two years later he entered the noviceship. The words of *The Month*, granted their highly coloured pious rhetoric, might describe Hopkins's situation:

He was ripe for that great and final venture of faith . . . No doubt the leading of exterior circumstances . . . had their weight . . . but it was far more the inmost and profoundest instinct . . . of his spiritual being which found its ultimate and only adequate satisfaction in the bands of the triple vows of that illustrious Company.[17]

Editor of *The Month* for sixteen years, where it was his unfortunate distinction to reject 'The Wreck of the Deutschland', he went on to write books and articles on religious subjects up to his death in 1893.

His first meeting with Hopkins was on 5 April 1868 when he came as has already been stated, to give the Oratory retreat. The previous December, Newman had advised Hopkins to bring an unspecified 'matter' (possibly the question of vocation) before the retreat priest. On 27 April, perhaps acting on Coleridge's advice, Hopkins began a ten-day private retreat at Manresa House, Roehampton, the home of the Jesuit novitiate; on 5 May he declared he had 'resolved to be a religious'; by 7 May he was choosing between the Jesuits and the Benedictines.[18]

His visit to the Provincial of the Society of Jesus on 19 May resulted in his being accepted for the Society on 30 May. He was 24 years old. It is usually assumed that much of the struggle of the previous few months, or even the previous two years, enters into the beginning of the 'Deutschland'. Yet apart from its recall there, there was no trauma attached to that period, no point in the future (after 'The Deutschland') when he looked back to those days with regret or scepticism.

His conversion and his realisation of his vocation were perhaps the greatest things in his life and certainly determined the rest of it. Within these decisions were the seeds of his future writing, as well as his reluctance to write, of joy and despair, of glory in Nature and loss of faith in himself. The new direction he had chosen was to turn him from minor to major poet (almost against his will) by enabling him to range and test depths of experience that would otherwise not have been his.

It was not simply a transition in the *matter* of his poetry that was being determined – indeed, as we have suggested, themes of his later verse were already implicit in the pre-Catholic period. The modes of mid-Victorian poetry offered no expression for his independent personality. He needed and developed a language and to some extent forms that were peculiarly his: 'A typical Hopkins poem seems to be using a currency of its own'.[19] But in the period of poetic abstinence from 1868 to the writing of 'The Wreck of the Deutschland', one vehicle of imaginative writing was not denied to him. The Journal, which had become a regular form of expression for him since the summer of 1866, continued to be written and to provide a practice-ground for his imaginative vision in language that was by no means traditional, a staging-post for the emergence of the new poet in 1875.

### Notes

1. *Further Letters of Hopkins*, p. 54.
2. *Essays of Fr. Ryder*, ed. F. Bacchus (London, 1911) p. 1. This essay was printed in *Nineteenth Century* (August 1885).
3. *Letters to Bridges*, p. 24.
4. *Further Letters of Hopkins*, p. 231.
5. But John Keble, the Anglican priest-poet, published his *Poems* in the

hope that 'the glory of God should be promoted . . . by this volume'
(2nd edn; London, 1857, Preface).
6. See Chapter 3, note 10.
7. Hopkins wrote to his father: 'I am most anxious that you shd. not think
of my future. It is likely that the positions you wd. like to see me in wd.
have no attraction for me' (*Further Letters*, p. 95).
8. Mrs Maxwell Scott, *Henry Schomberg Kerr* (London, 1901) p. 86.
9. Andrew Steinmetz, *The Novitiate; or, a Year among the English Jesuits*
(London, 1846) p. 8.
10. *Constitutions of the Society of Jesus*, ed. G. Ganss (St Louis, 1970) p. 95.
11. *Further Letters of Hopkins*, p. 51.
12. *Letters of Newman*, ed. C. Dessain (Nelson, 1972) vol. xxii, letter dated 15
April 1866, pp. 212–13.
13. *Letters of Newman* (Oxford, 1973) vol. xxiv, p. 247.
14. *Letters of Newman*, ibid.
15. *Further Letters of Hopkins*, p. 408.
16. *The Month* (May 1893) p. 162.
17. Ibid., p. 166.
18. *Journals of Hopkins*, pp. 164–5.
19. *Early Poetic Manuscripts and Notebooks of Hopkins*, ed. N. MacKenzie
(New York and London, 1989) p. 12.

# 5

# The Journal

Had Hopkins read the Jesuit house journal, *Letters and Notices*, for the previous year he might have hesitated at the information that those who entered the Society at the age of 24 (like himself) or less lived, on average, only to the age of 38, while the average age at death for all the 65 priests and scholastics who had died between 1844–65 was 44: 'The general result is that those who enter for the priesthood live in the Society about half the time that might have been expected from their age at entrance'.[1]

Although the research on which this prediction was based had to be withdrawn as faulty 14 years later,[2] it was ironically unerringly accurate about Hopkins's own life. Known to Hopkins or not, the earlier information might have appealed to many as another sign of the heroic nature of the Jesuit commitment and an encouragement to the personality who thrived on sacrifice and idealism. *Letters and Notices* was itself a testament to the devotion of the Order, with its contributors covering a wide range of Jesuit activity: priests in Rochdale and missionaries in Guyana; chaplains in the American Civil War or the notorious Millbank Prison; accounts of missions and miracles, converts and examination-results – for the excellence of which at Stonyhurst, their most prestigious school, the 'blessed Virgin' was to be thanked.[3]

To the Jesuit on probation like Hopkins the *Constitutions* allowed little leeway in earthly things. There must be no letter-writing, or conversation with unspiritual people, and 'All should take special care to guard with great diligence the gates of their senses . . . from all disordere'.[4] General literary studies were not allowable, and it would seem that only spiritual works were referred to in the requirement that 'One who has talent to write books useful for the common good and who has written them ought not to publish any writing unless the superior general sees it first, and has it read and examined'.[5]

While the few letters of Hopkins's noviceship reflect that the *Constitutions*'s injunction against writing them was more or less observed, the Journal, by whoever's advice, was continued and, as before, the sensuous external world figured far more than the spiritual. The colour, imagery and generally imaginative language by no means reflect a novice subdued by his training. Begun in 1862 with a single entry about an unsuccessful friendship, from 1863–65 this developed into a series of individual isolated entries, including many passages from his own poems and from the writings of others. Only from 1866 does it become fuller and more continuous, although there are still disappointing gaps and sparse entries.

At this time, the natural observation, especially of skies (like Ruskin he was a 'cloud-worshipper') is outstanding, and the painter's eye, as much as the poet's imagination, seems everywhere at work:

> Green windows of cabbages in sunshine. The roses: their richness, variety, etc, will no doubt always make them necessary to the poets. Take colour: there are some pink-grey or lilac a little way off upon their dead-green bushes, there are the yellow ones with packed pieces blushing yellower at the foot, the coupe d'Hebe pink outside and dry bright-grained rose-pink where the leaves turn out, etc. Then for shape, some flat and straggling have fissures twisting inwards upon the centre, some are globed and with the inner petals drawn geometrically across each other like laces of boddices at the opera with chipped-back little tight rolls at the edge.[6]

The painter's eye is seen in the emphasis on colour and shape, but the catholic and heterogeneous quality of 'green windows of cabbages' and 'like laces of boddices at the opera' is even more striking.

Many other original passages of this time are nevertheless surpassed by the quality of the writing about the pre-novitiate holiday in Switzerland in July 1868, a particularly emotionally charged occasion. It reflected both Hopkins's relief at having decided his vocation and the last fling of the artist which, by some appropriate coincidence, was to be in a country which denied entry to Jesuits. The choice of Switzerland and the Alps was fashionable, for the area had become a favourite for English visitors, for mountaineers like the critic Leslie Stephen, walkers like Samuel Butler, the author of *Erewhon*, and, most influentially, the artist Ruskin, Hopkins's particular idol.

Although Ruskin's interests were now moving to the social and economic scene, he and Hopkins shared an almost polymathic appetite for cultural experience: for the understanding of landscape, its flora and fauna, even in scientific detail, for architecture and the character of people who live in country and cities, for art which was not merely representational, for great writers like Keats and a belief in a Divinity which inspired the world. This passionate feeling for life in both men inspired moments of great exhilaration and, especially in later life, periods of profound melancholy.

*Modern Painters,* Ruskin's early and possibly greatest work, of which the fifth volume was published in 1860, seems to endorse much of Hopkins's thinking in its dynamic view of art, faith in originality as the supreme virtue and in its author's sense of 'the exhaustless living energy with which the universe is filled'.[7] Despite his insistence on the painter's need to *know* what he paints, Ruskin saw a picture as an 'interpretation' of Nature, not a 'substitute', and he was also aware, and like Hopkins became increasingly more so with age, that 'human calamity' and human toil must be taken into account by the artist. He believed in his own version of the Fall, that the physical world had long been in a state of decline.

Ruskin would have appreciated how Hopkins's descriptions seem to strive for line and shape, however 'odd' the subject-matter and (pedantically) precise the language:

> To mass at the church. It was an odd sight: all the women sat on one side and you saw hundreds of headdresses all alike. The hair is taken back and (apparently) made into one continuous plait with narrow white linen, which crosses the lock of hair not always the same way but zigzag (so that perhaps there must be more than one linen strip), and the alternation of lock and linen gives the look of rows of regular teeth.[8]

Although Hopkins up to this date had made few uses of the word 'inscape' (which first appears in the English language in one of his Oxford essays), a definition he later offered seems remarkably appropriate to his experience of the Swiss women at mass. Just as 'design' struck him in painting, he wrote to Bridges,

> so design, pattern or what I am in the habit of calling 'inscape' is what I above all aim at in poetry. Now it is the virtue of design, pattern, or inscape to be distinctive and it is the vice of distinctiveness to become queer. This vice I cannot have escaped.[9]

But 'inscape' also implied, in the widest sense, 'beauty' and, at another level of Hopkins's response, evidence of the divine individuality of the world as it may be experienced by humankind. In *Modern Painters* Ruskin explains that the artist *interprets*, not copies experience and should make us feel the 'wonder' of the universe. Hopkins sadly appreciated that however universally available inscapes were, the experience of them was personal:

> Stepped into a barn of ours, a great shadowy barn, where the hay had been stacked on either side, and looking at the great rudely arched timberframes . . . I thought how sadly beauty of inscape was unknown and buried away from simple people and yet how near at hand it was if they had eyes to see it and it could be called out everywhere again.[10]

In the first year of his novitiate at Manresa, the Journal, no doubt for good reason, was irregularly kept: the demanding timetable, let alone personal scruples about writing it, must have made him a tired man at the end of the day. But the summer of 1869 shows a resumption of the characteristic style, and this passage, from his second academic year, early in 1870, typically combines close observation and imaginative perception:

> In the Park [Richmond] in the afternoon the wind was driving little clouds of snow-dust which caught the sun as they rose and delightfully took the eyes: flying up the slopes they looked like breaks of sunlight fallen through ravelled cloud upon the hills and again like deep flossy velvet blown to the root by breath which passed all along.[11]

Contemporary with Hopkins's Journal is the *Diary* of Francis Kilvert, the Anglican parson who was curate of Clyro in Radnorshire and later of his father's parish in Wiltshire. Leading a much fuller social life than Hopkins, his sensitivity to Nature and affection for ordinary country folk nevertheless suggest their temperaments had much in common, and he writes with similar tenderness, if less originality of rural scenes:

> *17 May 1874* We shall not have a more lovely Sunday than this has been. The hawthorn bushes were loaded with their sweet May

snow, and in the glowing afternoon sun the sheets of buttercups stretched away under the bright elms like a sea of gold.[12]

The final clause is Hopkinsian in its emotionally arresting description of the elms as 'bright', but the rhetorical and artistic sensibility behind the passage is a world away from such a sentence as Hopkins wrote the year before at Stonyhurst: 'Meadows smeared yellow with buttercups and bright squares of rapefield in the landscape'.[13] The spirit of painter and poet is mingled in the daring connection between 'smeared' and 'butter' and the association of sounds in 'meadows' and 'yellow', 'rape' and 'scape'.

But what Hopkins was learning at Manresa was necessarily modifying the enthusiastic, idealistic Oxford graduate who had joined the Society in 1868. He was learning the nature of its discipline, the theory and practice of the religious life and acquiring a sense of the traditions and aspirations of a notable body of men. His Journal reflected the emotional and imaginative undercurrent that remained unquenched throughout the often hard years of training.

### Notes

1. *Letters and Notices*, III (Feb. 1867) p. 43.
2. Ibid., XIV (1881) p. 127.
3. Ibid., I (1863) p. 233.
4. *Constitutions of the Society of Jesus*, ed. Ganss, p. 155.
5. Ibid., p. 284. This passage occurs in the section describing full members of the Society, but a similar requirement was made of novices: see Part III, I, 18.
6. *Journals of Hopkins*, p. 143.
7. *Modern Painters*, I, 3rd edn (London, 1900) p. 251.
8. *Journals of Hopkins*, pp. 172–3.
9. *Letters of Hopkins to Bridges*, p. 66.
10. *Journals of Hopkins*, p. 221.
11. Ibid., pp. 195–6.
12. *Selections from Kilvert's Diary*, ed. W. Plomer (London, 1969) p. 245.
13. *Journals of Hopkins*, p. 231.

# 6
# The Jesuits

By 1868, the Society had been in existence for some 300 years, alternately the wielder of power and the victim of persecution. Some 10,000 Jesuits worked around the world, with 340 in the English Province; in 1859, there had been 250; in 1879, there would be 440. Flourishing numerically, then, in the first half of the nineteenth century, it became 'even more influential in the second half'.[1]

Its present (comparative) prosperity was remarkable for an order that had been suppressed worldwide in the latter part of the eighteenth century and persecuted in the one that followed in Spain, Portugal, Italy, France and Germany. Persecution was not seen by the Society as a sign of its own failings but rather as recognition of its opposition to questionable trends in modern life: one polemical convert to Catholicism writing in 1877 claimed that Jesuits were the 'only men who can successfully keep down Socialism' in a Europe 'now a mine charged with revolution'.[2]

Yet, at least in the spiritual sense, St Ignatius was a reformer. His *Spiritual Exercises* were based on the assumption that a man could come to know God through his own intellect and senses and without privileged visionary insight. These two faculties, harnessed by the imagination, were capable of recreating scenes from the Gospel, so making the retreatant's experience more vivid, and hopefully more spiritual.

The creative and personal aspects of their founder's approach were less evident in the Victorian period, however, than an emphasis on the role of self-denial. To quote a Jesuit writing in *The Month*, service of God meant 'self-sacrifice and heroism', and 'obedience' was essential to achieve perfection.[3] Military life was an obvious parallel: Hopkins admired the ideal of duty professed by soldier and sailor – 'the calling manly – and even in the First World War a Jesuit novice doing his army training described the experience as 'like the *Spiritual Exercises*'.[4]

But each age interprets in its own way, and the modern reader of the *Exercises* is more likely to be impressed by the tolerance of the recommendation to caution before condemning a 'proposition advanced by [one's] neighbour'[5] and by the flexibility of the suggestion that each week of the Exercises should be adapted in length according to the exercitant's needs. Ignatius's concern was that the giver of the Exercises should not impose his will and that the exercitant should be allowed time so that he might develop his 'natural faculties more freely'.[6]

The first and most basic principle of the *Exercises* is that the created world exists for the purpose of drawing man to God. This proposition has two implications: that man is, therefore, in a spiritual sense the centre of the universe, and that nothing in the universe need be alien to his progress to God. Yet, in the first of the four weeks into which the *Exercises* are divided, in which the Creation evokes a 'cry of wonder', Ignatius describes the soul coming to love 'no created thing on the face of the earth itself, but only . . . the Creator of them all'.[7]

Here lies the great conflict of Hopkins's heart, emerging in so much of his poetry and thinking: the great attraction of beauty on one hand, the call to subordinate it to spiritual and moral values on the other. The answer to the question posed by his poem, 'To what serves Mortal Beauty?' is that it can only serve as a clue to that deeper beauty of soul that really matters. Similarly, in 'That Nature is a Heraclitean Fire', which confronts the tragedy of the mortality of man and his achievements, Hopkins finds comfort in our immortality with Christ. The assertion of faith as an emotional, rather than intellectual experience makes these poems especially Ignatian.

Throughout the *Exercises* there is a repeated emphasis on 'composition of place': the exercitant is expected to create in the mind's eye a picture of the subject for contemplation, whether it be Christ suffering or Hell in all its physical horrors: 'Smell with an imaginary smell the smoke, the brimstone, the dregs and bilgewater of that pit, all that is foul and loathsome'.[8] It was with such a picture of Hell that the Jesuit retreat-giver overwhelmed Stephen Dedalus in *A Portrait of the Artist as a Young Man*.

With the help of these biblically inspired scenes, the exercitant is expected to make an Election, a choice of a state of life according to whether he feels a vocation to follow strictly the example of Christ or to continue the life of the world, doing good as he can in his own way. One might compare the situation of Hopkins's Jesuit contemporary, Henry Kerr, who, when he first told a priest that he felt a vocation, was dissuaded from going any further at the time by the argument of the good he was doing in his profession as ship's officer.[9]

Selfishness is particularly mentioned as a hindrance to spiritual progress.[10] 'Let each one reflect that his advancement in all spiritual things will be exactly in proportion to the degree in which he goes out from self-love, self-will, and self-interest', declared Fr Peter Gallwey, one of the great figures of the Society in the late nineteenth century, and a man who took a particular interest in Hopkins's progress. 'Self is anti-Christ: self is the real obstacle to the love of our Lord . . . One must go before the other can reign'.[11]

Typical of the selflessness required of the Jesuit was the giving up of family (as Christ had asked for in St Luke's Gospel), so that the novice was 'dead to the world and to self-love . . . and lives only for Christ our Lord'.[12] The path to such selflessness was encouraged by the notorious Jesuit insistence on obedience. The *Constitutions* declare:

> We ought to be convinced that everyone of those who live under obedience ought to allow himself to be carried and directed by divine Providence through the agency of the superior as if he were a lifeless body which allows itself to be carried to any place and to be treated in any manner desired, or as if he were an old man's staff which serves in any place and in any manner whatsoever in which the holder wishes to use it.[13]

Although St Ignatius did not exclude appeals against authority, he encouraged a view of the Superior of a Community as the voice of God. The obedience which Hopkins would not willingly give to Dr Dyne of Highgate, or to the wishes and creed of his father and mother, he had now promised to render to the Society, and the implications of this undertaking are evident at many points in his Jesuit life: his scruples over writing poetry, his doubts over taking holidays and making engagements with friends, his uncertainties over how long he was to hold an appointment were all the result of his interpretation of the concept of Jesuit obedience.

A reading of the correspondence exchanged in Hopkins's time between the higher ranks of the English Jesuits reveals that 'docile' is one of the key words used in praise of their colleagues (although it must be said that superiors spent more time worrying about manifestations of independent behaviour than might be imagined). Ideally, Ignatius saw obedience as internalised by the individual, who subordinated his personal feelings to his intellect. The old

Protestant image of the order caricatured it as a smoothly functioning machine in which each part mindlessly performed its role: thus, C. N. Luxmoore, once a friend of Hopkins at Highgate, wrote after his death: 'To get on with the Jesuits you must become on many grave points a machine, without will, without conscience'.[14]

In reality, not only was it a somewhat cumbersome organisation, struggling at times through relays of authority to fit more than one square peg into a round hole, with more jobs than Jesuits, but it held, even among its great men, characters who swam more or less discreetly against the general current. Reminiscences of Fr Gallwey (who died in 1906) recall a comment of his during a retreat: 'How anxious St Ignatius is that our intellectual faculties should have fair play'.[15] The same man reminded novices: 'Sanctification is the business of the individual and cannot be managed in companies under a drill-master, however useful and necessary drill may be in itself'.[16]

By all accounts, he was one who found obedience 'the most difficult of virtues',[17] yet he clearly knew where to draw the line, for he achieved the highest positions in the Society in England, as well as winning universal affection and respect. Alongside those, like Gallwey, who consciously subdued their individualism to the discipline of their vocation, were many who welcomed the regularity of the Jesuit life who might have said, as the 'docile' Augustus Law did of his novitiate days, 'It is such a capital thing . . . that we have never got an idle moment'.[18] The overall picture of the Society in the Victorian period, confirmed by both lay and Jesuit historians, is that 'at no other time in its history, before or since, [had it] displayed such a remarkably high degree of regular observance of rules and of the uniformity of practice and policy'.[19] Both Frs Roothaan, General until 1853, and Beckx, who followed him, emphasised literal adherence to St Ignatius's words, symptomatic of what one Jesuit critic has called the 'strange form of Jansenism' affecting the whole of the Catholic church in the latter part of the nineteenth century.[20]

George Tyrrell, the ultimate Jesuit rebel, who might have crossed the path of Hopkins in the later years of the latter's career in the Society and was finally expelled for his modernist views, declared defiantly that St Ignatius established an order 'whose first principle should be elasticity and accommodation'.[21] For him, the nineteenth-century Jesuit's 'methods of prayer and examination were wooden and mechanical and unreal,'[22] and the Society itself hopelessly un-self-critical.

If Hopkins ever toyed with such thoughts, he left no record of them in his 20 years in the Society. The modern reader may find much personal unhappiness in his life and work but he never attributed it to unreasonable demands or expectations made of him; whatever dissidence he might have been inclined to expressed itself in the form of 'eccentricity'[23] for which he gained a reputation – whether it was staring at the gravel at St Mary's Hall, the composition of 'The Wreck of the Deutschland' or climbing into his bedroom window at Stonyhurst.

The caution of the Jesuit body at this time was founded on historical experience and political expediency. It had been born and had grown up in exciting, dangerous times: 'Launched in a state of siege, the Society had thrived upon tension and political turmoil'.[24] The vanguard of the Counter-Reformation, its members had been educated to expect and seek out struggle and suffering, a prospect which was still placed before its nineteenth-century counterparts in the course of their training and in the pages of their private journal, *Letters and Notices*. Current politics were rarely mentioned for obvious reasons, although one suspects far more Jesuits supported the Tories than the Liberals, and Hopkins's dislike for Gladstone was to become almost obsessive in the last ten years of his life. 'Social policy', in the sense of a shared and coherent approach towards social problems, did not exist: charitable work may have been plentiful but the ultimate goals were always spiritual and set in eternity.

The image of the ideal Jesuit that Hopkins absorbed from his training was bound to have been modified and diluted by his real-life experience of them then and later, although there is never any serious criticism of his colleagues in his letters. But in the Farm Street Archives the letters between the English assistant to the General in Italy and the English Provincial or between the Provincial and the Rector of Stonyhurst paint a realistic picture of the trials and tribulations of the Society in England. We learn of the occasional dismissal of priests, of one who was now 'a most unsafe man in the Society',[25] of another who had run up debts and infringed the vows of poverty, of another with a 'tendency to madness'.[26] At the time when Hopkins was teaching at Stonyhurst in the 1880s, the Rector was in despair over school problems: 'Everything is disappointment and affliction of spirits'.[27]

Although the reservoir of suitable manpower was limited, the Jesuits still pressed ahead with their work in the third quarter of the nineteenth century. Important new buildings were erected at their schools in Liverpool, Stonyhurst, and Mount St Mary's near Sheffield, while a new school was established at Beaumont, Old Windsor. To accommodate the increasing numbers applying to join the Society, a new novitiate, Manresa House (named after Ignatius's place of retreat in Catalonia), was founded at Roehampton. New churches were built at Richmond in Yorkshire, Bournemouth, and Oxford and in northern industrial centres in Accrington, St Helens, and Manchester.

Abroad, the English Province forged ahead in British Guyana and Southern Africa, where schools and missions were established and heroic expeditions made to christianise the Zulu, Lobengula, culminating in the tragic death of Fr Law at Umzela's Kraal.

The variety of Jesuit activity contradicts any simple notion that they only had to do with the educated and the fashionable. As one writer pointed out, Farm Street church and its prosperous congregations might be well known, but the Fathers also worked in Horseferry Road where 'the locality is not very choice or the work pleasant'.[28] Hopkins's own work in Liverpool and Glasgow was to reveal to him the poverty and misery of many of his countrymen, for whom he and his colleagues tried to provide spiritual consolation and moral direction.

But the evidence remains that the Society was over-extending itself and taking on commitments that were making heavy demands on its numbers and their quality: a laudable sense of duty was not unmixed with a more human desire to strengthen the Society's influence, and Hopkins's many and often inappropriate appointments in the years following his training can in part be seen as the result of this policy of expansion. For an ex-Balliol man, hailing from the cultured middle classes, whose early poetry echoed the aesthetic ideals of Keats and Tennyson, the years learning to be a Jesuit were a new world in themselves. But it was the years that followed that were probably to be the more psychologically disruptive.

### Notes

1. E. Norman, *The English Catholic Church in the Nineteenth Century* (Oxford, 1984) p. 222.
2. W. Nevins, *A Popular Defence of the Jesuits* (London, 1877) p. 7.
3. T. M[eyrick], 'Ascetism and Modern Life', *The Month* (March 1870) pp. 308ff.
4. *Letters and Notices*, xxxiv (1917–18) p. 366.
5. *Spiritual Exercises*, ed. J. Rickaby (London, 1915) p. 1.
6. Ibid., p. 13.
7. Ibid., p. 68.

8. Hopkins's notes on the *Spiritual Exercises* in *Sermons of Hopkins*, ed. Devlin, p. 242.
9. Mrs Maxwell Scott, *Henry Schomberg Kerr*, op. cit., p. 78. Similarly, the evangelical William Wilberforce thought it 'a great pity that officers in the army and navy should upon becoming religious quit that line of life in which they had been engaged and enter into the Church' (quoted in D. Newsome, *The Parting of Friends* (London, 1966) p. 50.
10. *Spiritual Exercises*, p. 161.
11. Fr Gavin SJ, *Memoirs of Fr P. Gallwey* (London, 1913) p. vii.
12. *Constitutions of the Society of Jesus*, op. cit., p. 95.
13. Ibid., p. 249.
14. *Further Letters of Hopkins*, p. 396.
15. *Letters and Notices* (July 1914) p. 470.
16. Ibid. (January 1916) p. 302.
17. Gavin, *Memoirs of Fr Gallwey*, p. 18.
18. *Memoir of the Life and Death of Fr Augustus Law SJ*, 3 vols (London, 1882–3) III, p. 2. No author is given.
19. J. C. H. Aveling, *The Jesuits* (London, 1981) p. 304.
20. See Fr B. Bassett, *The English Jesuits* (London, 1967) p. 392.
21. Quoted in M. F. Petre, *Life of George Tyrrell*, 2 vols (London, 1912) II, p. 463.
22. Ibid., I, p. 191.
23. This, and similar words, are common in historical remarks about Hopkins. See, for example, his obituary in *Letters and Notices*, xx (March 1890) pp. 173–9.
24. D. Mitchell, *The Jesuits* (London, 1980) p. 8.
25. Weld Papers, Farm Street (London) Archives, letter dated 20 Feb. 1880.
26. Ibid., letter dated 26 Oct. 1880.
27. Eyre Papers, Farm Street Archives, letter dated 23 Sept. 1882.
28. Nevins, *A Popular Defence of the Jesuits*, p. 69.

# 7

# Towards the 'Deutschland'

Hopkins's eight years of training to be a Jesuit began, together with ten other novices, in a total community of 49, in the pleasant surroundings of Manresa House on the outskirts of South-West London, the Jesuit novitiate since 1861. His letters, such as there were, and the Journal entries reflect the secluded atmosphere of the fine eighteenth-century building which looked south over Richmond Park and was surrounded by 40 acres of private grounds. The aura of tradition, class and style presented an image of the Jesuits appropriate to the most respectable standards of Victorian society. Even in the often prosaic pages of *Letters and Notices* it was possible to be lyrical about the estate's natural beauty, savouring at the same time the power of the nation to which it belonged:

> No one standing at this front [the western], and surveying the wide extent of parkland stretched out before him, which seems to extend to his very feet, could possibly imagine he was on the very outskirts of the greatest city of the Empire; the countless deer of the park have taken the place of the myriads of human beings, and the din of London is hushed into the silence of the forest.[1]

The appeal of the solitude of natural beauty and achievements of civilised man in close proximity is a powerful paradoxical image, both mystical and patriotic, and one to which Hopkins himself would have been responsive. Once the first winter was passed, he wrote finely in the Journal:

> We were gathering mulberries in [the] tree a little before. The hangers of smaller but barky branches, seen black against the leaves from within, look like ship-tackle. When you climbed to the top of the tree and came out the sky looked as if you could touch it and it was as if you were in a world made up of these three colours, the green of the leaves lit through by the sun, the blue of the sky, and the gray blaze of their upper sides against it.[2]

The image of travel into a new world seems no coincidence in the context in which he was writing.

Hopkins's early silence is partly explained by the demands of the 30-day Retreat, based on the Spiritual Exercises, which began within a few days of his arrival. This crucial experience, in which the retreatant preserves silence throughout, except for the three Sundays of the Retreat, may be what was in Hopkins's mind, when he wrote at the beginning of the 'Wreck of the Deutschland':

> Thou [God] knowest the walls, altar and hour and night:
> The swoon of a heart that the sweep and hurl of thee trod
> Hard down with a horror of height,

but otherwise we learn nothing of its impact. Reticence on innermost spiritual matters is a feature of the Journal. The reader may discover how Hopkins is occasionally moved to tears, how Nature inspires him to praise God and of self-imposed acts of penance, but there is no analysis of the nature of his religious experience. It has been argued that there may have been a spiritual diary,[3] and there are many pages of retreat notes from the later part of his life now in print in the standard edition of his Sermons, but his reaction to the 30-day Retreat can only be guessed at.

Briefly, in view of the details already given, the *Spiritual Exercises* is the basis of the 30-day Retreat and consists of four separate periods, usually of a week each. It begins with the Principle that 'Man was created to praise . . . God,' and the first week is a meditation upon sin and hell, employing the pictorial approach peculiar to Ignatius. In the second week the most important feature is the making of an Election, that is, of the choice of a right way of life. The third week is centred on the life and death of Jesus and the final one concerned with His Resurrection.

We may not know how Hopkins reacted to the Long Retreat, but when another Victorian Jesuit, Fr Dignam, looked back to his, he recalled it as an emotionally overwhelming experience: 'I used to sit there, the tears running down my cheeks,' and again: 'The meditations were like revelations to me'.[4] Crucial to the success of the Retreat is the personality of the Novice-Master who gives it,[5] and here it may not be that Hopkins was as lucky as Fr Dignam. His Novice-Master was Fr Christopher Fitzsimon, an Irishman who had entered the Society at the age of 19, and for ten years been Spiritual Father at Stonyhurst. He had a somewhat schoolmasterly manner, and when at the end of Hopkins's first year at Manresa he 'left suddenly and without a Goodbye,'[6] it brought no more comment from Hopkins than that he was supposedly 'broken with hard work'.[7]

Sympathy and good humour were always likely to be more successful with Hopkins than the authoritarian approach, and it must have been a particular pleasure to him that Fr Fitzsimon's replacement, in October 1869, was the genial Fr Gallwey, whose dictum, 'How anxious St Ignatius is that our intellectual faculties should have fair play',[8] contrasted with the reputed punctiliousness of his predecessor. Three pages of Hopkins's Journal are devoted to Fr Fitzsimon's term of office, eight to Fr Gallwey's. The passage describing him in the mulberry-tree was written in the month of the latter's arrival, while it was a month or so later that he suddenly 'began to cry and sob and could not stop'[9] in the refectory, listening to an account of the Agony in the Garden – he must have been treated sympathetically by Fr Gallwey who was himself moved to tears by the songs of his native Ireland.[10]

Of the usual daily timetable at Manresa, there is a long account by a Fr Clarke in the monthly *The Nineteenth Century* in 1896, quoted in Fr Thomas's *Hopkins, the Jesuit* (London, 1969, pp. 31–3). As this was specifically intended for a mainly Protestant public, it represents what may be called an ideal order, yet what strikes the modern reader is the lack of academic content and the emphasis on the precise timings of each period of activity. The day began at 5.30 a.m. and ended at 10 p.m., and by all accounts it was a tiring one, but whether it also stimulated the mind and spirit of Hopkins must be more doubtful.

At the end of two years, in September 1870, along with three other novices, he made his vows to the Society:

> I, Gerard Hopkins, make profession, and I promise to almighty God, in the presence of his Virgin Mother, the whole heavenly court, and all those here present, and to you Reverend Father Gallwey, representing the Superior General of the Society of Jesus and his successors and holding the place of God, perpetual poverty, chastity, and obedience . . .[11]

Now officially described as a scholastic, he went on to St Mary's Hall at Stonyhurst in Lancashire to study Philosophy, a three-year course, more comprehensive than its name suggests. If intellectual matter had been lacking at Roehampton, the Seminary provided good, solid, if somewhat stodgy content. Logic and Mathematics were taught in the first year, psychology, ethics, metaphysics and theology in the last two. During term-time, called 'schools', for there were regular holiday periods, Hopkins attended two one-hour lectures in the morning and did three hours of study from five until eight o'clock in the evening. Religious duties and recreation periods were fitted in around these fixed times.

There is always the danger that an existence devoted to following a regular timetable – and that laid down by someone else – will have a negative effect on personality. Initiative, the ability to appreciate new departures and retain a freshness of spirit, can be lost in the process of the repetition of daily routine. Apart from holidays with his family or with the community, from 1868–77 Hopkins was never far from a punctually carried-out organisation of his daily external life. There is no record that the impression he made in three years was anything like the picture painted by Wilfred Blunt, once a Catholic and partly educated at Stonyhurst, of the William Kerr who entered Manresa in 1867:

> The Jesuit novitiate is the most mentally crushing process ever invented, and I remember well meeting William Kerr on the first day of his release from I forget how many years of absolute seclusion. It was at some function of the Redemptorist Convent at Clapham, and I walked back with him from it across the Common, I think to Putney, and he told me something of his life as a novice. He was like an owl that had wandered out into the daylight, an absolutely different man from what I had known him before his experience.[12]

Nevertheless, at St Mary's Hall, to judge from a few references, he found his studies wearisome. In his first year he lamented a 'hard course of scholastic logic' which made life 'painful to nature'.[13] In his third year, with typical wry humour, he described his teachers as 'having at me with ethics and mechanics. Today is a whole holiday: I spent a miserable morning over formulas for the lever'.[14]

Thomism seems to have been the dominant philosophy taught in Jesuit establishments and, in 1878, Pope Leo XIII officially declared the system of St Thomas Aquinas to be the basis of Roman Catholic thought. But there were factions within the camp, and another influential figure was the sixteenth-century Jesuit theologian Francisco Suarez whose interpretation of Acquinas was probably in vogue at

St Mary's Hall during Hopkins's time there. The refinements of neither thinker, however, are much to the purpose of the present study, and it is typical that Hopkins was personally fired not by them, but by the unconventional Scotus who was not regarded with official favour.[15]

In lighter moments at the Seminary there were the weekly meetings of a new literary society, the English Academy, with talks on 'The Prussian Army' and 'The Principles of the Art of Painting' and sometimes debates ('Secular Education is no Education at all'), although we do not know how far Hopkins was involved on these occasions.

Out of doors, to judge by the Journal, was perhaps the greatest source of pleasure. Place was always important to Hopkins, whether it was the dignity of Oxford as he had recently known it or the dreadful squalor of Liverpool where he was to be assigned in 1880. St Mary's Hall, a functional building of local stone, nevertheless stood next to the imposing mass of Stonyhurst College in splendid countryside. The natural surroundings were 'bare and bleak but the rivers . . . beautiful',[16] and the room he occupied overlooked a 'beautiful range of moors dappled with light and shade'.[17] It was a panorama that included the 'world-wielding shoulder' of Pendle Hill, whose varying moods of sun, shadow and even snow never failed to find an appreciative 'beholder' in Hopkins.

The people too impressed him. His regard for the simplicity of the locals now strikes us as naive, but as a born and bred Londoner he could only have found rural Lancashire a totally different world. Part of this distinctiveness he celebrates by recording examples of dialect:

'Of all the wind instruments big droom fots me best'.

He called felly/*felk* and *nave* short like *have*. *Wind* he pronounced with the *i* long.

Mr Vaughan took off Cornelius the philosopher's servant – 'a-bullockin', ay and a-bullyraggin' tëoo', that is bullying, using abusive words.[18]

From his experience here, and later in industrial Lancashire, he acquired at least one phrase that was to enter his poetry: 'All road ever he offended' in 'Felix Randal'.

He was also acquiring a social conscience:

I am afraid some great revolution is not far off. Horrible to say, in a manner I am a Communist. Their ideal bating [i.e. excluding] some things is nobler than that professed by any secular statesman I know of. . . . It is a dreadful thing for the greatest and most necessary part of a very rich nation to live a hard life without dignity, knowledge, comforts, delight, or hopes in the midst of plenty – which plenty they make . . . England has grown hugely wealthy but this wealth has not reached the working classes.

(2 August 1871)[19]

These were remarkable sentiments from a Victorian Jesuit scholastic, whose French colleagues had suffered in the Commune from those who espoused similar sentiments, but it also reflected a radicalism that was to be imbibed from the English air. As long ago as 1843, in *Past and Present*, Thomas Carlyle had deplored the same inequality in Victorian society: 'In the midst of plethoric plenty, the people perish',[20] and for Carlyle Hopkins had a good deal of respect, albeit mixed with caution. 'Genius' though he called him,[21] it was in curiously critical contexts, where the strength, rather than the content of Carlyle's vision is praised: the latter's prose-style, with its lists, coinages, compounds and general air of excitement and energy reflects a man possessed like Hopkins by the power of language.

He could also share, in principle, in Carlyle's admiration for heroes and in the ideals of duty and obedience (rather than a thoughtless worship of democracy). Carlyle's vision of modern English society in the grip of an exploiting and polluting industry and a working class coarsened by the selfishness of its bosses became, at least for a time, the view of Hopkins. This letter of August 1871 embodies, too, the social criticism of Ruskin: '[The] masters have set [the workers] to do all the work, and have themselves taken all the wages',[22] and may even have been immediately inspired by one of his monthly letters to the workmen of Great Britain, in *Fors Clavigera*, where in the number dated 1 July 1871, after exclaiming 'I am myself a Communist of the old school – reddest also of the red', Ruskin went on:

The guilty thieves of Europe . . . are the Capitalists . . . the Real War in Europe, of which this fighting in Paris is the inauguration, is between these and the workmen, such as these have made him.

They have kept him poor, ignorant, and sinful, that they might, without his knowledge, gather for themselves the produce of his toil.[23]

But apart from any literary influences, Hopkins's letter may also have been prompted by discussion among the Stonyhurst community. Teaching at the College, just a short walk away, was Joseph Rickaby, a good scholar with a strong interest in social affairs, later to be ordained at the same time as Hopkins at St Beuno's. In a pamphlet, *Socialism*, published by the Catholic Truth Society in 1885, Rickaby described the miserable domestic conditions of the poor workman ('Lazarus') and his sense of injustice:

Lazarus can read; he has had some education; he can think; and he does think the division of this world's goods between himself and Dives desperately unfair; and in his weakness he growls to his comrades in misery, 'We will right this injustice some day'.[24]

Rickaby went on to attack the 'undeniable wretchedness and iniquity of the capitalist system and its present working',[25] and ended with an impassioned plea for democracy and the right of the common people to choose their rulers. In 1871, Hopkins had concluded his letter with a grim warning: 'The more I look, the more black and deservedly black the future looks', a reflection on the 'probability of revolution' which had been vexing Fr Purbrick, the Rector of Stonyhurst, at about this time:

Many currents . . . are quietly sapping the foundations of our English Constitution. . . . One day will come from without a war which will come in aid of their work, and seem to accomplish what has in fact been their doing. When will that day come? Perhaps not in '70 or '71, but sooner or later come it must . . .[26]

Bearing in mind his own privileged background, one wonders whether Hopkins would have ever developed a social conscience if he had not joined the Jesuits. Such colleagues and the many migrations he was to endure from one racially and socially diverse part of the British Isles to another equipped him, however unwittingly, with a wider perspective of society than could have been available to most Victorians.

At St Mary's Hall his sense of inscape also grew in response to the world around him. Watching the clouds over Kemple End, a local landmark, he noted one standing out from the rest and filling the 'zenith with a white shire of cloud':

> I looked long up at it till the tall height and the beauty of the scaping – regularly curled knots springing if I remember from fine stems, like foliation in wood or stone – had strongly grown on me. It changed beautiful changes, growing more into ribs and one stretch of running into branching like coral. Unless you refresh the mind from time to time you cannot always remember or believe how deep the inscape in things is.[27]

This is an aesthetic experience where the emphasis is on the 'beauty' and pattern of what is seen; there is no attempt to analyse the why and the how of these feelings. The same could be said of the famous account of the Stonyhurst barn, where the precise detail of the impression of the roof is followed by a lament at the blindness of the many:

> I thought how sadly beauty of inscape was unknown and buried away from simple people and yet how near at hand it was if they had eyes to see it and it could be called out everywhere again.[28]

There is something here of the Paterian spirit at the conclusion of *The Renaissance* with its talk of catching 'at any exquisite passion . . . that seems . . . to set the spirit free for a moment'.

This was a period in Hopkins's life when many things appeared to confirm his sense of the uniqueness of phenomena. He had started to read the medieval philosopher, Duns Scotus, whose dynamic view of individuality seemed to complement his own. John Pick summarises the Scotian philosophy as proclaiming the 'sharp singularity of inner form which necessarily expresses itself in unity with outward distinctiveness'.[29] Individuality, too, is not only itself, but it is a confirmation of the divine.

There were few regrets for lack of literary outlet, although reading Euripides's *Iphigenia in Aulis* he told a correspondent: 'I wish I could have more of such reading'.[30] He wrote some Greek verses in honour of the visit to Stonyhurst of a distinguished Old Boy, Bishop Vaughan of Salford, in November 1872, and the following May is the date ascribed to the English lines *Ad Mariam*:

We have suffered the sons of Winter in sorrow
And been in their ruinous reigns oppressed,

a clear imitation of Swinburne's style and rhythms, and a somewhat odd choice in view of the latter's reputation for impropriety. The verses were presumably intended for display in the College as part of the traditional May celebrations of the Virgin Mary, and Hopkins might simply have wished to cut a poetic dash – but anonymously, as was the custom. The following month he did indeed teach at the College in the absence of a member of staff, but he was required for only a few days and says nothing of the experience, which was followed by two much longer spells in the years to come.

At St Mary's Hall it was usual to spend part of the summer vacation with the other Philosophers at one or other of the British resorts. That year it was the Isle of Man, where his descriptive skill was as evident as ever in the Journal, although the return journey brought on a characteristic fit of melancholy when he reached Stonyhurst:

Things not ready, darkness and despair. In fact being unwell I was quite downcast: nature in all her parcels and faculties gaped and fell apart, *fatiscebat*, like a clod cleaving and holding only by strings of root. But this must often be.[31]

His health may have worried his superiors – he had earlier had an operation for piles – and for the academic year 1873–4, with his Philosophy course successfully concluded, he was sent on the relatively easy assignment of teaching the so-called Juniors (novices without higher education) at Manresa. With the grand title of Professor of Rhetoric and the humdrum responsibility of teaching Latin, Greek and English to a wide range of intelligences, it might have been the time and place to return to verse of his own, but the personal resolve he had made six years before held firm. Perhaps he took some vicarious pleasure in composing his lectures, although, like all newcomers to the teaching profession, finding the right wavelength could not have been easy:

Verse is speech having a marked figure, order of sounds independent of meaning and such as can be shifted from one word or words to others without changing. It is *figure of spoken sound*.[32]

His meticulous analysis of rhythm and metre must have made him a difficult teacher for the uninitiated, and even the initiated might have been puzzled by the remark that sound in verse is independent of meaning – Hopkins's own poetry manifestly demonstrates that stress follows meaning. Later he declared: 'I taught so badly and so painfully,'[33] and at the end of the twelve months he did not hide his general dissatisfaction:

Altogether perhaps my heart has never been so burdened and cast down as this year. The tax on my strength has been greater than I have felt before. . . . But in all this our Lord goes His own way.[34]

Yet the Journal writing produced its customary magic, and the richness of image and idea in this passage already suggests a poem:

At the end of the month hard frosts. Wonderful downpour of leaf: when the morning sun began to melt the frost they fell at one touch and in a few minutes a whole tree was flung of them; they lay masking and papering the ground at the foot. Then the tree seems to be looking down on its cast self as blue sky on snow after a long fall, its losing, its doing.[35]

If the seeds of 'Spring and Fall' are in this October scene, it has to be balanced with the puritanical scruples that were all too ready to deny him sensuous pleasure:

July 23 – To Beaumont: it was the rector's day. It was a lovely day: shires-long of pearled cloud under cloud, with a grey stroke underneath marking each row; beautiful blushing yellow in the straw of the uncut ryefields. . . . All this I would have looked at again in returning but during dinner I talked too freely and unkindly and had to do penance going home.[36]

But men, as well as landscapes, had their influence on Hopkins at Manresa, and two individuals must be noted among the Community who, then or later, were significant to him. Prefect of Studies for the Juniors was Fr John Macleod, a Scotsman in his late forties, who was to become *scriptor*, house-writer, in communities he later moved to, and eventually editor of the Jesuits' own *Letters and Notices* from 1894–1907. It was he who in 1906 published extracts from the Journal and recalled the author as a man whose 'views and opinions . . . tended to that form of eccentricity which is closely allied to a touch of true genius'.[37]

The most unusual character in the house was probably Thomas Harper, a convert from the Anglican ministry and brilliant preacher, but a man who lived on his nerves. He was an enthusiast of scholasticism ('Dear, dear Tommy!' he used to say as he stroked his Acquinas), often above the heads of his students and totally involved to the point of nervous collapse when he delivered his sermons. He feared madness and ended his life in a Surrey asylum.

Fr Harper was not the only member of the Society whom Hopkins encountered whose later life was marred by mental breakdown. Madness was a secret fear of the century, associated sometimes with melancholia, sometimes with religious doubt after an earlier period of religious enthusiasm.[38] It was a fear Hopkins himself was to admit to, some ten years later.[39]

However, on 26 August 1874, he learnt that he was to go to St Beuno's College in North Wales to do his Theology, the final stage of his training. It was also where the poet was to be reborn.

### Notes

1. *Letters and Notices*, I (1863) p. 10.
2. *Journals of Hopkins*, p. 192.
3. See ibid., Preface, p. xiv.
4. *Memoir of Fr Dignam*, ed. Fr Purbrick (London, n.d.) pp. 15 and 16.
5. See *Spiritual Exercises*, ed. Fr Rickaby, p. 17.
6. *Journals of Hopkins*, p. 191.
7. *Further Letters of Hopkins*, p. 108.
8. *Letters and Notices*, XXXII (July 1914) p. 470.
9. *Journals of Hopkins*, p. 195.
10. *Letters and Notices*, XXXIII (January 1916) p. 305.
11. See *Constitutions of the Society of Jesus*, p. 238.
12. W. S. Blunt, *My Diaries* (London, 1932) p. 785.
13. *Further Letters of Hopkins*, pp. 234–5.
14. Ibid., p. 238.
15. See Ch. 2, note 9.
16. *Letters of Hopkins to Bridges*, p. 26.
17. *Further Letters of Hopkins*, p. 112.
18. *Journals of Hopkins*, pp. 211, 227, 232.
19. *Letters of Hopkins to Bridges*, pp. 27–8.
20. Carlyle, *Past and Present*, Book 1, Ch. 1.
21. *Correspondence of Hopkins and R. W. Dixon*, pp. 59, 75.
22. Ruskin, *Crown of Wild Olive* (1869) para. 136.

23. Ruskin, *Fors Clavigera* (1896 edn) I, pp. 126, 140–1 (Letter VII).
24. J. Rickaby, *Socialism* (Catholic Truth Society, 1885) p. 2.
25. Ibid., p. 8.
26. *The Month* (July–December 1926) p. 207.
27. *Journals of Hopkins*, pp. 204–5.
28. Ibid., p. 221.
29. John Pick, *Hopkins, Priest and Poet*, 2nd edn (Oxford, 1966) p. 156.
30. *Further Letters of Hopkins*, p. 239.
31. *Journals of Hopkins*, p. 236.
32. Ibid., p. 267.
33. *Letters of Hopkins to Bridges*, p. 30.
34. *Journals of Hopkins*, pp. 249–50.
35. Ibid., p. 239.
36. Ibid., p. 249.
37. *Letters and Notices*, vol. XXVIII (April 1906) p. 390.
38. See Ann Colley, *Tennyson and Madness* (1983).
39. See *Letters of Hopkins to Bridges*, p. 216.

# 8

# The Return to Poetry

*A style may be fatiguing and faulty precisely by being too emphatic,*
*forcible and pointed; and so straining the attention to find its*
*meaning, or the admiration to appreciate its beauty.*
John Sterling, letter to Carlyle on *Sartor Resartus*[1]

The course in Theology had a daunting reputation: 'Hours of study
very close – lectures in dogmatic theology, moral ditto, canon law,
church history, scripture, Hebrew and what not',[2] wrote Hopkins to
his father at the beginning of it. The account written by Fr Clarke for
*The Nineteenth Century* some years later does not minimise the
difficulties:

> The work is certainly hard, especially during the first two years.
> On three days in the week, the student . . . has to attend two
> lectures in the morning and three in the afternoon. The morning
> lectures are on moral and dogmatic theology; and those in the
> afternoon on canon law or history, dogmatic theology, and Hebrew.
> . . . Besides this, on each of these afternoons there is held a circle
> or disputation. . . .
>
> During the third and fourth years of the course of theology,
> lectures in Scriptures are substituted for those on moral theology
> and Hebrew. At the end of the third year the young Jesuit (if a
> man of thirty-four or thirty-five can be accounted young) is
> ordained priest.[3]

Like St Mary's Hall, the students and community of St Beuno's
lived their virtually self-contained existence in a rural setting, some
ten miles south-east of Rhyl in the Vale of Clwyd. The total community
of about 50 naturally varied from year to year with the influx of new
faces and the departure of ordained priests. In such circumstances,
as at Manresa and St Mary's Hall, it was inevitable that Hopkins

would meet many whom he would also come across later in his career.

The situation was not unlike that which once applied, and perhaps still does apply to students at the older public schools and universities, where reputations are made and survive long after, perpetuated and perhaps amplified by memory and hearsay. The Rickaby's, MacLeod's, Barraud's and countless other Jesuits would naturally spread each other's names throughout the province, fixing labels which a lifetime would not easily alter. The man who wept uncontrollably one mealtime at Manresa, whom Jesuit brothers found peering intently at the gravel at St Mary's Hall ('A strange yoong man . . . that Mr 'opkins'[4]), whose poetry Clement Barraud was to hear with such surprise, was already building the legend that would follow him all his Jesuit life.

With the possible exception of some verses on St Winefred, the Welsh saint, his poetic exile continued during his first year and a half at St Beuno's. The verses themselves are not important, but his devotion to this twelfth-century saint, niece to St Beuno, supposed founder of the well associated with her at Holywell, reflects the strongly emotional element in his temperament and spirituality.

He was particularly moved by the active manifestation of her in the spring at Holywell:

> The strong unfailing flow of the water and the chain of cures from year to year all these centuries took hold of my mind with wonder at the bounty of God in one of His saints, the sensible thing so naturally and gracefully uttering the spiritual reason of its being . . . and the spring in place leading back the thoughts by its spring in time to its spring in eternity.[5]

The spiritual simplicity – and the wordplay – are entirely characteristic of one side of Hopkins, whose companion on the expedition to Holywell had been another Jesuit student with poetic ambitions. Clement Barraud was born in 1843 and lived to be 82, and his reminiscences of Hopkins, published in *The Month* in 1919, reflect affection for his character but puzzlement at his verse. He had joined the Jesuits in 1862, having been educated partly at Stonyhurst. Much of his career was spent as a priest in the West Indies, but he wrote plays of a historical-religious interest which received approving notices in *The Times*, and his poetry (*Lays of the Knights*, 1898) is marked by the predictable diction and imagery of minor Victorian verse. Like Hopkins, he was a patriot ('Up, England! up and chant God save the Queen'), he wrote on the sea ('The Loss of the Victoria'), he shared some common religious themes ('St Winefride'), and responded to the beauty of Nature: in 'Tell me where' he writes:

> Oh, the stars – the stars so bright,
> Shimmering through the frosty night!
> Angel eyes they seem to me.[6]

Hopkins was shortly to write:

> Look at the stars! look, look up at the skies!
> O look at all the fire-folk sitting in the air.[7]

Barraud's image is presented almost apologetically, whereas the repetition, alliteration and sprung rhythm of Hopkins's lines are symptomatic of his energy and directness.

The richness of his own response to Nature is apparent in a description of a sunset which occurred shortly after he had attended the ordination of sixteen priests and received minor orders himself, when he was 'by God's mercy deeply touched';[8] the sensuous artist was clearly still unspoilt by the Jesuit experience:

> A lovely sunset of rosy juices and creams and combs; the combs I mean scattered floating bats or rafts or racks above, the creams, the strew and bed of the sunset, passing north and south or rather north only into grey marestail and brush along the horizon to the hills. Afterwards the rosy field of the sundown turned gold and the slips and creamings in it stood out like brands, with jots of purple.[9]

But he found the first year of Theology hard work. He wrote to Bridges in February 1875:

> The close pressure of my theological studies leaves me time for hardly anything: the course is very hard, it must be said. Nevertheless I have tried to learn a little Welsh, in reality one of the hardest of languages.[10]

For someone who had excelled in Greats at Oxford, his formal studies both at St Mary's Hall and at St Beuno's must have been a grind. Learning Welsh was a pleasant diversion but it was not to the taste of the authorities. Fr James Jones, the Rector, had to point out that serious study of the language could only be justified if Hopkins felt a genuine vocation to work among the people, and he had to admit he did not. Still, he did not give up reading and writing the language and kept an affection for Wales throughout his life.

But if Fr Jones brought one diversion to a halt, he was the immediate cause of reviving another that was to ensure his student's name, as well as his own, for posterity. Hopkins's Journal had come to an end, in mid-sentence, in February 1875; in December of the same year he began writing 'The Wreck of the Deutschland'. The German passenger-ship, sailing from Bremen to New York, was carrying over 200 passengers and crew when it went aground in appalling conditions at the mouth of the Thames in the early morning of 7 December. Sixty lives were lost before rescue could be attempted, the victims including five Franciscan nuns who were fleeing Bismarck's persecution of religious orders. It is their deaths which are the inspiration of the poem.

According to what Hopkins told his Anglican poet-friend, Canon Dixon, some years later:

> I was affected by the account and happening to say so to my rector he said that he wished someone would write a poem on the subject. On this hint I set to work and, though my hand was out at first, produced one. I had long had haunting my ear the echo of a new rhythm which now I realised on paper.[11]

The new rhythm, of course, was what he elsewhere called sprung rhythm, and which he had already been teaching to the (no doubt bemused) Juniors at Roehampton, calling it there 'beat-rhythm', of which the 'essential principle' was that 'beat is measured by stress or strength, not number' of syllables.[12]

The finer detail can be read in his own words in the 'Preface on Rhythm', written 1883–4, or in Edward Stephenson's modern exposition, *What Sprung Rhythm Really Is*,[13] but the essential features are the primacy of the heavy stress in determining the number of feet in a line and the absence of a regular order of light and heavy stresses:

> Thóu mástering mé
> Gód! gíver of bréath and bréad;
> World's stránd, swáy of the séa;
> Lórd of líving and déad.[14]

Simple regularity is eschewed and the poet is faced with the challenge of a freer and more sensitive system of scansion, while the reader has to assess for himself each line as he reads it. To Robert Bridges (who doubted his friend's wisdom but practised his own form of sprung rhythm), he wrote:

> Why do I employ Sprung Rhythm at all? Because it is the nearest to the rhythm of prose, that is the native and natural rhythm of speech . . . combining markedness of rhythm . . . and naturalness of expression.[15]

The shock of sprung rhythm is intensified by all the aural devices with which Hopkins accompanies it:

> It dates from day
> Of his going in Galilee;
> Warm-laid grave of a womb-life grey;
> Manger, maiden's knee.

Besides the half-rhymes: *da*tes, *day*; *go*ing, *in*; *gra*ve, *grey*; *ma*nger, *ma*iden's; there is assonance in *la*id, *gra*ve, and alliteration occurs in every line.

It is clear, then, even from this small extract, that sound is very important in the poem (as it is, as every reader will know, in all Hopkins's mature work). From his study of Welsh he also knew and utilised the art of *cynghanedd*, a complex system of vowelling and alliteration.[16] Perhaps, in the end, it is hardly surprising that the confidence of his theorising and the power of his examples influenced Bridges, who, in *Poems* (3rd Series, 1880) acknowledged his debt to a 'friend', which is apparent, for instance, in the sprung rhythm of 'London Snow'.

But in this concern for sound there is always the danger of what the poem is saying being overwhelmed by the aural rhetoric: rhythmic energy and aural devices are a two-edged weapon if they dictate, rather than share in the growth of a poem, and Hopkins, one feels, often delights in letting this happen. Need 'the', for example, have been omitted before 'day' in the verse above except to lend the line a more urgent sound (and at the same time a more eccentric flavour)? The third line is obscure because its rhetorical and aural balance were irresistible to the poet.

These sound dangerously like the strictures Bridges was to make on Hopkins in the posthumous first edition, but in their enthusiasm for Hopkins modern readers have perhaps too easily been swept from one extreme to the other. 'The Wreck of the Deutschland' is a great poem, but there are many sorts of great poem, and if one is to isolate in this one the supremacy of its sound and rhythm, it must also be to acknowledge that all gains are not without some losses.

The author signalled one of the latter when he admitted the poem's weakness as a narrative, and its mixture of personal, confessional and meditative elements with story make the nature of its form and structure difficult to judge. Part the First recalls more than one religious crisis in the poet's life – certainly conversion, and perhaps moments of stress on his way to becoming a Jesuit – and ends on the note of willing subjection to the Christ who had himself suffered the pain of being man.

In Part the Second we are told that our recognition of God's power must include our awareness of mortality, and the story of the 'Deutschland' is one experience of that. Now the poet recounts the wreck of the ship, the agonies of its passengers and the 'martyrdom' of the five nuns. (Thus, dominating his first Jesuit poem, is his life-long preoccupation with the idea of heroic sacrifice and the question of the value of the individual sacrifice in the unheeding world of the selfish and faithless.)

But, the poem goes on, it is not only from moments of extreme danger that deliverance may come through Christ, but also from the tediousness of ordinary life with all its disappointments. In the death of these nuns we can see again the meaning of the Redemption: may they intercede with Christ for the conversion of England:

> Our King back, Oh, upon English souls!
> Let him easter in us, be a dayspring to the dimness of us.

The amalgam of thoroughly Victorian patriotism and piety is not much to modern taste, but Hopkins was by no means alone among Catholics and Protestants of his time in suggesting God's special concern for England. Michael Moore in the *Hopkins Quarterly*[17] has suggested parallels in theme and imagery with both the 'Wreck of the Deutschland' and its successor 'The Loss of the Eurydice' in Newman's two sermons on the restoration of the hierarchy in Britain, 'Christ upon the Waters' and 'The Second Spring': 'both writers share the conviction that God has chosen to retire from England only to come again in time'.

That we may find Victorian ideas difficult to accept is not a decisive reason for withdrawing the effort at sympathetic identification and honest engagement with the text. Moreover, the rhetorical and emotional power of the verse, the daring imagery and dramatic rhythms work at their own level, regardless of our agreement with the argument. The mood swings from the peace of:

> Away in the lovable west,
> On a pastoral forehead of Wales,
> I was under a roof here, I was at rest,
> And they the prey of the gales

to the excited, semi-incoherence of:

> But how shall I . . . make me room there:
> Reach me a . . . Fancy, come faster –

Pindaric elements, too, have been identified in the personification, exclamation and coining of words and phrases.[18]

If we find these things strange, what would contemporary Jesuits (who made up a high proportion of Hopkins's readers!) have thought of the embarrassing egotism of

> I kiss my hand
> To the stars . . .

or the apparently meaningless repetition in

> Since, tho' he is under the world's splendour and wonder,
> His mystery must be instressed, stressed.

These matters, together with the markings that he felt necessary on the manuscript to indicate the rhythm, were too much for the editorial department of *The Month*, to which he submitted the poem. Although the editor was Fr Coleridge, one of his first acquaintances in the Society, the poem was finally classified, after a good deal of hesitation, as 'unreadable'.[19]

He wrote in the following September, 'I am glad now it has not appeared',[20] but his concern in the previous month, 'It has cost me a good deal of trouble',[21] and his lengthy defence of the poem to Bridges more probably reflect the real state of affairs and his deep disappointment. Indeed, for someone who had published as a young man and led so successful a career at Oxford, the rejection must have been a shock to an ego that still yearned for achievement.

It is probably useless to speculate what reception the poem would have received had it been published, whether in *The Month* or in a purely secular publication. Fifteen years later, shortly after Hopkins's death, another great religious poem *had* been printed, in another Catholic magazine, *Merry England*:

> I fled Him, down the nights and down the days;
> I fled Him, down the arches of the years;
> I fled Him down the labyrinthine ways
> Of my own mind; and in the midst of tears
> I fled from Him, and under running laughter.

Thompson's 'Hound of Heaven' was an immediate popular and critical success, yet it too was the confession of a man haunted by God, intense, passionate, full of urgency. Its rich imagery and language is mingled at times with the directness of Herbert, but it is a diction with which, on the whole, the Victorian reader would have felt at ease, recognisably 'poetic', Keats the ultimate master.

The poem is also detached from any actual circumstances: it might be dealing with any man (or woman), Catholic or Protestant or neither, forced to take stock of their spiritual position. There are no nuns, no ship, no storm and no poet on a Welsh hillside. The reader of 'The Hound of Heaven' can feel as private in his experience of the poem as the real Francis Thompson in composing it. Hopkins's offence against good taste is to expose himself and the seemingly extraordinary style merely underlines this:

> Is out with it! Oh,
> We lash with the best or worst
> Word last! How a lush-kept plush-capped sloe
> Will, mouthed to flesh-burst,
> Gush!

With writing as openly emotional as this one feels that only the similarly open-hearted reader can respond.

Bridges – naturally enough for Bridges – complained about the unintelligibility. Had Hopkins been egotistic he might have answered with Ruskin's assertion that 'Excellence of the highest kind without obscurity cannot exist',[22] but he did offer him advice which all later readers have found useful: 'If it is obscure do not bother yourself with the meaning but pay attention to the best and most intelligible stanzas.' If he had to read the difficult parts, then:

> Sometimes one enjoys and admires the very lines one cannot understand, as for instance 'If it were done when 'tis done' sqq., which is all obscure and disputed, though how fine it is everybody sees and nobody disputes.

Finally it was a question of getting used to something different, and with more reading, 'You would have got more weathered to the style and its features'.[23]

It is not the best Hopkins poem to read first, a fact which Bridges realised by the time he came to write the 'Notes' to his edition of Hopkins's poems in 1918. However, his honesty in admitting his own shortcomings in appreciating the 'Wreck' reveals him at his best:

> This editor advises the reader to circumvent him [the poem] and attack him later in the rear; for he was himself shamefully worsted in a brave frontal assault, the more easily perhaps because both subject and treatment were distasteful to him.[24]

Hopkins was particularly anxious that the poem should be read aloud: 'My verse is less to be read than heard,'[25] for, as he was later to say of the 'true nature of poetry' in general, '*till it is spoken it is not performed*'.[26] Indeed, the glory (and challenge) of sprung rhythm is its sensitivity to the reader's interpretation of the poem; this 'acting-out' element would not have appealed to so correct a reader as Bridges, nor, perhaps, to many Victorians.

We have no means of knowing whether Hopkins regarded Fr Jones's encouragement to write the 'Wreck of the Deutschland' as freeing him from his general resolve to write no more poetry, but there was certainly no opening of the flood-gates as a result. His second poem, 'Penmaen Pool', was not composed until August 1876, and its light-hearted subject-matter and treatment are in complete contrast with the 'Wreck'.

In September 1876, Fr Jones was appointed Provincial, and his replacement as Rector was the ubiquitous Fr Gallwey, whose arrival brought a tightening-up of house discipline, such as his popularity could easily afford: 'His reverence drew attention to the rule of silence and of speaking Latin.'[27] Gallwey's presence, increasing affection for St Beuno's, and impending ordination might all have contributed to the outburst of poetry from Hopkins that finally began in the late spring of 1877. This series of sonnets has become his best-loved work, reflecting, so it would seem, the happiest period of his Jesuit life. Their general mood is summed up by a Journal entry made some years before when he was on holiday in Devonshire:

> As we drove home the stars came out thick: I leant back to look at them and my heart opening more than usual praised our Lord to and in whom all that beauty comes home.[28]

Their exultant descriptions of the countryside are combined with a profound sense of God's presence in Nature, but Hopkins is equally conscious of a society which does not share this vision and is content with its materialism. This element of melancholy, combined with the sacramental, helps to give them a special place in the great Nature poetry of the nineteenth century from Wordsworth to Hardy.

'God's Grandeur' illustrates characteristically this perception of a beautiful God-filled world inhabited by uncaring man. After a triumphant opening, the octet turns into a lament for man's headlessness, and the brilliant dazzle of silver foil 'shook' is lost in the greyness of modern working life. Alliteration, half-rhyme and assonance underline the heavy rhythm in which the poet's disgust is manifested:

> And weárs mán's smúdge and sháres mán's mélll: the sóil . . .

The image for man's loss of contact with Nature, 'nor can foot feel, being shod', anticipates the letter which Hopkins wrote to the *Stonyhurst Magazine* in November 1888, advocating that pupils should imitate the Irish and 'play football and other games barefoot . . . on grass'.[29] It was a suggestion that a later correspondent treated with some mockery: like other opinions of Hopkins, it hardly seems so eccentric to us today.

But the sestet offers an optimistic conclusion (in 'The Sea and the Skylark' the order is reversed and the poem ends pessimistically). The eternal repetitiveness of the order of things in the natural world is a sure sign of God's care, and the virtually unpunctuated sweep of the final four lines (compare the full stops, colons, etc of the octet) reflects the confidence of the poet's belief.

It is a confidence which also marks the choice and organisation of language, the responsive rhythms and handling of lines: the completion of a sense unit by an adjective in the following line:

> It gathers to a greatness, like the ooze of oil
> Crushed,

or the subject at the end of a line and its predicate in the next one:

> . . . the soil

> Is bare now,

or an adjective separated from its noun:

> Because the Holy Ghost over the bent
> World broods.

'God's Grandeur', of course, is not an argument; like all the great Hopkins poems, it is a personal (and emotional) expression of beliefs and values, in which optimism is finally triumphant. A similar awareness of a world which is not at one with itself is expressed in 'Spring'. A glowing succession of images from Nature fill the octet – the thrush's eggs 'look little low heavens', the peartree leaves 'brush the descending blue' and birdsong through the 'echoing timber does so rinse and wring'. But these pictures recall the innocence of a world that was, not the one that is (for Hopkins is rarely content to accept beauty unalloyed by moral values). He experiences the sadness of loss, where he should feel joy, and must have felt with Ruskin that, 'It is not good for man to live among what is most beautiful . . . he is a creation incapable of satisfaction by anything upon earth.'[30] Just as Hopkins harks back to 'Eden garden', Ruskin asks: 'Is this . . . the earth's prime into which we are born: or is it, with all its beauty, only the wreck of Paradise?'[31]

The poem's conclusion is a depressing one: unless Christ can enter the hearts of the young before sin becomes habitual, they will be lost to Him for ever. Youthful innocence is the state of greatest impressionability to Christ – a point of view which explains the tendency in a number of Hopkins's poems towards a somewhat sentimental idealisation of young people.

'The Starlight Night' has less serious things to say about the human condition, although again, through the imagery of Nature, the fragility of material beauty is suggested. The brilliance of the night sky, of the woods, and of spring and summer are to be interpreted as signs of the greater beauty of Christ:

> These are indeed the barn; withindoors house
> The shocks.                                 [*stooks*

Emotion and excitement characterise the usual tone of the St Beuno's sonnets, but 'In the Valley of the Elwy' is meditative in atmosphere. Hopkins draws a contrast between a house with hospitable owners set in beautiful surroundings and the equally lovely land of Wales which unhappily is inhabited by the unconverted Welsh. He prays that God may 'Complete thy creature dear O where it fails': his natural affection for the Welsh does not allow him to forget his religious scruples.

Pessimism of a more universal character appears in 'The Sea and the Skylark', which takes up a favourite Victorian theme of modern decadence.[32] Partly because he felt that he had exploited Welsh *cynghanedd*, 'consonant-chime', to excess, he was not happy with the poem. He apologised to Bridges for the 'sense' getting 'the worst of it' as a result and after a paraphrase of part of the poem added: 'There is, you see, plenty meant; but the saying of it smells, I fear, of the lamp.'[33]

In the sonnet the poet hears the natural sounds of the tide on the shore and the skylark, putting to shame the artificiality of modern life which declines further and further from original innocence:

> We, life's pride and cared-for crown,
>
> Have lost that cheer and charm of earth's past prime.

Man is returning to dust, his 'first slime', a word that he had already used in his Oxford notes on Parmenides.[34]

This pessimism, no doubt, had its personal sources, but the

troubled political and social background of the time may also have prompted it: unemployment, socialism, industrial power moving from England to Germany seemed to justify Ruskin's remark that Britain was 'likely to perish, as a power, from the face of the earth'.[35]

By contrast 'The Windhover' is one of his most joyous, as well as most discussed pieces and although Elisabeth Schneider has said, 'As is so true in Hopkins the plan is simple and straightforward, only the execution is complex,'[36] the multitude of books and articles it has prompted reflect the ambiguities many readers have found. These cannot be dealt with here: the familiar danger of Hopkins scholarship is a concern with the finer details at the expense of the overall aesthetic impact and we should heed the author's own warning that obscurity is a necessary part of poetry and no necessary hindrance to appreciation.

The extraordinary octet is based on one rhyme, hyphenated at first as 'king-dom', and this, together with remarkable effects of internal rhyme, alliteration and assonance, conveys sensations of exhilaration and excitement associated with both the movement of the bird and the emotions of the onlooker. But the latter watches 'in hiding', his feelings repressed (like the Stranger 'unseen' in the later 'Epithalamion'[37]), as if to show them or himself would frighten away the cause. Or is it, at another level, a consciousness of unworthiness before Christ symbolised by the bird?

In the sestet one meaning of 'buckle' is 'brought together', a reference to man's recognition of Christ as the source of all power, a mastery which is 'dangerous', perhaps, because it includes the temptation of merely sensuous beauty to the unwary. As if to temper the overwhelming impression we may have of Christ, the last lines also tell us that his own earthly experience, and ours, of daily toil have their own glory, and the poem concludes with a picture of agricultural labour as such an act of devotion.

Another poem of praise is the 'curtal' sonnet, 'Pied Beauty', its octave and sestet 'curtailed' into three-quarters of the normal length. The first six lines consist of a series of (qualified) nouns, a miscellany of mainly rural images that exemplify the glory of God. The second and final sentence of the poem lists a succession of opposing adjectives . that suggest the power and variety of God's creativeness:

> With swíft, slów; swéet, soúr; adázzle, dím.

The metrical energy mimics the creative. The poem seems to exemplify the remark of the Victorian scientist, James Joule, that we find on the earth

> a vast variety of phenomena connected with the conversion of living force and heat into one another, which speak in language which cannot be misunderstood of the wisdom and beneficence of the Great Architect of Nature.[38]

Hopkins's description of 'Hurrahing in Harvest' as 'the outcome of half an hour of extreme enthusiasm'[39] is an apt summing-up of the first impressions made by the best poems of this remarkable year: their spontaneity and sincerity seems to belie the great art which has gone into their making and the succession of simple statements, exclamations and questions in the octet of 'Hurrahing in Harvest' rushes us into the immediacy of the poet's feelings. The poet finds fulfilment for his sense of Christ in the beauty of Nature, but knows this is not true for all:

> These things, these things were here and but the beholder
> Wanting.

It is only when the 'beholder' is spiritually in tune with the Divine in Nature that he finds his consummation in Christ,

> The heart rears wings bold and bolder
> And hurls for him, O half hurls earth for him off under his feet.

Far less successful are the final sonnets from this period, 'The Caged Skylark' and 'The Lantern out of Doors', in which Nature is secondary to the tedious working-out of the moral. In the first, the skylark and the fells seem forced into rhetorical duty to illustrate the theme that man's dual nature is acceptable to Christ:

> Man's spirit will be flesh-bound when found at best,
> But uncumbered.

In 'The Lantern out of Doors' the poet reproves himself for assuming that the worst will befall the good and the beautiful:

> Men go by me whom either beauty bright
> In mould or mind or what not else makes rare,

but Christ has them in His care, and the poet's forebodings are misplaced. Again, the opening image of a lantern being carried into darkness seems an inadequate structure for the laboured moral that follows. The optimism of both poems is too studied to be memorable.

The appeal of the sonnet form to Hopkins reflects both its general nineteenth-century popularity and its personal suitability to a poet of his temperament. Wordsworth and Keats had distinguished the form, and although it also attracted a host of minor poets of little distinction, sonnet anthologies were common. Hopkins was invited to contribute to a prestigious one, edited by Hall Caine, in 1882, but was fortunately rejected (in view of the mediocrity of the other contributors) on the grounds of his original use of the form.

Some thirty of his most important poems are sonnets and offered him a pattern and discipline within which he could execute original variations in overall length, length of line, rhythm, and rhyme-scheme. The emotional and impulsive quality of Hopkins's temperament was well served by having to adapt itself to, and sometimes to adapt, the basic recognised structure.

Meanwhile, life in St Beuno's went on much as usual. There were debates in which he took part, adopting recognisable Hopkins positions: he proposed that 'Eminence in arms is a better object of national ambition than eminence in commerce', and that 'It is never lawful to tell real untruth.' Spelling-bees brought him mixed fortunes: he won one, but was floored in another by 'allegiance'. His health remained uncertain and he was allowed the privilege of rides in a pony and trap to improve it.

But the academic year ended in disappointment when he failed to pass his Theology exam, an unexpected blow and one which deprived him of the extra year at St Beuno's to which he had been looking forward. The failure has been kept secret from the pubic until recent years, Jesuit writers having an understandable reluctance on dwell on the implications, whether for their examination system or the intellectual abilities of their greatest poet. Fr Joseph Rickaby, who had known Hopkins and went on to a distinguished career in the Society, wrote in 1929 to the poet's first Jesuit biographer, 'Don't tell *externs* [the general public] about his failure in theology' (his correspondent did not) and gave the reason: 'He was too Scotist for his examiners.'[40]

A fourth year in Theology was a necessity if a Jesuit was to be appointed to any of the senior positions, from Superior upwards. Hopkins never suggested a wish to rise higher, nor does there seem much evidence that he would have made a good leader of men. The result, therefore, in the end was probably to his benefit and that of posterity.

His ordination as a priest took place on 23 September 1877, when none of his family seem to have been present, although he had kept in regular contact while at St Beuno's and enjoyed a holiday with them the previous month. In October he was sent out into the world to do 'nondescript' work at a Jesuit boarding school, Mount St Mary's, near Sheffield. The post combined teaching, administrative and religious functions, the sort of appointment suitable for a new recruit whose particular talent was not yet evident. Nobody mentioned poetry.

### Notes

1. Carlyle, *Sartor Resartus* (London, 1896) p. xxii.
2. *Further Letters of Hopkins*, p. 124.
3. Fr. R. Clarke SJ, 'The Training of a Jesuit', in *The Nineteenth Century* (August 1896) pp. 211–25. Passages are quoted in Fr. A. Thomas's *Hopkins: The Jesuit*, as here, pp. 155–6.
4. Denis Meadows, *Obedient Men* (London, 1953) p. 143.
5. *Journals of Hopkins*, p. 261.
6. Clement Barraud SJ, *Lays of the Knights* (London, 1898) 'Tell Me Where', pp. 114–16.
7. *Hopkins: Poems*, ed. Gardner and MacKenzie, p. 66.
8. *Journals of Hopkins*, p. 260.
9. Ibid., p. 260.
10. *Letters to Bridges*, p. 231.
11. *Correspondence of Hopkins and R. W. Dixon*, p. 14.
12. *Journals of Hopkins*, p. 278.
13. Published by the International Hopkins Association (Ontario, 1987).
14. 'Wreck of the *Deutschland*', verse 1.
15. *Letters of Hopkins to Bridges*, p. 46.
16. See D. McChesney in the *Casebook* of Hopkins criticism, ed. M. Bottrall (London, 1975) p. 209.
17. Moore, 'Newman and the "Second Spring" of Hopkins's Poetry', *Hopkins Quarterly*, vi: 3 (Fall, 1979) pp. 119ff.
18. See R. V. Schoder in *Hopkins: New Essays* (1989).
19. Quoted in *Journals of Hopkins*, notes, p. 382.
20. *Further Letters of Hopkins*, p. 141.
21. Ibid., p. 139.
22. Quoted in A. Sulloway, *Hopkins and the Victorian Temper* (London, 1972) p. 100. Compare Hopkins's own remarks in *Letters to Bridges*, pp. 54 and 46.
23. *Letters of Hopkins to Bridges*, p. 50.

24. *Poems of Hopkins*, 2nd edn, ed. C. Williams (London, 1944) p. 104.
25. *Letters of Hopkins to Bridges*, p. 46.
26. *Hopkins: Selected Prose*, ed. Roberts (Oxford, 1980) p. 137. The italics are Hopkins's.
27. Fr A. Thomas, *Hopkins the Jesuit*, p. 172.
28. *Journals of Hopkins*, p. 254.
29. *Stonyhurst Magazine*, vol. III, no. 40 (November 1888) p. 236.
30. Ruskin, *Modern Painters*, vol. IV, p. 167, in *Works of Ruskin*, ed. Cook and Wedderburn (London, 1904) vol. VI.
31. Ruskin, ibid., p. 177.
32. See J. H. Buckley, *The Triumph of Time* (Cambridge, Mass., 1967).
33. *Letters of Hopkins to Bridges*, p. 164.
34. *Journals of Hopkins*, p. 130.
35. Quoted Buckley, *The Triumph of Time*, p. 72.
36. E. Schneider, 'The Windhover', in *Hopkins Casebook*, p. 182.
37. *Hopkins: Poems*, 4th edn, p. 198.
38. Quoted Buckley, *The Triumph of Time*, p. 45.
39. *Letters of Hopkins to Bridges*, p. 56.
40. Lahey Papers, Farm St Archives, letter from Rickaby dated 29 June 1929.

# 9

# The Poet and the Priest

*The obedient man ought joyfully to devote himself to any task whatsoever in which the superior desires to employ him to aid the whole body of the religious Institute.*

*Constitutions of the Society of Jesus*[1]

It was unlikely that Hopkins himself was preoccupied with the question of his poetry at a time when his recent ordination and new responsibilities brought more pressing obligations. It was not the time to worry about a hobby when he had the needs of a school to consider and when, in any case, the readership of his own poetry was so tiny and so sceptical.

First established in 1842, Mount St Mary's College had originally been a feeder establishment to Stonyhurst, which provided a more advanced education, but in 1866 it began to enter into direct competition with its rivals by taking pupils beyond the middle-school level. By 1874, its numbers had risen to 150, making new buildings necessary by the time of Hopkins's arrival.

However, the academic standards were not high and one reason for his appointment might have been the need for a top-quality Classics teacher.[2] He complained of a 'mess of employments' in January 1878, but matters then improved and he was given more teaching including one or two of the cleverer (and older) boys. It is not surprising, perhaps, that he always seems to have enjoyed taking the more able pupils and in this case his star pupil, Herbert Berkeley, won prizes in the competitions that took place between Jesuit schools.

Another shipwreck set him writing again. The merchant navy training ship, the *Eurydice*, returning from a voyage to the West Indies, was sunk in a sudden storm off the Isle of Wight in March 1878, with the loss of almost all the 300 young sailors on board. Set as the subject of the Mount St Mary's Verse Prize, it was treated in the country as a whole as a national catastrophe and attracted many would-be poets. Edmund Gosse was inspired to write on it; Sir

Joseph Noel Paton, the artist, produced an account which appeared in *The Scotsman* the day after the tragedy:

> The training-ship Eurydice –
> As tight a craft I ween . . .

and the young Conan Doyle, in all the enthusiasm of his recent Stonyhurst education, wrote of the fatal squall:

> It broke in one moment of blizzard and blindness;
>    The next, like a foul bat, it flapped on its way.
> But our ship and our boys! Gracious Lord, in your kindness,
>    Give help to the mothers who need it today![3]

It must have been a challenge to Hopkins to write on a secular subject which was a greater tragedy in human terms than the Wreck of the Deutschland, but lacked any obvious opportunity for a confessional element, and most readers find it difficult to reconcile the last 34 lines of Catholic discourse on the conversion of England with the rest of the poem. Although this was his second major poem on shipwrecks in two and a half years, it was an interest shared with many other Victorians including novelists, poets, and painters; as the son of a marine loss adjuster Hopkins had particular reason to be aware of such catastrophes.

Compared with the other versions to which reference has been made, Hopkins, as ever, remains distinctively individual, but whereas 'The Wreck of the Deutschland' would have been, in his own words, 'more generally interesting if there were more wreck and less discourse',[4] 'The Wreck of the Eurydice' suffers from the reverse failing and reads at times like an unconventional newspaper report. An initial difficulty is the verse form:

> The Eurydice – it concerned thee, O Lord:
> Three hundred souls, O alas! on board,
>    Some asleep unawakened, all un-
> warned, eleven fathoms fallen
>
> Where she foundered!

For an elegy – which is what, in effect, the poem is – the sprung rhythm and short rhyming lines, together with the usual artillery of

Hopkins's sound effects, create an inappropriately lively mood. Moreover, the poet himself emphasised the importance of reading the poem aloud: 'You must not slovenly read it with the eyes but with your ears, as if the paper were declaiming it at you.'[5] He might have quoted:

> Sharp with her, shórten sáil!
> Too láte; lóst; góne with the gále.

As the imitation of a tragic moment it verges on bathos, which is perilously close at other moments in the poem:

> Marcus Hare, high her captain,
> Kept to her – care-drowned and wrapped in
> Cheer's death, would follow
> His charge through the champ-white water-in-a-wallow,
>
> All under Channel to bury in a beach her
> Cheeks.

The personification of her bows as 'Cheeks' – particularly in a stressed position – only succeeds in being ludicrous.

The transition to a more personal and Catholic conclusion comes at line 85, where the death of the Protestant sailors inspires a lament for England's loss of the Faith and its Catholic shrines; he begs the grieving mothers to pray to Christ for their sons. In April, Hopkins had told Bridges that his muse had turned 'utterly sullen in the Sheffield smoke-ridden air'[6] until 'the foundering of the Eurydice worked on me', but the final impression of the poem remains that of a miscalculation in judgement and taste.

After some preaching at the Mount, including High Mass on Easter Sunday (suggesting his sermons were well thought of), he learnt from the Provincial that he would be needed for teaching at Stonyhurst in the summer term before proceeding to Farm Street where Fr Gallwey 'has some time asked to have me'.[7]

As Hopkins knew, such rapid movements were not uncommon with the Jesuits and he gave every indication of being pleased with these. He went to Stonyhurst on 27 April, explaining to his mother that he was there for the purpose of 'coaching some people . . . for their degrees at the London University'.[8] The College prepared students for exams at matriculation and degree levels as an alternative to attendance at Oxford and Cambridge, which were unacceptable to Catholics for religious reasons. Most of the boys in Rhetoric, the traditional name for the class taught by Hopkins, were entered for matriculation and in the June examination one of them gained fourth place in the country overall. An even greater distinction was achieved at a higher level by Herbert Lucas (with whom Hopkins had talked Scotus six years before on the banks of the Hodder): taking his MA in Classics and Philosophy, he came first in one and second in the other.

It was no doubt pleasing for Hopkins to be working in a school where the academic year 1877–8 was described by a correspondent in *Letters and Notices* as 'one of the most successful we ever had',[9] even when the Prefect of Studies admitted, 'Some people think the boys study too hard.'[10] Perhaps the hard-working atmosphere explains Hopkins telling Bridges, 'I shall never have leisure or desire to write much.'[11] However in June the subject of poetry was raised in a letter to another poet, Canon Richard Watson Dixon, of the Anglican Church, who had taught Hopkins for a brief period at Highgate many years before. He was now a country vicar near Carlisle, working on the five-volume *History of the Church of England* which occupied the last thirty years of his life, but still writing poetry and, in Hopkins's opinion, deserving a higher place than literary fashion had given him:

> if I had written and published works the extreme beauty of which the author himself the most keenly feels and they had fallen out of sight at once and been . . . almost wholly unknown; then, I say, I should feel a certain comfort to be told they had been deeply appreciated by some one person, a stranger . . . [12]

Dixon could not have guessed the sympathetic self-identification that lay behind this letter, for Hopkins did not tell him for almost a year that he, too, wrote poetry. Had he known, he would have detected the undertone of personal experience behind a further remark by his former pupil that 'Disappointments and humiliations embitter the heart and make an aching in the very bones'.[13]

Hopkins had time to write only one poem in his term at Stonyhurst, another of those May verses which he had first composed while at St Mary's Hall some years earlier. This time the model is not Swinburne; the lines are authentic Hopkins, albeit in the romantic mode: May is associated with Mary because of:

Growth in everything –

Flesh and fleece, fur and feather,
Grass and greenworld all together;
Star-eyed strawberry-breasted
Throstle above her nested

Cluster of bugle blue eggs thin
Forms and warms the life within.

The *final* criteria by which Hopkins selects his diction is not meaning
but music, and over and above the memorable series of images in
these lines is the striving for richness of sounds, in alliteration,
internal rhyme, assonance and variety of vowels. The witty energy
of the verse-form is as appropriate as that of the 'Loss of the Eurydice'
was not: in one of the final verses we have a six-word compound
adjective describing a noun in the following line and some surprising
familiarities: 'Well but there was more than this'. It must have been
too much for Stonyhurst tradition: the verse did *not* appear on the
Virgin's statue outside the Boy's Chapel. Hopkins went on to London,
perhaps leaving another puzzled community behind him.

He came to Farm Street Church in early July in the specific role of
preacher. This was both a compliment and a challenge for, lying
between Berkeley Square and Park Lane, this church attracted a
sophisticated congregation and had built up a reputation for its
sermons. Established in 1849, the first Jesuit church in London, it had
recently had the benefit as preacher of Fr James Clare (whom Hopkins
was later to be under in Liverpool), who had drawn large and
fashionable audiences in the period 1866–77.

The Provincial's headquarters had been established nearby in
1873, so that Hopkins was directly under the eye of his superiors.
More comfortably, he was also close to the family home and all the
cultural attractions that the West End offered. What he apparently
did not know at the time was how long the appointment might last,
nor do we know whether his success as preacher would be regarded
as deciding the length of his stay.

He prepared three sermons for delivery in August, not Mayfair's
busiest time, and none survives in full, but on one of them, that for
4 August, we have both his comments and those of Bridges who
came to hear him. Hopkins wrote modestly: 'I was very nervous at
the beginning and not at all after. It was pure forgetting and flurry.

The delivery was not good, but I hope to get a good one in time.'[14]

Perhaps surprisingly, Bridges was impressed. He told a correspondent:

> Gerard Hopkins is in town preaching and confessing at Farm Street. I went to hear him. He is good. He calls here; and we have sweet laughter, and pleasant chat.'

He added: 'He is not at all the worse for being a Jesuit. . . . His poetry is magnificent but 'caviare to the general'.[15]

But he was allowed only four months at Farm Street; the needs of St Aloysius, the Jesuit parish in Oxford, were apparently greater. With the suggestion of tight-lipped despair he told Bridges on a postcard: 'I am to leave London. . . . I daresay we may not meet again for years.'[16]

As if Oxford were a Jesuit mission in Guyana!

### Notes

1.  *Constitutions of the Society of Jesus*, ed. Ganss, p. 249.
2.  F. E. Keegan SJ, 'Hopkins at Mount St Mary's College, 1877–8', *The Mountaineer* (the school magazine of Mount St Mary's) vol. XL, no. 211 (July 1977) pp. 14ff.
3.  Conan Doyle, *Poems* (London, 1922) p. 67.
4.  *Letters to Bridges*, p. 49.
5.  Ibid., pp. 51–2.
6.  Ibid., p. 48.
7.  *Further Letters of Hopkins*, p. 150.
8.  Ibid.
9.  *Letters and Notices*, XII (1879) p. 205.
10. Ibid., X (1875) p. 83.
11. *Letters of Hopkins to Bridges*, p. 54.
12. *Correspondence of Hopkins and R. W. Dixon*, p. 2.
13. Ibid., p. 9.
14. *Letters of Hopkins to Bridges*, p. 57.
15. *Selected Letters of Robert Bridges*, ed. D. Stanford (Newark, 1983) I, p. 127.
16. *Letters of Hopkins to Bridges*, p. 58.

# 10
# Oxford

*How alien it was, how chilling*
Hopkins, *Further Letters*[1]

It might have been no accident that he was sent back to the university town where he had been so happy and so successful: someone of his scholarly interests and possible university contacts could make an important contribution to the reputation of the new Jesuit church recently set up in Oxford. Although the Society had been in the town since 1750 and had a church at St Clements, this was in an unfashionable area, whereas the new one, St Aloysius, built in 1875 at the very top of St Giles, was convenient for North Oxford in general and the central university area in particular.

The Catholic Church had no representation in the Colleges which actively discouraged undergraduates from attending Catholic services, just as the English Catholic hierarchy officially forbade members of their Church from going to either Oxford or Cambridge. But many Catholics had once been Oxford students and, like Hopkins, their memories of their old university were dear. One of these converts, Cardinal Manning, sadly declared at the opening of St Aloysius: 'We are strangers in Jerusalem, and to be strangers in our home is full of pain. We know its every street, and love its every stone.'[2]

Hopkins felt the same sensations of alienation and affection, although he typically refrained from expressing his feelings during his spell at St Aloysius. Later, he told an old Balliol friend, Alexander Baillie:

Not to love my University would be to undo the very buttons of my being and as for the Oxford townspeople I found them in my 10 months' stay among them very deserving of affection – though somewhat stiff, stand-off, and depressed. And in that stay I saw very little of the University. But I could not but feel how alien it was, how chilling, and deeply to be distrusted. I could have wished, and yet I could not, that there had been no one that had known me there. As a fact there were many and those friendly, some cordially so, but with others I cd. not feel at home.[3]

The friends included the Baron de Paravicini, once a fellow student, now a Fellow of Balliol, and his old tutor, Walter Pater, a Fellow of Brasenose, with a house in North Oxford. The friendship with the Paravicini's was life-long and on his death they presented St Aloysius with a holy-water font in his memory. Pater offered a different sort of tribute in his greatest work, *Marius the Epicurean* (1885), whose hero with his 'almost morbid religious idealism, and . . . healthful love of the country' seems partly modelled on the Hopkins he had known.[4]

Now, in 1878, Hopkins was involved in a more public religious conflict, with the Jesuits making converts amongst both town and gown, but it was 'far harder to set the Isis on fire than the Thames', he reported to Bridges.[5] In March, *The Tablet* had given the names of 'seven members of the University' who had 'just gone to Rome',[6] while the leading article of an Oxford newspaper in June declared:

Unless something is done . . . to counteract the subtle persuasiveness of Roman Catholicism as represented by a company of clever and polished controversialists . . . the reception of large numbers of undergraduates every term into the Roman Communion may be taken for granted.[7]

'Polished' might have been the word to describe Hopkins's Superior, Fr Parkinson ('suave . . . almost to demureness' was the phrase used in his obituary[8]). Once an Anglican parson, his own *alma mater* was Cambridge, which he always regarded as the better place. Again, looking back to his time in Oxford, Hopkins was to say that he 'did not quite hit if off with Fr Parkinson'[9] and being his sole assistant had a great deal of work put on him, especially when his Superior fell ill and needed two periods of convalescence. The burden on Hopkins can be judged by what happened after he left St Aloysius, when, in 1880, the parish was granted *four* assistants.

Yet, despite the parish work, there must have been something congenial in the Oxford air, for he composed a number of poems between November 1878 and October 1879. In contrast with the exuberance of St Beuno's, most of them are characterised by a mood of gentle melancholy. 'Binsey Poplars' nostalgically evokes a lost natural beauty and seems to symbolise the sadness of the passing of time itself.

The first verse paints beautiful pictures of the shadows once cast by trees, falling like the thongs and buckles of a sandal across river and grass, but not one of these trees has been spared the axe. In the second verse the poet laments the thoughtlessness of attempts to improve the countryside, which, however well-meaning, destroy its special character, 'unselve / The sweet especial scene'. (The melancholy recalls the felling of an ash-tree in his St Mary's Hall days when 'I wished to die and not to see the inscapes of the world destroyed any more.'[10])

All Hopkins's skill in rhyme and alliteration is employed in evoking a gentle sense of loss and pain and in a verse-form which was original to him. It is illuminating to compare this environmental plea with the later 'Inversnaid', written after he had been pent for two years in the dreadful cities of Liverpool and Glasgow. The driving energy and rhythms of the Scottish poem reflect both the change in landscapes, from quiet river-meadow to bleak moorland torrent and the contrasting biographical context of the controllable unhappiness of Oxford and the impending liberation of the return from Scotland to Manresa for his tertianship.

Hopkins's success may be compared, too, with Bridges's failure on a similar subject: in one of the latter's collections,[11] the concluding verse of a poem describes the fall of an oak-tree:

> Anon a sound appalling,
> As a hundred years of pride
> Crashed, in the silence falling:
> And the shadowy pine-trees sighed.

With due recognition for Bridges's traditional views on poetic diction, it is difficult in these lines to see any more than a token attempt to convey a sense of loss at the tree's destruction: from the abstractness of 'A hundred years of pride' to the conventional 'pine-trees sighed' we have the impression of a purely literary exercise in which feeling is almost intentionally avoided.

But it must be said that the poetry of the Oxford period – or, more properly, the second Oxford period – lacks the excitement and intensity of Hopkins's best work. 'Duns Scotus's Oxford' seems a poem looking for, rather than finding a theme, at first, like 'Binsey

Poplars', lamenting how the city's modern suburbs have upset the traditional and charming mingling of urban and pastoral, and then, in its second part, celebrating Scotus's association with the university.

In 'Henry Purcell' weight of rhetoric overwhelms the content, requiring two letters of explanation to Bridges in May 1879 and January 1883. Hopkins declares in the poem that his particular interest in Purcell's music is aroused when it, by chance, reveals the composer's individuality, the 'forgèd feature', and he draws an elaborate comparison with a great 'stormfowl' whose flapping wings as he takes off for flight may attract our admiration, although the action is only incidental to the bird's purpose.

'The Candle Indoors' is a companion-piece to the later 'Lantern Outdoors', both poems suggesting the dangers in excessive concern over the conduct of others, the Oxford poem recommending our own self-examination first, 'Mend first and vital candle in close heart's vault'. In 'The Handsome Heart' the popular theme of children's innocence is again explored and the supremacy of natural virtue declared over sensuous and aesthetic beauty:

> Mannerly-hearted! more than handsome face –
> Beauty's bearing or muse of mounting vein.

He wrote to Bridges about this time: 'If we care for fine verses how much more for a noble life,'[12] and the theme of the three beauties – of body, mind, and soul – was to become a sermon at his next posting.[13] Of the corruption of innocence by the adult world he had said at St Beuno's:

> Have, get, before it cloy,
> Before it cloud, Christ, Lord, and sour with sinning,
> Innocent mind and May day in girl and boy,

and uttered the same warning in one of his Irish poems, 'On the Portrait of Two Beautiful Young People', where he anticipated the work of the 'dark tramplers, tyrant years'.

These feelings are important in 'The Bugler's First Communion', composed at Oxford and based on an experience at the Cowley Barracks which was part of his pastoral responsibilities in the district. Both theme and style make it a thoroughly representative poem. Its opening mixes colloquial and mannered writing:

A bugler boy from barrack (it is over the hill
There) – boy bugler, born, he tells me, of Irish
Mother to an English sire (he
Shares their best gifts surely, fall how things will)

but the variants on normal order and diction are minimal, in keeping with the simplicity of the subject, a young bugler taking his first communion in all humility of spirit. The poet consigns him to God's protection, although fearing the corrupting influence of a soldier's life (in a letter to Bridges he wishes for him a soldierly death rather than loss of innocence[14]):

> . . . may he not rankle and roam
> In backwheels though bound home?

There is an unashamed, and no doubt unconscious sexual suggestion in the poem's carefully alliterated descriptions of the young man: 'Breathing bloom of a chastity in mansex fine', 'Yields tender as a pushed peach' and 'fresh-youth fretted in a bloomfall' and nowhere else does Hopkins come so close to the warm, sensual spirit of Whitman. Yet it is not erotic: the basis of the affection remains moral and religious, and duty and service are ideals for both priest and soldier. In an aggressive imperial period, when British arms were active in Afghanistan and Southern Africa, Hopkins's high valuation of the British soldier would have been shared by many Victorians.

'Morning, Midday, and Evening Sacrifice's is a simple but sensuous exhortation to devotion to God at all stages of one's life and had the distinction of appearing during Hopkins's life-time in Canon Dixon's *Bible Birthday Book* in 1887. On the other hand, the more characteristic 'Andromeda' (August 1879) was rejected by Hall Caine for the sonnet anthology he published in 1882. Its Catholic didacticism – if Caine understood the message – could have been reason for its refusal. Greek myth disguises the theme of the plight of the Roman Catholic Church (Andromeda) threatened by the socialism and atheism of contemporary Europe, from which it will be saved by the eternally vigilant Christ (Perseus).

Hopkins was not normally respectful of classical myth in modern poetry and its use here may conceal a deeper disquiet about the precariousness of his own sense of vocation. It was in Oxford that he confessed to Bridges a cooling-off in religious feeling and where the 'patience' of the last lines of 'Andromeda' became a necessary state of mind. 'Let him who is in desolation,' said St Ignatius, 'labour to hold on in patience, such patience as makes against the vexations that harass him.'[15]

This state of mind forms the subject of 'Peace', his last poem at Oxford, whose title expresses a wish, not an achievement. Like 'Pied Beauty', it is, in its author's terminology, a 'curtal' sonnet of eleven lines of Alexandrines and despite the deceptively soothing image of 'wild wooddove, shy wings shut', quickly speaks of the restlessness of the poet's heart:

> When, when, Peace, will you, Peace? I'll not play hypocrite
>
> To own my heart . . .

This dramatic, questioning self, with its colloquialisms (as well as plays with language) and overriding of line endings is a voice that becomes more familiar in the Dublin sonnets, where it is even the same tranquillising patience that is asked for:

> Patience, hard thing! the hard thing but to pray,
> But bid for, Patience is!

In the Oxford sonnet Patience is seen as the first crucial stage to Peace, a Peace characterised not by inactivity but, for the poet, by work.

In February 1879, the question of publication arose: Bridges made some suggestion that the rising critic, Edmund Gosse, might be prepared to write a comment which could prepare the way for publishing some of Hopkins's poems. Hopkins was not impressed:

> If I were going to publish, and that soon, such a mention would be 'the puff preliminary', which it wd. be dishonourable of me to allow of. . . . If I did, a mention in one article of one review would do very little indeed, especially as publishing now is out of the question.[16]

The latter was so because he had not asked for authority from his Jesuit superiors to publish, but, if some one in authority knew of my having some poems printable and suggested my doing it I shd. not refuse, I shd. be partly, though not altogether, glad. But that is very unlikely.

The conditions and qualifications – 'if' used three times, the conditional tense, the cautious 'partly, though not altogether' – reflect his indecisiveness. Yet he is definite on one point: the poems should be kept:

All therefore that I think of doing is to keep my verses together in one place . . . that, if anyone shd. like, they might be published after my death. And that again is unlikely, as well as remote.

After more excuses – if he were to publish, more would be expected, and how could he in his position promise more? – he concludes his apology:

I cannot spend time on poetry, neither have I the inducements and inspirations that make others compose. Feeling, love in particular, is the great moving power and spring of verse and the only person I am in love with seldom, especially now, stirs my heart sensibly and when he does I cannot always make capital of it, it would be a sacrilege to do so.

The 'only person' is Christ, and the confession helps to explain the melancholy tone of his Oxford poetry, although he also adds 'I have of myself made verse so laborious'. The picture given of a scruple-ridden, artistically punctilious poet is a sad one, although something has to be conceded to his life-long tendency to react to experience by going to emotional extremes. Like other melancholics, such as Edward Thomas and Ivor Gurney, Hopkins knew both high exhilaration and deep depression; the 'real' Hopkins is a complex figure, whose individual statements and moods should always be cautiously judged in assessing the character that lies behind them.

Not a great deal can be said of the few sermons that survive from this time. One preached on the Feast of the Precious Blood in July 1879, with its play on literal and metaphorical senses of 'blood', might have been found hard going in the workaday atmosphere of St Clements. More to the listeners' understanding, perhaps, was the sermon preached in September on the obligation of going to Sunday mass; reminding them of the usual duties, Hopkins yet takes care to explain that good reason may exempt attendance at mass:

> you are to know that in the Church's laws any really reasonable cause excuses. And mark this: a reasonable cause makes it no sin at all to break the commandment.[17]

This appeal to the priority of reason over tradition and convention contrasts with a more authoritarian impression of his moral views that we sometimes receive from his writing.

After ten months at Oxford, he was again on the move. Although we know he was not entirely happy there, we do not know whether it was considered he had given satisfaction or not. He was told that his next appointment was to work on a city centre parish in Liverpool, but before that he was needed for a short period to help in another northern industrial parish. It was here that he enjoyed some of his happiest months in the Society.

## Notes

1. *Further Letters of Hopkins*, p. 244.
2. Quoted in a letter to *The Tablet* (15 December 1877) p. 750.
3. *Further Letters of Hopkins*, p. 244.
4. Pater, *Marius the Epicurean* (Oxford, 1986) p. 17.
5. *Letters of Hopkins to Bridges*, p. 61.
6. *The Tablet* (March, 1878) p. 407.
7. Quoted in *Letters and Notices*, vol. xii (1879) p. 115.
8. *Letters and Notices*, vol. xxvii (1903–4) p. 556.
9. *Letters of Hopkins to Bridges*, p. 97.
10. *Journals of Hopkins*, p. 230.
11. Bridges, *Shorter Poems* (1890), Book iv, no. 12.
12. *Letters of Hopkins to Bridges*, p. 61.
13. *Sermons of Hopkins*, ed. Devlin, pp. 34ff.
14. *Letters of Hopkins to Bridges*, p. p. 92.
15. *Spiritual Exercises*, ed. Rickaby, p. 70.
16. *Letters of Hopkins to Bridges*, pp. 65–6.
17. *Sermons of Hopkins*, ed. Devlin, p. 237.

# 11
# At Bedford Leigh

*Is Industry free to tumble out whatever horror of refuse it may
have arrived at into the nearest crystal brook? Regardless of gods
and men and little fishes. Is Free Industry free to convert all our
rivers into Acherontic sewers; England generally into a roaring,
sooty smith's forge? Are we all doomed to eat dust, as the Old
Serpent was, and to breathe solutions of soot?*

Carlyle, *Shooting Niagara*[1]

*The air is charged with smoke as well as damp; but the people are
hearty.*

Hopkins to Bridges[2]

It was early in October 1879 that Hopkins came to the parish of
Bedford Leigh, some twelve miles to the south of Manchester, his
first extensive acquaintance with the industrial North, as compared
with the rural surroundings of Stonyhurst and Mount St Mary's. His
Jesuit predecessors had worked at Leigh since the early seventeenth
century, building up a remarkable reputation for their devoted work
in the parish. Fr Middlehurst, who had been parish priest from 1845
until his death in 1877, had been so popular that when the Provincial
had wished to send him elsewhere for a change, Protestants and
Catholics had signed a petition which had succeeded in keeping him
in Leigh. The same priest's funeral brought 20,000 mourners on to
the streets.

Fr Middlehurst's replacement was Fr James Fanning, Hopkins's
superior, who had worked with schools and guilds for seven years
in Glasgow. Spoken of as a man of energy and efficiency, his
contemporaries sometimes complained of his off-hand treatment of
people and 'pronounced opinions',[3] but he is never mentioned by
Hopkins during the two and a half months of his stay.

Only one poem was written while Hopkins was at Leigh, the
celebratory 'At the Wedding March', whose only interest to posterity

may be the innocent frankness with which he anticipates the prospect of marital fecundity:

> God with honour hang your head,
> Groom, and grace you, bride, your bed
> With lissome scions, sweet scions,
> Out of hallowed bodies bred.

We do not know whether the Lancashire couple concerned read or heard the poem: if they were embarrassed by it, they would not have been the first or last audience of his to be offended by his disregard of convention.

Leigh was not the place for poetry, a town 'in a flat [hollow]; the houses red, mean, and two storied; there are a dozen mills or so, and coalpits also; the air is charged with smoke as well damp',[4] yet if the appearance was grim, the people more than made up for their blighted environment, as he was soon to notice when he favourably compared them with the 'unsatisfactory' population of Oxford where 'every prospect pleases and only man is vile'.[5] 'In the Valley of the Elwy' had deplored that so beautiful a country as Wales housed such unredeemed inhabitants as the unconverted Welsh, and sweeping conclusions about the relationship between character and environment had to be further qualified at Leigh. If it was true that the place was 'bleared, smeared with toil', could its present parishioners be blamed for causing the contamination? And they had certainly not lost their 'cheer and charm'. 'The place is very gloomy but our people hearty and devoted.'[6]

The 'education' of Hopkins at Bedford Leigh anticipated a similar experience for another Jesuit, George Tyrrell, who served in a parish not far away at St Helens in 1893–4. That area was described by Hopkins as

> probably the most repulsive place in Lancashire or out of the Black Country. The stench of sulphuretted hydrogen rolls in the air and films of the same gas form on railing and pavement.[7]

Judging by Tyrrell's friend and biographer, Maud Petre, the place made a similar impression on the later Jesuit:

> It was hardly the ideal post for an imaginative and highly strung Irishman, with a specially fastidious sense of smell, a keen love of

Nature, and a delicate appreciation of the importance of trifles and the value of words and manner'.[8]

His feeling for Nature was as sensitive as Hopkins's:

Dead calm, vertical smoke, moist but bright atmosphere. Cloud continents with blue skies and lakes; green-gold fields here and there amid the general shadows. Cows, birds, dogs audible, and men in the distance; and the mysterious rustle of autumn decay.[9]

Yet, like Hopkins at Bedford Leigh, his brief time at St Helens was one of the happiest periods of his life, when he absorbed himself in the life of the parish and put on one side his doubts about the Jesuits and their interpretation of St Ignatius's teaching. That peace was short. A natural rebel, his published views soon brought him into conflict with his colleagues and the Church; expelled from the Society and in effect excommunicated, he died an early death at the age of 48.

For all his originality, Hopkins was no rebel in spiritual matters; Tyrrell's way could not have been his, but it was the busy run of life that occupied him at Bedford Leigh and the gratitude and simple faith of the parishioners that moved him: masses, sermons, confessions, duty at the workhouse gave him no time for worrying about poetry and the state of his vocation.

Apart from Liverpool, Bedford Leigh offered him the best opportunity for developing the range and technique of his homilies, but changing tastes and the question of oral delivery make it virtually impossible for later readers to judge how successful they might have been. Hopkins would have been the first to recognise that his primary purpose was to instruct, not entertain, and the Leigh sermons give every impression of care in the selection of language and imagery. He told Bridges that he felt happy in delivering them, and the characteristic touches of quirkiness in style and idea do not affect their general simplicity and directness.

We have ten of these sermons, preached at regular intervals from 5 October (the week of his arrival in Leigh) to 14 December (two weeks before his departure). The first is a delightful one on Christ's ability to cure both physical and spiritual ills and is based on the story in the New Testament of the man sick of the palsy:

Imagine the surprise of those assembled, the sound of feet

scrambling on the tiles, the light of heaven breaking in, a mattress coming through swung by four ends of rope, and a man that had for many years perhaps been confined to one room now dangling between heaven and earth over the heads of a crowd of strangers.[10]

One hopes this ludicrous picture appealed to the congregation as it deserved. On the other hand, the opening of the sermon for 9 November with a characteristically outré image mixing odd and familiar might have caused a few puzzled expressions:

In this Gospel two miracles, not one after the other, but first the beginning of one, then the other, then the end of the first: as when you drive a quill or straw or knitting needle through an egg, it pierces first the white, then the yolk, then the white again.[11]

These passages illustrate the qualities of narrative, originality and humour which he employed with his Leigh congregation. The homely and familiar is also associated with a surprising realism in this attack on drink:

Drunkenness is shameful, it makes the man a beast; it drowns noble reason, their eyes swim, they hiccup in their talk, they gabble and blur their words, they stagger and fall. . . . Times may be good, wages may abound, and yet in the house is seen want and slovenly disorder, for gold and silver and clothes and furniture and all are gone one way, down the belly.[12]

He adopts the role of the ironic narrator:

Bad company seem hearty friends, goodnatured companions and such as a man should have: must not a man have his friend, his companion, unbend from his work at times, see company and life? Must he sit mum? must he mope at home?[13]

The more solemn tones of his sermon of 23 November on Christ as Hero are anticipated in a letter written in October[14] in which he consoles Bridges who had been experiencing doubts about himself as a poet. In reassuring him, he defined three sorts of beauty: 'beauty of the body' ('But this kind of beauty is dangerous'); 'beauty of the mind'; and finally 'more beautiful than the beauty of the mind is beauty of character' – which Bridges had.

These distinctions, at greater length, are introduced into the sermon on Christ 'Our Hero' (Carlyle had written that 'The greatest of all Heroes is one – whom we do not name here!'[15]), which perhaps comes nearest to modern expectations of Victorian religious oratory – laudatory, incantatory, sentimental. For all that, it has a direct personal quality which lends it a certain power:

> You know how books of tales are written, that put one man before the reader and shew him off handsome for the most part and brave and call him My Hero or Our Hero. Often mothers make a hero of a son; girls of a sweetheart [Hopkins was to be forbidden to use the word in Liverpool] and good wives of a husband. Soldiers make a hero of a great general, a party of its leader, a nation of any great man that brings it glory. . . . But Christ, he is the hero.[16]

At a time when he was fulfilling most obviously his vocation as a priest, it must have been at least irritating to find he was still expected to interest himself in being published as a poet. The well-intentioned Dixon had suggested as far back as April that he should make an appreciative mention of Hopkins as a poet in an 'abrupt footnote' in his *History of the English Church* and in October that he would try to get 'The Loss of the Eurydice' published in a Carlisle paper.

Hopkins refused both offers, the second as vehemently as he had ever spoken to Dixon ('To publish my manuscript . . . is a breach of trust'), and the disagreement blew over without any harm done or poem published. He had no inclination to test article 273 in the Jesuit Constitutions: 'It will not be permissible to publish books without the approval and permission of the superior general.' 'Want of fame as a poet,' said Hopkins, was the least of his 'mortifications'.[17]

When he came to Leigh, he had known that it was only a temporary posting and that his final destination was the Jesuit parish in Liverpool, and by 30 December 1879 he was in the city. Intellectually, he had accepted the 'gingerbread permanence' of the Society's postings and proudly explained to his Mother that 'ours can never be an abiding city nor any one of us know what a day may bring forth'.[18] Emotionally he developed strong attachments to places – Oxford, Manresa, Stonyhurst, North Wales – and the pain of uprooting he describes when moving from Manresa to St Mary's Hall must have been repeated more than once in his life: 'I feel the strangeness of the place, and the noviceship after two years seems like a second home.'[19]

When George Tyrrell left St Helens in 1894, with a year of devoted work behind him, he had resisted invitations to continue in the parish. He felt that for such a man as himself it would have meant the evasion of his personal destiny, a 'sort of moral suicide'.[20] For how long would Hopkins, too, have continued to feel a fulfilled parish priest? His career is full of such unanswerable questions. Like his own Caradoc, who slew the one he loved, he was destined to cry, 'My heart, where have we been? What have we seen, my mind?'[21] and find rest neither in place nor spirit.

### Notes

1. 'Shooting Niagara', in Carlyle's *Critical and Miscellaneous Essays* (London, 1894) IV, p. 240.
2. *Letters of Hopkins to Bridges*, p. 90.
3. *Letters and Notices*, XXVI (1901–2) obituary of Fr Fanning, p 431.
4. *Letters of Hopkins to Bridges*, p. 90.
5. Ibid., p. 90.
6. *Correspondence of Hopkins and R. W. Dixon*, p. 29.
7. *Letters of Hopkins to Bridges*, p. 90.
8. M. D. Petre, *Life of Tyrrell* (London, 1912) II, p. 35.
9. Quoted in Petre, ibid., p. 136.
10. *Sermons of Hopkins*, ed. Devlin, p. 26.
11. Ibid., p. 30.
12. Ibid., p. 41.
13. Ibid., p. 41.
14. *Letters of Hopkins to Bridges*, p. 95.
15. Carlyle, *On Heroes and Hero-Worship* (London, 1894) p. 16.
16. *Sermons of Hopkins*, p. 34.
17. *Correspondence of Hopkins and R. W. Dixon*, p. 28.
18. *Further Letters of Hopkins*, p. 142.
19. Ibid., p. 112. Compare the impression of Fr Eyre, the Rector, when Hopkins moved from Stonyhurst to Dublin in 1884: 'This good father felt leaving very much' (quoted Chapter 14 *post*).
20. Petre, *Life of Tyrrell*, II, p. 35.
21. *Hopkins: Poems*, 4th edn, p. 189.

# 12
# Liverpool

*Even the little children of our cities and towns look care-worn, as,
indeed they well may, while snatching a brief precarious breathing
time from the primitive toil in the workshop or manufactory. . . .
[There are] large sections of the community who, rightly or wrongly
. . . are animated by a deep spirit of discontent with, and mutiny
against, the existing social order. . . . History shows clearly enough
that the decay of patriotism among the masses is ever a grave
symptom of national sickness.*

*The Tablet*, March 1879[1]

If St Joseph's at Bedford Leigh was a benign example of a northern
industrial parish, St Francis Xavier's in Liverpool could only be
characterised as its opposite, its problems all too evident to its
hardworking priests:

> I am brought face to face with the deepest poverty and misery in
> my district.
>     The drunkards go on drinking, the filthy, as the scripture says,
> are filthy still: human nature is so inveterate. Would that I had
> seen the last of it.[2]

The church itself had been built in 1848 in Salisbury Street, three-
quarters of a mile north-west of the present Lime Street Station, a
part of the city which even then was down-at-heel:

> The district extending from Islington to Everton Crescent was one
> vast piece of waste ground . . . a mere dumping-place for refuse,
> a horse-training place for livery stable keepers, and was the great
> theatre of war for lads of all sizes, creeds, and nationalities.[3]

The original small and struggling school, at which the ubiquitous
Fr Gallwey, when he was a scholastic, had polished desks to save

money, had grown to 400 pupils by Hopkins's time, although teaching at it was not to be part of his responsibilities. In a large community of eleven Jesuits, his role was to share the parochial tasks of his colleagues, preaching, visiting, attending the work-house, hearing confessions (which might mean hours at a time in the confessional) and sometimes saying mass at nearby Lydiate where a local benevolent family, the Lightbounds, lived.

For one who admired the elegance of London's West End, the city architecture of Liverpool must have been a shock; not unlike Bedford Leigh, perhaps, but multiplied endlessly, 'Miles of dull, monotonous and ugly streets in which not only the poor but the middle classes of the town are condemned to live',[4] helping to produce the criminality and ill-health for which the city was notorious. In December 1877, under the heading of 'The Liverpool Black Book', the *Tablet* printed a review of the annual report of the Chief Constable of Liverpool, remarking, 'Anything more gloomy we never read.' Pointing to the vast number of arrests and the preponderance of female prisoners, it noted that drink, 'this monster evil', was a major cause of convictions, with most arrests taking place on a Saturday or a Sunday after the pubs had closed. Almost a thousand of these served half-a-million people at a time when nineteenth-century England was consuming record quantities of beer and spirits.[5]

If Hopkins had been aware of the drink problem at Bedford Leigh, how much more must it, and worse matters, have come home to him as he did his long hours of visiting to 'Jenkinson Street and Gomer Street and Back Queen Ann Street and Torbock Street and Bidder Street and Birchfield Street and Bickerstaffe Street'.[6] The grinding repetition of words and syntax reflect all too plainly that 'the parish work of Liverpool is very wearying to mind and body'.[7]

Neither he nor the *Tablet* directly refers to a yet more unpleasant social phenomenon (though his complaint to Bridges that 'the filthy . . . are filthy still' perhaps conceals what he had in mind): the rampant prostitution of the area. One rector of St Francis Xavier calculated that there were 400 'bad houses' in the district and in 1887 the Jesuits felt impelled to establish a local society to try and suppress them. Catholics were encouraged to do all they could to 'preserve their children from the evil influence of such foul contagion'.[8]

Coming from Bedford Leigh with its fine community spirit and homely Catholicism, this abuse of women encouraged by women themselves was a ghastly milestone in the human experience of a man whose view of them in his poems and letters was normally so idealistic. 'I have a kind of spooniness and delight over married people,' he wrote to Bridges shortly after the latter's wedding, 'especially if they say "my wife", "my husband", or shew the wedding ring.'[9]

To be expected to write poetry in such a 'hellhole' as Liverpool[10] seemed blasphemy, and time in any case always seemed lacking:

> When you have a parish you can no longer . . . have intellectual interests.

> No time for writing anything serious.

> I shall have less time than ever.[11]

The letters are full of complaints and regrets: excessive work, tiredness and illness, political and social disaffection . . . little mention of friends and virtually none of the Jesuit community. Whatever happened, a demanding and monotonous round of duties had to be carried through. There was something thoughtless about expecting him to deliver a sermon within six days of his arrival on 30 December; in this parish of 10,000 souls, congregations had got used to the best, whether it was from the famous Dominican Tom Burke or the silver-tongued Fr Clare himself, the community Superior, whose 'somewhat rough and unadorned eloquence' helped to drive home religious truths, assisted by an 'expressive countenance' and a 'commanding presence'.[12]

It was said of him that he 'expected too much of [his staff] . . . [and] seemed to think all ought to be as ready in the pulpit as he was',[13] but for his first sermon Hopkins rose to the occasion on a subject very close to him: this was the nature of God's love which, so he had said, had lost its power of stirring his heart at Oxford a year before. The words are directed at all those who feel the inadequacy and insincerity of their feelings for God. Dramatically, and significantly, he adopts the first person:

> I have searched my conscience, I have with whatever shame told all my sins, I have heard my absolution at the priest's lips spoken, I have done the penance enjoined, and I have no peace . . .[14]

We recall his worries to Dixon that he had spent too much time on poetry and not enough on his life as a priest, and we may look ahead, too, to his harsh self-searching about motive and achievement in his Irish retreats and poems. What solution could he offer the Liverpudlian congregation (and himself)? It was to practise duty and obedience, for since 'All love is seen in the doing the beloved's will,' then the conclusion must be that 'Willing obedience is a subject's love to his sovereign.' 'Duty is love.'[15] It has a chilling sound.

Scruples, lack of time and lack of inspiration meant little verse. In May 1880 he told Canon Dixon: '26 lines is the whole I have written in more than half a year, since I left Oxford'[16] (he was refering to 'At the Wedding March' and the incomplete 'St Winefred's Well'). In June he lamented to Bridges that he had written only two poems in nine months and enclosed 'Spring and Fall' with the observation that 'Liverpool is of all places the most museless'.[17] And finally, in April 1881, he declared, 'Every impulse and spring of art seems to have died in me.'[18]

It is, of course, paradoxical that he can complain about lack of time for poetry and as frequently of his waste of priestly time upon it. He engaged in a two-way traffic of verse with Bridges and took up Dixon's suggestion to send some earlier sonnets – which were rejected – for Hall Caine's anthology. These and other subjects ensured no shortage of literary discussion while he was at Liverpool. The Jesuit priest and the Catholic poet were forced to co-exist, and whether such a partnership (or conflict) can be called tragic or creative must remain open to debate in terms of our own assumptions about the working of the human psyche.

To Fr Clare he must have seemed an exotic cuckoo in the workaday community nest, with little in common personally with his colleagues, and we know of only one fellow-priest of whom he made a friend. A certain Father Hilton was 'yokemate' with Hopkins for nearly two years on that 'laborious mission'.[19] 'He used to come up to me and say, "Gerard, you are a good soul" and that I was a comfort to him in his troubles.' Near the end of 1881, he visited a sick family in Jenkinson Street, caught typhoid and died.

If endings like this were tragic, they were also inspirational and in the heroic mode of Jesuit martyrdom. Another death with a strong human interest moved Hopkins to write 'Felix Randal' (April 1880), said to be based on a parishioner who died of tuberculosis at the age of 31.[20] His occupation as farrier links him as much to the countryside as to the town, and the picture of a once proud and lusty man brought low by sickness is touched by both compassion and nobility. The element of dialect, 'Being anointed and all' and 'God rest him all road ever he offended' fits uneasily into the general style of the poem, but overall there is an almost Tolstoyan feeling for both the beauty and corruptibility of human strength.

But the sermons had not been going well. His second, on God's Kingdom, had drawn a comparison with the English political structure, on the rightness of which, he declared, 'We have no two thoughts about the matter':

> we find the queen on her throne, houses of parliament, judges sitting or going, the army, the police, the postoffice at work; the common good is being provided for, we share it more or less, we share the common weal.[21]

It smacks of complacency and, what is worse, Hopkins can hardly have believed it. He had said in 1871: 'England has grown hugely wealthy but this wealth has not reached the working classes,'[22] and re-affirmed that radical view sixteen years later in 'Tom's Garland': 'The curse of our times is that many do not share [in the Commonwealth]'.[23] Neither the poor nor the Liverpool Irish could have listened happily to this sermon.

By the end of it, Hopkins seems to have noticed the unresponsiveness of his congregation:

> But, brethren, that I may not be too long and weary you, here against my first purpose I have resolved to give over for tonight.[24]

(The colloquialism comes too late to bring the subject down to earth.) Confessing he has taken on too much, he adds: 'The heavenly Jerusalem will not be huddled in a corner' and promises that next week he would consider the 'famous and fatal fall of Man', an alluring alliteration which raised the doubts of Fr Clare, for Hopkins put a note before the text of the following week's sermon, explaining:

> I was not allowed to take this title and on the printed bills it was covered by a blank slip pasted over. The text too I changed . . . and had to leave out or reword all passages speaking of God's kingdom as falling.

Here follows what eventually becomes a broadly narrative (and often moving) treatment of the Fall, Miltonic in some of its rhetorical quality ('What flower, what fruitful tree, what living thing was there in Paradise so lovely as Eve?'), completely traditional in its view of man's first disobedience.

After this, there fell a silence of two months from the pulpit, perhaps as welcome to Hopkins as to the congregation. It must have been some comfort in March to be told by Canon Dixon that he had read copies of poems sent him by Hopkins 'with the greatest admiration', and Dixon commented on their power of 'carrying one out of one's self with healing' – presumably he meant some Aristotelian cathartic effect. With characteristic sensitivity he noted that 'The Wreck of the Deutschland' had 'such elements of deep distress in it' that one read it with particular interest.[25]

On 25 April it was back to the rack of the pulpit with a disquisition on the role of the Paraclete, the Holy Spirit, the 'one who encourages', and for which he found an analogy in a traditional English game:

> One sight is before my mind, it is homely but it comes home: you have seen at cricket, how one of the batsmen at the wicket has made a hit and wants to score a run, the other doubts, hangs back, or is ready to run in again, how eagerly the first will cry 'Come on, come on'.[26]

Perhaps cricket was no more familiar to this inner city parish than plays on words, but in any case the sermon began plaintively (in manuscript): 'Notes (for it seems that written sermons do no good)', followed almost immediately by another parenthesis, 'however, the Rector wishes me to write'. Clearly there was disagreement why Hopkins's sermons had not been successful.

On the next two sermons he noted they were not preached at all, whereas on Friday 16 July he preached at half an hour's notice. ('Fr Clare,' said a Jesuit obituarist, 'risked a good deal at times in sending fathers out in haste and unprepared to preach.'[27]) Of this one, he wryly remarked that he thought the congregation had been weeping, but it turned out to be perspiration they were wiping away because of the hot weather.[28]

It was after a sermon on 24 July that one of his hearers came up to him and intimated that Fr Clare was the better preacher, confessing at the same time that he had been 'sleeping for parts of it'.[29] As this particular homily only survives in note form, it is difficult to know with whom to be more sympathetic, Hopkins or his audience.

Surprising perhaps that in the midst of these disappointments, and in one of the hottest summers for years, during which he was unwell, he could write during his annual eight-day retreat in August some of his finest reflections on the opening words of St Ignatius's Principle and Foundation, 'Man was created to praise, reverence, and serve God':

> I find myself with my pleasures and pains, my powers and my experiences, my deserts and guilt, my shame and sense of beauty, my dangers, hopes, fears, and all my fate, more important to myself than anything I see.[30]

This selfhood comes from God, thus giving divine sanction to individuality and the uniqueness of personal experience. The Paterian suggestion of the supremacy of the passing moment, however, is definitively limited by the moral and religious basis of Hopkins's thinking.

One may associate with this fine passage the poem 'As Kingfishers catch fire', which has no manuscript dating and has been ascribed to the period 1877–81. Orthodox in form, the sonnet is a joyful exposition of Scotist selfhood, the individuality of things which is also celebrated in 'Pied Beauty'. The later exposition is more philosophical, but no less energetic:

> I say more: the just man justices;
> > Keeps graces: that keeps all his goings graces;
> Acts in God's eyes what in God's eyes he is –
> > Christ.

Whereas in 'Hurrahing in Harvest', God is present in the 'world-wielding shoulder' of the hills, Christ in this poem may be experienced through the actions of men. If this is a poem of 1881, it reflects the change of emphasis in Hopkins's outlook from the world of Nature to the lives of men. The poet had, after all, seen Christ in Felix Randal and the parishioners of Bedford Leigh.

The only other poem inspired in Liverpool (more accurately, Lydiate, just outside), was 'Spring and Fall', 'not founded on any real incident'.[31] This was one of the poems included in the small selection made by Bridges soon after Hopkins's death for the authoritative collection of Victorian poetry, *The Poets and the Poetry of the Century* (1893) and has remained one of his best loved pieces.

Earthly impermanence is a sombre theme which recurs throughout Hopkins's work, yet the experience of it is common to all, a part of real life that is regularly recreated in art.

The choice of a young child whose innocence intuitively recognises this tragic truth is characteristic of Hopkins's perception of the child as one whose insight into reality is finer than that of the coarsened adult. The central character determines the simplicity of form and style, for if lines 3–4 rely on distortions of syntax, both these lines and much of the rest of the poem suggest the tones of the speaking voice. The rhyme, including internal and half-rhyme, assonance and alliteration, build a web of musical effect, for which the stage is set in the opening lines: *Mar-, gar, are* begin the poem, and *O*-ver, *Go*-lden and -*grove* suggest an 'oh' of grief which echoes through almost all of it.

There was no saving, however, of the stodgy text-based sermon of 12 September, but it was followed a month or so later by the dramatic and impressive Monday evening sermon of 25 October. This was the piece in which he used the word 'sweetheart' – he'd already done so at Bedford Leigh – in suggesting that God 'takes more interest . . . in a lover's sweetheart than the lover [does]'.[32] 'In consequence of this word 'sweetheart,' noted Hopkins, 'I was in a manner suspended'; at any rate he was told not to preach in future without having his sermons read first by Fr Clare (although with typical inconsistency Fr Clare refused to bother when he brought his next sermon to him).

It was fortunate that his Superior was not able to see the sermon in time to censor it because it contains some of Hopkins's most appealing writing. He begins by dealing with one of his favourite ideas, that of a world in all its pied-beauty which is made for man: 'The songs of birds, flowers and their smells and colours, fruits and their taste for our enjoyment.' He then faces the fact that 'providence is imperfect':

> At night the moon sometimes has no light to give, at others the clouds darken her; she measures time most strangely and gives us reckonings most difficult to make and never exact enough; the coalpits and oilwells are full of explosions, fires, and outbreaks of sudden death, the sea of storms and wrecks . . . everything is full of fault, flaw, imperfection.[33]

His conclusion is that if God did give us what we wanted, we would neither pray to, nor glorify Him, a piece of realism which might have consoled him over his own disappointments with British politics at this time, ranging from a disagreement with a local liberal in a railway carriage to much depression over news of military setbacks in South Africa. Personal depression is rarely unassociated with the sufferer's larger perspective of the world. Granted what may be called a chemical tendency to melancholy, the depressive still has to feed on the apparent failures of his own life and the tragedies, as he sees them, of the world at large. Beyond the joyless parish life of Liverpool lay a country controlled by Gladstone who was losing the Empire in defeats like Majuba in the Transvaal in February 1881, 'a deep disgrace . . . a stain upon our arms. . . . The effect will, I am afraid, be felt all over the Empire.'[34]

As at St Beuno's, and now confirmed by city living, he believed implicitly that industrial and urban development was destroying English character and physique. After witnessing the annual procession of horses in Liverpool in May 1880, he told Bridges:

> While I admired the handsome horses I remarked for the thousandth time with sorrow and loathing the base and besotted figures and features of the Liverpool crowd. When I see the fine and manly Norwegians that flock hither to embark for America walk our streets and look about them it fills me with shame and wretchedness.[35]

The economic background to these reflections was the peak in unemployment reached in 1879 and the fact that 70 per cent of the population lived in towns in 1881 compared with 48 per cent in 1841. When General Gordon declared that British arms were in decline because of the lack of men of 'tall stature, sinewy frame, well-chiselled features, clean glance, and elastic figure', he echoed the historian James Froude's lament over England's present state that no 'nation can long remain great which does not possess . . . a hardy and abundant peasantry'.[36]

Hopkins must have felt ill-equipped to deal with the social misery he saw around him in Liverpool. Whereas today one can talk of the Jesuits' 'option for the poor', their Victorian counterparts depended on individual and parochial initiatives, with no general policy as their mainspring. In traditional Catholic circles, too, all talk of Socialism was regarded as implying anti-Church attitudes. The papal encyclical of 1878, *Concerning Modern Errors*, denounced the evil of all forms of revolution, and Socialists, Communists and Nihilists were all lumped together as preaching the unacceptable doctrine of the 'perfect equality of all men in regard to rights alike and duties'.

There is little deviation from this uncompromising line in the *Christian Constitution of States* pronounced in 1885, which, although admitting 'Government should be administered for the well-being of the citizens', chooses to attack the desire for material wealth, rather than recommend its more equal distribution.

Fr Joseph Rickaby, who had been a colleague of Hopkins at St Beuno's, seems to have been the only significant social critic writing for the Society. His pamphlet 'Socialism' (1885)[37] represented the working classes as victims of society, haunted by unemployment and dying in poverty. At least Socialism seemed to offer an answer to the 'undeniable wretchedness and iniquity of the capitalist system in its present form'. But this was a solitary voice and it lost its reforming edge in his later years at Oxford when he turned to religious and ethical writing.

An insight into the generally jaundiced state of Hopkins's mind is provided in a long letter to Dixon which he began on 22 December 1880 and finished on 16 January 1881. It analyses, with reference to poetry, the 'loss of relish for what once charmed us', a sensitive subject for someone as conscious as Hopkins of the effects of the passage of time on mortal things.

He cites four reasons for our disenchantment with verse that we once found a pleasure to read. First, our maturer judgement may correct our earlier one; second, what seemed fine on first experience is lessened in its effect by repetition; third, we have a greater awareness of technical shortcomings; and fourth, there is a Wordsworthian effect, our

> insight is more sensitive, in fact is more perfect, earlier in life than later and especially towards elementary impressions: I remember that crimson and pure blues seemed to me spiritual and heavenly sights fit to draw tears once; now I can just see what I once saw, but can hardly dwell on it and should not care to do so.[38]

To adopt a Wordsworthian metaphor, there had passed away a glory from the earth, and the effort of recall, nostalgia, brought pain. A personal sense of disillusion seems to underlie these reflections.

He was turning more to music, 'the only Muse that does not stifle in this horrible place',[39] and writing about his enthusiasm to Bridges in June 1880, he claimed he had invented a 'new style, something standing to ordinary music as sprung rhythm to common rhythm'.[40] Less than a year later, scruples over this recreation were worrying him: 'I am afraid it may be Almighty God who is unwilling,' but the fear appears to have had no significant effect on the part that music continued to play in the rest of his life.

A modern verdict on Hopkins as a composer is that he possessed a talent which did not progress beyond the early stages of development and that criticism from well-meaning academic experts when he was in Dublin tended to repress his originality.[4] One cannot, in any case, avoid the reflection that writing music, by its very abstractness, provided him with what he felt as a priest to be a more permissible, as well as aesthetic escape from the scrupulous worries and apparent decline in inspiration that beset his poetry.

1881 saw the disappointment about publication in Hall Caine's anthology, *Sonnets of Three Centuries*. To the three poems submitted by Hopkins, Caine responded first with an 'effusive postcard', then followed a period of silence and finally a refusal on the grounds that his collection was intended to show that the traditional sonnet form could not be bettered. Hopkins thought this an excuse, since in 'Andromeda', one of the sonnets he submitted, 'one cannot say there is any novelty in rhythm',[42] but he philosophically accepted what he had already become used to from his own Jesuit editors: perhaps no one would print him anyway.

On 26 June 1881, in commemoration of the Feast of the Sacred Heart, he delivered his last sermon in Liverpool. It pulls no punches in its readiness to deal literally with the subject and to explain to the more delicate-minded in the congregation why it is *not* 'repulsive . . . to have one piece of Christ's flesh . . . nakedly thrust upon their mind's eye'.[43] At a more personal level, the sermon reflects the profoundly conservative view of life taken by Hopkins:

men may travel, but do not change their minds with change of latitude. We write to one another a hundred times as fast and often as our forefathers could, but we do but say fast and often what we should still have said seldom and slowly. And learning, the knowing more or knowing less, leaves us with our characters, our passions, and our appetites much what they were.[44]

By now, at the age of 37, and after twelve years in the Society, it must have seemed to the speaker that no transformation was likely in his life, nor had any achievement so far marked it, whether as priest or poet. His sermons in Liverpool would not be remembered by a Jesuit historian writing in *Letters and Notices* in 1911–12, although a contemporary's, Fr Dubberley, were recalled with enthusiasm, as were the two delivered by the famous Dominican Tom Burke in October 1880. He got instant attention by declaiming at the beginning of one of them: 'To hell with the Jesuits!'[45] – while Hopkins had not got away with 'sweetheart'.

It was a relief to learn that in September 1881 he was to go to Manresa to complete the final stage of his Jesuit training. In the interval, however, he was needed to help out in Glasgow.

## Notes

1. *The Tablet* (29 March 1879) p. 390.
2. *Further Letters of Hopkins*, p. 245 and *Letters of Hopkins to Bridges*, p. 110.
3. *Letters and Notices*, xxxi (July 1911) p. 150.
4. Ramsey Muir, *A History of Liverpool* (London, 1907) p. 304.
5. James Treble, *Urban Poverty in Britain 1830–1914* (London, 1979) p. 113.
6. *Letters of Hopkins to Bridges*, p. 100.
7. *Correspondence of Hopkins and R. W. Dixon*, p. 33.
8. See N. Ryan SJ, *St Francis Xavier's Church Centenary 1848–1948* (Liverpool, 1948) p. 49.
9. *Letters of Hopkins to Bridges*, p. 198.
10. *Further Letters of Hopkins*, p. 63.
11. See *Further Letters*, p. 246; *Correspondence with Dixon*, p. 42; and *Letters to Bridges*, p. 99.
12. *Letters and Notices*, xxvi (1901–2) p. 500.
13. Ibid., vol. xxxv, p. 269.
14. *Sermons of Hopkins*, p. 50.
15. Ibid., pp. 52–3.
16. *Correspondence of Hopkins and R. W. Dixon*, p. 33.
17. Ibid., p. 42.
18. *Letters of Hopkins to Bridges*, p. 124.
19. *Further Letters of Hopkins*, p. 162.
20. A. Thomas SJ, article in the *Times Literary Supplement*, 19 March 1971, pp. 331–2.
21. *Sermons of Hopkins*, p. 56.
22. *Letters of Hopkins to Bridges*, p. 28.
23. Ibid., p. 273.
24. *Sermons of Hopkins*, p. 62.
25. *Correspondence of Hopkins and R. W. Dixon*, pp. 32–3.
26. *Sermons of Hopkins*, p. 70.
27. *Letters and Notices*, vol. xxvi, p. 501.
28. *Sermons of Hopkins*, p. 81.
29. Ibid., p. 83.
30. Ibid., p. 122.

31. *Letters of Hopkins to Bridges*, p. 109.
32. *Sermons of Hopkins*, p. 89.
33. Ibid., p. 90.
34. *Further Letters of Hopkins*, p. 158.
35. *Letters of Hopkins to Bridges*, p. 35.
36. See G. Roberts, 'The Countryman as Hero', in the *Hopkins Quarterly* (Summer 1982) pp. 79ff.
37. See p. 50, note 24.
38. *Correspondence of Hopkins and R. W. Dixon*, p. 38.
39. *Letters of Hopkins to Bridges*, p. 126.
40. Ibid., p. 103.
41. See Appendix II, 'Gerard Manley Hopkins as Musician' by John Stevens in the House and Storey edition of the *Journals*, pp. 457ff.
42. *Letters of Hopkins to Bridges*, p. 128.
43. *Sermons of Hopkins*, pp. 101–2.
44. Ibid., p. 104.
45. Quoted, ibid., p. 11.

# 13
# Glasgow

The original temporary posting to Glasgow, where the Jesuits had a parish, at St Joseph's, North Woodside, within the city, was for the last two weeks of August 1881, but it was extended to two months, perhaps to give more respite to the priests who belonged to this notably hard-working community.

Despite the district's name, it was an area of urban squalor, 'in part a very slum-land', the presbytery without a garden and 'closely hemmed in at the back by the unsavoury tenements of Lyon Street'.[1] A Jesuit describing it soon after Hopkins's time gives the impression of another Liverpool:

> The work is hard and incessant, allowing no rest from early morn until late at night, and requiring men of exceptionally strong fibre to withstand the fatigue; the people are nearly all of the poorer class, very many of them obliged to live in crowded 'closes', where the air is thick with fetid exhalations, and the sights that meet the eye too often revolting.[2]

The parish priests here, as at Liverpool, died of the same typhoid that struck down their flock, or were unable to stay the demanding pace. The Superior from 1881 to 1884 was Fr Joseph Jackson who broke down from overwork and had to be sent to Rhyl to recuperate, while his successor retired and died from ill-health two years later.

Such personal tragedies reflected the burden of work the Society had taken on: true though it was that their numbers were increasing, needs were still exceeding suitable manpower. Of the 800 Jesuits of all ranks and status who were in the United Kingdom in 1880 only 200 were priests, and these had to cover more than 30 parishes and nine schools (where they usually provided, together with those still unordained, all the staff). Moreover, an average of one student a year was dying before ordination.[3]

St Joseph's may have been hard work for its priests, but distinguished churchmen had passed through its doors. The future

Cardinal Manning had preached one of his first sermons there after entering the Church; the ubiquitous Tom Burke had occupied its pulpit; Fr Clare had given his first mission at St Joseph's and felt great affection for it. Most who worked there soon came to realise that the city, like Liverpool, had a serious drink problem. In February 1878 a priest characterised Glasgow as 'one of the most drunken, if not the most drunken city [*sic*], in one of the most drunken countries in the world'.[4] Nevertheless, perhaps because he'd known such problems before, perhaps because he was soon to enjoy the peace of Manresa, Hopkins was able to tell Bridges that he got on 'better' in Glasgow than in Liverpool. Although it was a 'wretched place . . . like all our great towns',[5] there were 'alleviations':

the streets and buildings are fine and the people lively. The poor Irish, among whom my duties lay, are mostly from the North of Ireland. . . . They are found by all who have to deal with them very attractive; for, though always very drunken and at present very Fenian, they are warm-hearted and give a far heartier welcome than those of Liverpool. I found myself very much at home with them.[6]

He told Bridges that he still found it difficult to write verse, and warned him to expect nothing while he was doing his tertianship, but in 'Inversnaid', inspired by a brief visit to Loch Lomond, he returned to the theme of 'Binsey Poplars', his love of the inviolability and uniqueness of Nature. But the sweetness and melancholy of the Oxford poem is replaced by the driving rhythms and direct statement of a man who is now possessed by his convictions. The drabness of the city is anti-life, whereas the 'wet' and 'wildness' of Inversnaid express what Ruskin called the 'exhaustless living energy with which the universe is filled'.[7] The sprung rhythm engages with the most important words:

Dégged with déw, dáppled with déw
Are the gróins of the bráes that the bróok tréads through,

and the alliteration follows the stresses:

Of a *p*ool so *p*itch-black, *f*ell-*f*rowning,
It rounds and rounds *D*espair to *d*rowning.

Man is excluded from this sombre but powerful scene: Hopkins had seen too much of him and his town and cities of late to wish for anything less than the healing force of solitude.

There was a brief, if rather painful exchange of correspondence at this time with Bridges, who had complained that he had found his friend's poetry more difficult to appreciate than usual during a debilitating illness that he had been suffering from. Hopkins wrote a hurt reply that 'your mind towards my verse is like mine towards Browning's: I greatly admire the touches and details, but the general effect, the whole offends me, I think it repulsive.'[8]

Like all their disagreements, it was a passing one, and Hopkins left the world of the big cities anxious for the peace of Manresa: 'I feel that I need the noviceship very much and shall be every way better off when I have been made more spiritual minded'.[9] Writing poetry formed no conscious part of his intentions over the next ten months.

### Notes

1. *Letters and Notices*, xxx (1909–10) p. 97.
2. Ibid.
3. B. Bassett, *The English Jesuits*, p. 422.
4. *The Tablet* (16 February 1878) p. 316.
5. *Letters of Hopkins to Bridges*, p. p. 135.
6. *Further Letters of Hopkins*, pp. 248–9.
7. *Modern Painters*, 3rd edn (London, 1900) I, 251.
8. *Letters of Hopkins to Bridges*, p. 137.
9. Ibid., p. 135.

# 14
## Training Completed

*The question . . . for me is not whether I am willing . . . to make a sacrifice of hopes of fame . . . but whether I am not to undergo a severe judgment from God for the lothness I have shown in making it, for the reserves I may have in my heart made, for the backward glances I have given with my hand upon the plough, for the waste of time the very compositions you admire may have caused and their preoccupation of the mind which belonged to more sacred or more binding duties.*

Hopkins to Canon Dixon[1]

*The persona is a complicated system of relations between individual consciousness and society, fittingly enough a kind of mask, designed on the one hand to make a definite impression upon others, and, on the other, to conceal the true nature of the individual. . . . Society expects, and indeed must expect, every individual to play the part assigned to him as perfectly as possible, so that a man who is a parson must not only carry out his official functions objectively, but must at all times and in all circumstances play the role of parson in a flawless manner. Society demands this as a kind of surety; each must stand at his post, here a cobbler, there a poet. No man is expected to be both. Nor is it advisable to be both, for that would be 'queer'. Such a man would be different from other people, not quite reliable. . . . He would always be suspected of unreliability and incompetence, because society is persuaded that only the cobbler who is not a poet can supply workmanlike shoes. . . . Obviously no one could completely submerge his individuality in these expectations; hence the construction of an artificial personality becomes an unavoidable necessity. . . . This painfully familiar division of consciousness into two figures, often preposterously different, is an incisive psychological operation that is bound to have repercussions on the unconscious.*

C. G. Jung,
*The Relations between the Ego and the Unconscious*[2]

On 8 October 1881, he was back at Roehampton, the leafy Manresa of happy memory, to begin the ten months of practical and spiritual experience that finally brought his training as a Jesuit to an end. Canon Dixon corresponded with him under an illusion both about the tertianship itself and Hopkins's feelings towards the Jesuits. He was mistaken in thinking that Hopkins was still in any sense a probationer who could withdraw from the Society, and mistaken, too, in concluding that because he often expressed his unhappiness it was a sign that he no longer felt a vocation: many others apart from Dixon have found it difficult to understand fully the complex personality of the poet-priest.

Dixon wrote: 'I suppose you are determined to go on with it: but it must be a severe trial – I will say no more',[3] yet a 'severe trial' was probably what Hopkins had come to regard as a necessary part of his experience of the religious life, and happiness as occasional and accidental. The element of moral masochism in his character meant that for him the figure of the suffering Christ loomed larger than the 'achieve of, the mastery of . . . my chevalier', and the acceptance of unhappiness merged into the expectation of it.[4]

But he hastened to explain what the tertainship was:

I see you do not understand my position in the Society. This Tertianship or Third Year of Probation or second Noviceship . . . is not really a noviceship at all in the sense of a time during which a candidate or probationer makes trial of our life and is free to withdraw. At the end of the noviceship proper we take vows which are perpetually binding and renew them every six months (not *for* every six months but for life) till we are professed. . . . It is in preparation for these last vows that we make the tertian-ship . . .[5]

Dixon might be forgiven if he had interpreted the tone of the next remark to suggest that his friend *had* thought of leaving the Society:

As for myself, I have not only made my vows publicly some two and twenty times but I make them to myself every day, so that I should be black with perjury if I drew back now. And beyond that I can say with St Peter: to whom shall I go?[6]

But the letter ends with a moving statement of his sense of being at peace with God in the surroundings of Manresa, expressed with a sincerity which seems undeniable.

A convenient account of the life of the tertian is given in Fr Clarke's article already referred to:

> [The tertian] has to sweep and dust the rooms and corridors, to chop wood, to wash plates and dishes, besides going over again the spiritual work of the novice, the long retreat of thirty days included. He has also during this year to study the institute of the Society, and during Lent to take part in some one of the public missions which are given by the various religious orders in the large towns.[7]

For Hopkins, the four-week retreat began on 7 November, and he was determined to deal with all lighter matters before it started, including comments on poems in manuscript which Dixon sent him. This clearing of the decks gave him the opportunity to write at length his views on the sonnet, and he pointed out that, although in theory the Italian and English forms seem equal in size, the elisions and pronunciation of the former language allow the Italian sonnet to be in practice longer by a ratio of 13:10. He claimed the effectiveness of his remedy, the '"outriding" feet I sometimes myself employ, for they more than equal the Italian elisions and make the whole sonnet longer, if anything, than the Italian is'.[8]

Dixon would not give up the question of his friend's poetry, and Hopkins felt forced to reply – before the delayed start of his retreat – that at least for the moment the question of his verse was to be relegated to the back of his mind, if not dismissed entirely. His answer should be read in full:

> The question then . . . is not whether I am willing . . . to make a sacrifice of hopes of fame, but whether I am not to undergo a severe judgment from God for the lothness I have shewn . . . for the reserves I may have in my heart made . . . for the waste of time the very compositions you admire may have caused. . . . I shall, in my present mind, continue to compose, as occasion shall fairly allow, which I am afraid will be seldom.[9]

The 'I am afraid' is a characteristic reflection of the contradictory nature of Hopkins's mind on the question and the matter did not end there. On one of the three 'repose' days when the restrictions of the Retreat were lifted, he told Dixon that it was for God to decide the fate of his poetry; his correspondent was not satisfied:

> The day will come, when so health-breathing and purely powerful a faculty as you have been gifted with may find its proper issue in the world. . . . [I] am certain that as a means of serving, I will not say your cause, but religion, you cannot have a more powerful instrument than your verses.[10]

Hopkins never answered this plausible criticism of his scrupulousness. His life as a Jesuit bears out Jung's view that 'the life of the individual is not determined solely by the ego and its opinion or by social factors, but quite as much, if not more, by a transcendent authority'.[11] Like the Jesuit General, Fr Roothan who declared: 'What pleases me must be rejected for the sole reason that it pleases,'[12] self-abnegation was the quality he most admired and he noted on 19 November the words of Fr Whitty, his tertian-master, that,

> the hidden life at Nazareth is the great help to faith for us who must live more or less an obscure, constrained, and unsuccessful life. . . . And sacrificing, as he [Christ] did, all to obedience his very obedience was unknown.[13]

It was a message that stuck in his mind because in another retreat two years later he recalled Fr Whitty 'teaching how a great part of life to the holiest of men consists in the well performance, the performance, one may say, of ordinary duties'.[14]

Ironically, he had the pleasure of a minor success with his poetry when he learnt that *The Month* (at least!) was going to publish, alongside the original text, his modern English version of the Middle English hymn to the Blessed Virgin, which Nicholas sings in Chaucer's *Miller's Tale*. He was then displeased to discover, when the magazine was printed, that the original music was no longer there: 'What a thing it is that even in publishing an antiquity, a piece of music every note interesting and precious from its date, people must change, adulterate, and modernise!'[15]

A few years before he might have used the word 'inscape' to describe the originality he meant, but it was a piece of vocabulary that had died with his (comparative) youth, an aesthetic experience no longer felt in the melancholy of middle age.

What remained of his time at Manresa was taken up with personal and spiritual matters. During Lent he preached on a mission in Cumberland and met Canon Dixon for the first and only time (if one excludes the period when Dixon was teaching at Highgate). The two had dinner in Carlisle, but the meeting was an anti-climax with Dixon later apologising for something that he was hardly to be blamed for: 'I have an unfortunate manner: and am constantly told that I am too quiet.'[16]

Hopkins welcomed Bridges to a Corpus Christi procession at Manresa in June. Hardly surprisingly Bridges did not like it and said so. It upset Hopkins, but they made it up – or, at least, as usual, Hopkins did: he needed Bridges too much as a cultural and emotional confidant to sacrifice him on the altar of ceremonial Catholicism.

On 15 August, the Feast of the Assumption, when St Ignatius and his companions three centuries before had pledged themselves to poverty, chastity and obedience, Hopkins and his colleagues repeated their vows. A week later, he left to teach at Stonyhurst College.

A year had passed since his last poem, but Manresa appeared to have given him the peace and time for reflection that he felt he needed. He added many pages of notes to his commentary on the *Spiritual Exercises*, 'very professional,' he told Bridges, and they would 'interest none but a Jesuit'.[17] Perhaps material for poetry was accumulating in that sub-conscious reservoir which Mark Twain suggested was always re-filling in the seemingly inactive writer, but the difference, apparently, in Hopkins's case was his deliberate desire to avoid composition. He was a priest–poet who wished *not* to write.

## Notes

1. *Correspondence of Hopkins and R. W. Dixon*, p. 88.
2. Jung, 'The Relations between the Ego and the Unconscious', in *Jung: Selected Writings*, ed. Storr, p. 94.
3. *Correspondence of Hopkins and R. W. Dixon*, p. 70.
4. That Hopkins had neurotic *tendencies* seems to me undeniable. See Karen Horney's *The Neurotic Personality of our Time* (London, 1937) where her remark that 'The neurotic . . . is not only a very unhappy person . . . but he does not see any chance of escaping his misery' (p. 227) is particularly appropriate to the later Hopkins.
5. *Correspondence of Hopkins and R. W. Dixon*, p. 75.
6. Ibid.
7. Quoted in Thomas, *Hopkins the Jesuit*, p. 187. See Ch. 7, n. 3.
8. *Correspondence of Hopkins and R. W. Dixon*, p. 87.

9. Ibid., p. 88.
10. Ibid., p. 100.
11. *Jung: Selected Writings*, ed. Storr, p. 359.
12. *Sermons of Hopkins*, p. 176. Quoted in P. Endean, 'The Spirituality of Gerard Manley Hopkins', *The Hopkins Quarterly* (Fall 1981) p. 110.
13. *Sermons of Hopkins*, p. 176.
14. Ibid., p. 253.
15. *Further Letters of Hopkins*, p. 162.
16. *Correspondence of Hopkins and R. W. Dixon*, p. 104.
17. *Letters of Hopkins to Bridges*, p. 150.

# 15

# At Stonyhurst

*I see no grounded prospect of my ever doing much not only in poetry but in anything at all.*

Hopkins to Dixon[1]

His appointment to the Society's most famous school, established nearly three centuries ago in penal times at St Omers and driven to England by the Revolutionary armies of 1792, was to teach, as he put it, 'our philosophers (like undergraduate students) Latin, Greek . . . for the London B.A. degree'. As Catholics were forbidden to attend Anglican universities, colleges such as Stonyhurst, Oscott and Ushaw prepared their lay students for the external degrees of the University of London.

At best, Hopkins would be teaching young men following university Classics courses, as in the case of his favourite scholar, Bernard O'Flaherty, a regular College prize-winner, who went on to gain his BA with honours, but at worst he might find himself teaching foreign students with little English whose interests were social, rather than academic. The standard of the London University exams was not, in any case, reckoned to be as high as that of Oxford and Cambridge and the letters he wrote from Stonyhurst during his sixteen months stay do not suggest he led an intellectually demanding life, despite the College's high reputation as a Catholic school.

His appointment to the post by the Provincial, Fr Purbrick, had not been made with a great deal of confidence. The latter had written to Fr Delaney in Ireland who was on the lookout for Jesuit talent to teach at University College, Dublin:

Fr Hopkins is a very clever and a good scholar . . . but I should do you no kindness in sending you a man so eccentric. I am trying him this year in coaching B.A.'s at Stonyhurst, but with fear and trembling.[2]

115

Purbrick was wise enough to realise the limitations of his own judgement, and later more charitably added that, 'Sometimes what we in Community deem oddities are the very qualities which outside are appreciated as original and valuable',[3] and there is every reason for believing that Purbrick, like Gallwey before him, was invariably sympathetic in his dealings with Hopkins.

According to Hopkins, it was in an interview with the Provincial, before coming to Stonyhurst that the latter had suggested he might write 'one or other of the books I had named to him',[4] presumably on one of those classical subjects that Hopkins toyed with to the end of his life with no real confidence that anything would come of it. A scholarly work would have come very appropriately from Stonyhurst, the pride of the Jesuits' educational crown, and given first place in the official (Latin) *Catalogue*, the printed list of their establishments and staff in Great Britain. Its excellent exam results, notable contributions to astronomy and the vast and impressive building helped to generate an impression of solidity and tradition:

> a fine library, museums, MSS illuminated and otherwise, coins, works of art . . . an anemometer, a sunshine guage [*sic*], a sundial, an icosihedron, statuary, magnetic instruments, a laboratory . . . studio, fine engravings . . .[5]

Hopkins, of course, already knew the school from working visits in 1873 and 1878 and had lived next to it for the two years of his Philosophy course. The Headmaster in 1882 was Fr William Eyre, a former Prefect (or Housemaster) of Philosophers, and a man of intelligence rather than learning. His letters to the Provincial, which are held in the Jesuit archives at Farm Street, suggest an emotional temperament, not well suited to the tensions of a lively school and individualistic staff. He, and the Society, were currently involved in a lawsuit with his brother, Archbishop Eyre of Glasgow, who was challenging Fr Eyre's right to dispose of money left by their father for the benefit of the College. The building work which Hopkins saw around him was to be paid for by the money and the uncertainties made it a worrying time.

On 23 September, a few days before Hopkins wrote his enthusiastic description of the Stonyhurst estate to Bridges, Fr Eyre was writing to Fr Purbrick that 'Fr Gerald [*sic*] Hopkins seems to me far more mad than Fr Harper was' (this was the convert who had taught brilliantly at St Mary's Hall, but ended his life in an asylum). Queried on what exactly he meant by this, for Fr Purbrick had his own views on the impulsiveness of Fr Eyre's judgement, Eyre had replied three days later: 'I meant that Fr Hopkins was mad in the 'Pickwickian' sense. Goes about saying his last day of happiness was spent before he came here; – he knows nothing; – he is unfit to teach; &c, &c, &c.'[6]

Fr Eyre also repeats (25 October) a story of Hopkins getting into his room through the window and another of his supposedly being in his bath with his clothes on! But this repetition of hearsay tells us more about Fr Eyre than the mental condition of one of his teachers. What is beyond dispute is that at times at Stonyhurst Hopkins was a desperately unhappy man. In January 1883 he wrote to his ex-Balliol friend, Alexander Baillie:

> I like my pupils and do not wholly dislike the work, but I fall into or continue in a heavy weary state of body and mind. . . . I make no way with what I read, and seem but half a man. It is a sad thing to say. I try, and am even meant to try . . . to write some books; but I find myself so tired or so harassed I fear they will never be written.[7]

In other letters the mood is so different that the same man is not recognisable, the cheerfulness for example of the letter of 18 May 1883 to Bridges or the balanced common-sense analysis of the concept of the gentleman on 3 February the same year. But among the more sombre aspects stands out the self-denigration which emerges in the mysterious comparison with Walt Whitman:

> I always knew in my heart Walt Whitman's mind to be more like my own than any other man's living. As he is a very great scoundrel this is not a pleasant confession. And this also makes me the more desirous to read him and the more determined that I will not.[8]

According to Hopkins in the same letter, he had read a few pieces by Whitman which had impressed him by their 'marked and original manner and way of thought and in particular of his rhythm'. He also recalled that nearly ten years before he had come across a review by the eminent critic George Saintsbury of *Leaves of Grass*, from which he must have learnt of Whitman's celebration of sex and drawn his own conclusions from the reviewer's discreet comment on the American poet's belief in love between men, that, 'Socrates himself seems renascent in this apostle of friendship'.[9]

On the other hand, he may well have felt more sympathetic towards what Saintsbury described as Whitman's faith in the 'necessity of the establishment of a universal republic, or rather brotherhood of men' and towards his philosophy of 'universality', or faith in the goodness of things. In some respects, this is also the philosophy of the priest who wrote 'Pied Beauty' and declared that all things glorify God and although he argued against any resemblance between sprung rhythm and Whitman's writing, the free rhythms of the latter are often similar:

> Cóme úp from the fíelds fáther, hére's a létter from our Péte,
> And cóme to the frónt dóor móther, hére's a létter from thy
>    déar són.

The language of self-denigration becomes fiercer in January 1883 when he denounces his own 'blackguardry' to Baillie because he, Hopkins, had called the philosopher Swedenborg a 'humbug', and in March when he told Bridges that if 'I had wanted a conspicuous instance of a blackguard I should have taken myself.'[10]

This self-repugnance reflects some profound emotional tension that was to emerge both more tragically and more creatively in Dublin. At Stonyhurst the mixed and sparse bag of verse is seen at its best in 'The Leaden Echo and the Golden Echo', whose nostalgic sadness is more reminiscent of the mood of Oxford and repeats Hopkins's favourite theme of the mortality of earthly things:

> How to keep . . .
> Back beauty, keep it, beauty, beauty, beauty . . . from
>    vanishing away.

The words of the Leaden Echo are answered by the Golden Echo:

> Give beauty back, beauty, beauty, beauty, back to God,
>    beauty's self and beauty's giver.

Whatever the familiarity, and even conventionality of the sentiment, the music and imagery are Hopkins at his finest:

> O is there no frowning of these wrinkles, ranked wrinkles deep,
> Down? no waving off of these most mournful messengers, still
>    messengers, sad and stealing messengers of grey?

The musical effects come through repetition, rhyme, half-rhyme and alliteration: the line-lengths signal sense- rather than musical-units, as in this consonant-dominated representation of depression:

> O then, weary then why should we tread? O why are we
>   so haggard at the heart so care-coiled, care-killed, so fagged,
>   so fashed, so cogged, so cumbered,
> When the thing we freely forfeit is kept with fonder a care.

This tone of languid protest is continued in 'Ribblesdale', written at Stonyhurst, but taking up one of the central themes of the St Beuno's poems: Nature as a witness of God's goodness. But in North Wales Hopkins felt the intimate identification of the physical world and its Creator:

> The world is charged with the grandeur of God
> ... the azurous hung hills are his world-wielding shoulder.

At Stonyhurst the role of Nature is seen as an intermediary:

> Thou canst but be, but that thou well dost; strong
> Thy plea with him,

and man is now the all-important centre:

> And what is Earth's eye, tongue, or heart else, where
> Else, but in dear and dogged man?

and this recognition of man's centrality brings sadness, the bleakness of reality.

A happy contrast is the wholly delightful 'The Blessed Virgin compared to the Air we Breathe' which was pinned up on the statue of the Virgin Mary at the College in commemoration of the month of May. Its three-stress couplets are appropriately simple for the poem's intention, and the sprung rhythm, the occasional interruption of the colloquial – 'that's fairly mixed with', 'merely a woman', 'O marvellous!' – reflect Hopkins's individuality without exaggeration:

> Again, look overhead
> How air is azurèd;
> O how! Nay do but stand
> Where you can lift your hand
> Skywards: rich, rich it laps
> Round the four finger gaps.

'A Trio of Triolets' was published in the *Stonyhurst Magazine* in March 1883, and includes the joke at Wordsworth's expense, 'The Child is Father to the Man'. Even Bridges, not normally amused by his friend's humour, liked this example and, whether it appeals to the modern reader or not, it is an important reminder of the comic touches that are everywhere in the letters: Hopkins has the humble man's gift of being able to laugh at himself, as well as the true humorist's ability to catch and describe what is usually called the 'funny side of things'. The story of the drunken organist at Liverpool,[11] recalled in the sombre atmosphere of Dublin, is an ideal example of this comic gift.

In the best traditions of the Victorian polymath, Hopkins also made several appearances in the periodical *Nature* between November 1882 and October 1884 (by which time he was in Dublin). This magazine had been published by Macmillan since 1869 and was devoted to the purpose of covering recent developments in science. One of its contributors was Fr Stephen Perry, the Stonyhurst astronomer, who had been in charge of the Stonyhurst Observatory since 1868 and whose distinction in the field led to his taking part in important scientific expeditions for astronomical observation to other parts of the world (he died in 1889 while returning from such an expedition to Kerguelen Island in the Indian Ocean).

Perhaps because of his encouragement, Hopkins wrote these four letters which included extraordinary poetic descriptions of the sunsets of the time which had been gaining universal attention in the second half of 1883. The cause – finally identified as the Krakatoa eruption of August 1883 – was at first a matter of speculation, but the phenomena drew writing from Hopkins which is reminiscent of the best in the Journal (and a tribute to the liberal editorial policy of the scientific paper that printed it):

> A bright sunset lines the clouds so that their brims look like gold, brass, bronze, or steel. It fetches out those dazzling flecks and spangles which people call fish-scales. It gives to a mackerel or

dappled cloudrack the appearance of quilted crimson silk, or a ploughed field glazed with crimson ice.[12]

The passage recalls his verse – the 'blue-bleak embers' which 'fall, gall themselves, and gash gold-vermillion', the 'wind-walks' of 'silk-sack clouds' – in a style of celebration of Nature which looks to the past. It needed the functional context of the pages of a scientific journal to allow Hopkins the luxury of reviving a sensuousness of writing which in priestly middle-age he almost entirely rejected.

Hopkins's third great poetic friendship began at Stonyhurst when the Rector asked him to look after the Catholic poet, Coventry Patmore, who came for prize-giving at the beginning of August 1883. Also a convert, but now in his sixties, Patmore had achieved a period of great popularity, some twenty years before, with a sequence of poems on married life, *The Angel in the House*. By the 1880's, although still known to the public for his right-wing journalism, he had become, like Canon Dixon, a minor figure in contemporary poetry.

He shared with Hopkins a strong interest in prosody, and both took a high moral line in their views of art and life. The meeting began a relationship in which Hopkins gave his friend's verse the same meticulous criticism as he devoted to Bridges and Dixon, but when Patmore read Hopkins's work in manuscript in the Spring of 1884 he had to confess apologetically that it was too original for his tastes:

> It seems to me that the thought and feeling of these poems, if expressed without any obscuring novelty of mode, are such as often to require the whole attention to apprehend and digest them; and are therefore of a kind to appeal only to the few. But to the already sufficiently arduous character of such poetry you seem to me to have added the difficulty of following *several* entirely novel and simultaneous experiments in versification and construction, together with an altogether unprecedented system of alliteration and compound words.[13]

He was the third 'professional' poet to have read Hopkins in manuscript and, of the three, his verdict was the most unfavourable.

Another disappointment for him was a further publishing rejection in October of 1883. Bridges's mother was editing a book of prayers and Hopkins had been asked for one that was as near interdenominational as possible; what he produced, unfortunately, was deemed too Catholic and rejected: he took the humiliation with cynical irony:

> I regret . . . that [the public] can no longer be trusted to bear, to stomach, the clear expression of or the taking for granted even very elementary Christian doctrines. I did not realise this well enough, did not realise that distinct Christianity damages the sale and so the usefulness of a well meant book.[14]

By September 1883 Stonyhurst numbers were flourishing. The 275 pupils were a record and were to reach 300 in the following year. For Hopkins, however, events beyond his control were to turn his stay at the College into yet another temporary stopping-place in his career as a Jesuit. Fr Delaney, President of University College, Dublin, had not given up his search for new staff, and spent the night of 3 December at the College, probably to discuss with Hopkins the details of the appointment of the Chair of Classics that he wished to offer him. Fr Purbrick had told Delaney on 29 November that he had no objection to his approaching Hopkins and had the 'highest opinion of his scholarship and abilities – I fancy also that University work would be more in his line than anything else'.[15]

The matter, however, was not settled until 29 January 1884, when, after considerable manoeuvring on Delaney's part in the troubled waters of Irish university politics, he was able to telegraph Stonyhurst that Hopkins's appointment had been ratified by the Senate. By 18 February Hopkins was in residence in Dublin.

It is difficult to be sure how he had originally responded to Delaney's offer. Later, in March, he told Bridges he felt 'unworthy and unfit for the post', a conclusion characteristic of the self-denigration and lack of confidence he had now become victim to and, looking back several years after, he recalled he found the posting 'inconvenient and painful'.[16] On the other hand, the impression given of his state of mind at Stonyhurst is so mixed that it is difficult to see what he would have gained by continuing there.

'This good father,' remarked Fr Eyre of his departed member of staff on 19 February, 'felt leaving very much. As usual they have stoned the prophet, and now will want to build him a monument!'[17] It would take posterity to confirm the truth of these words, but in ways that Fr Eyre could hardly have foreseen.

**Notes**

1. *Correspondence of Hopkins and R. W. Dixon*, pp. 108–9.
2. Quoted in *Hopkins: Selected Prose*, ed. Roberts, p. 9.
3. Quoted in N. White, 'Gerard Manley Hopkins and the Irish Row', *Hopkins Quarterly* (Fall 1982) p. 98.
4. *Letters of Hopkins to Bridges*, p. 150.
5. Ibid., p. 151.
6. Eyre Papers, Farm St Archives, letters dated 23 and 26 September 1882.
7. *Further Letters of Hopkins*, pp. 251–2.
8. *Letters of Hopkins to Bridges*, p. 155.
9. The review is printed in *Letters of Hopkins to Bridges*, pp. 311ff.
10. *Further Letters of Hopkins*, p. 251, and *Letters of Hopkins to Bridges*, p. 177.
11. Ibid., p. 264.
12. *Correspondence of Hopkins and R. W. Dixon*, p. 164.
13. *Further Letters of Hopkins*, p. 352.
14. *Letters of Hopkins to Bridges*, p. 186.
15. Quoted in N. White, 'Gerard Manley Hopkins and the Irish Row'.
16. *Letters of Hopkins to Bridges*, p. 190.
17. Eyre Papers, Farm St Archives. But on 20 November 1883, Fr Eyre had written: 'Father Gerard Hopkins may, at any time, go stark-staring mad, and as (1) it would be well to take him out of himself and as (2) it is better the dénouement should not be when George the third is King, alias, when I am in charge, I shall strongly recommend his being handed over to Father William Delaney SJ.' Fr Eyre, as his Provincial realised, was an impulsive man.

# 16
# Heraclitean Fire

*All creativeness in the realm of the spirit as well as every psychic advance of man arises from the suffering of the soul, and the cause of the suffering is spiritual stagnation, or psychic sterility.*

Jung[1]

Hopkins arrived in Dublin to find university and country in a state of ferment. On one side agricultural outrage and political protest by Parnell and his colleagues; on the other, disagreement amongst the hierarchy and the lay and Jesuit authorities of University College about the conduct of the establishment. Like almost every Irish question the University argument was a political one and went back to 1854 when the original Catholic University of Ireland had been established under Newman's leadership. He left four years later after many difficulties over funding and disagreement by the Irish bishops about his policies, compounded by the fact of his nationality as an Englishman.

The University, which had been intended as a Catholic answer to the wealthy, Protestant-dominated Trinity, endured a period of uncertainty and falling numbers after Newman's departure. Not without misgivings, the Irish Jesuits agreed to take over the College buildings in St Stephen's Green and become the new administrators: the material omens were not promising, the Irish Provincial describing the buildings as a 'dingy old barrack that would require a vast outlay',[2] while Hopkins in his own time commented on the inadequate academic facilities, 'poor, all unprovided to a degree that outsiders wd. scarcely believe'.[3]

But the new President, Fr Delaney, had behind him the highly successful headmastership of Tullabeg, the Jesuit boarding school in the centre of Ireland, which he had brought to the forefront of examination success, and from October 1882 he had begun the task of improving the University staff by seeking recruits from the English Province. It was a controversial policy: the Irish Provincial, Fr Tuite, was very apprehensive 'on account of the present feeling in the country, and particularly English converts who are sometimes – well let us say – unsuited to this country and its thoroughly Catholic people'.[4]

In fact, Hopkins was the only Jesuit Fr Purbrick could spare from the distinguished list Delaney had prepared – one draws the obvious conclusion from Hopkins's perceived dispensability as far as the English Society was concerned – and it was, in the end, only by some sharp practice on Delaney's part that even Hopkins was appointed to the Classics Fellowship and the Chair that went with it: one University committee's vote against his election was diplomatically ignored by Delaney at a crucial moment and then overturned by another on the following day.

Delaney was concerned that all the salaried fellowships, paid for by government money, should go to post-holders who would teach only at St Stephen's Green; other colleges and schools in Ireland also prepared candidates for the University exams (as Stonyhurst did for London University) and there was competition amongst other Irish educational establishments for some of these fellowships. Delaney's achievement in concentrating these salaried posts in the College at St Stephen's Green strengthened its academic prestige and its finances. He was so successful with the academic results in 1884, Hopkins's first year in Ireland, that he received congratulations from the General of the Society for showing 'what Jesuit education can produce, in a manner perhaps never surpassed in the whole course of our history'.[5]

Hopkins produced no poetry in that year, which seems to have continued and even intensified the melancholy he had felt at Stonyhurst. Within days he was writing to Newman with the customary greetings on the latter's birthday and describing himself as 'sent by the hand of providence' to University College despite his 'unfitness'.[6] In March, Bridges learnt that he was 'not at all strong, not strong enough for the requirements' of the work, although he felt it only fair to add 'I have been warmly welcomed and most kindly treated'.[7]

Throughout the spring his depression continued, a mixture of low spirits and poor health: 'WHAT DOES ANYTHING AT ALL MATTER?' he capitalised in April,[8] culminating later the same month in the confession that he was 'recovering from a deep fit of nervous prostration . . . I did not know but I was dying'.[9] This recovery, if it was one, was helped by a holiday in Galway in July that included a dangerous and almost fatal sea-trip to the mighty Cliffs of Moher, which may have provided him with the image for spiritual despair, 'cliffs of fall / Frightful, sheer', in the 'terrible sonnets' of the following year.

When Bridges blamed the Society for neglecting his gifts as a poet, Hopkins roundly defended it: 'Our society cannot be blamed for not valuing what it never knew of' (more truthfully, it 'knew', but could not value) and he expressed no regret for whatever he might have lost in personal recognition:

> It always seems to me that poetry is unprofessional, but that is what I have said to myself, not others to me. No doubt if I kept producing I should have to ask myself what I meant to do with it all; but I have long been at a standstill, and so the things lie.[10]

He often found himself fully occupied with his professional work as a teacher, principally in setting and marking six examinations a year, which on one occasion produced 557 scripts from one examination alone! It was notorious that the professors of University College had neither the time, nor the facilities for any personal research.[11]

At the same time, he found friends in the Jesuit community: Fr Delaney, 'as generous, cheering, and openhearted a man as I ever lived with'; Fr Maillac, an emigré French priest who lived at Stephen's Green; and particularly Robert Curtis SJ, who held the Fellowship in Mathematics and had been one of Trinity's best mathematical scholars, but was never to be a priest because of epilepsy: for Hopkins he was a 'kind of godsend I never expected to have'.[12]

But the clouds of melancholy never lifted for long. In April 1885, his friend Alexander Baillie received a letter from him which ranged over the subjects of death, suicide, insanity, uncompleted work, the wickedness of Gladstone and the despair of Hopkins himself: news of a college friend's suicide by drowning reminded him that 'Three of my intimate friends at Oxford have thus drowned themselves' and that a 'good many more' of his contemporaries had met their end by their own hand'.[13]

When the letter moved to his own condition, he remarked:

> The melancholy I have all my life been subject to has become of late years not indeed more intense in its fits but rather more distributed, constant, and crippling . . . when I am at the worst,

though my judgment is never affected, my state is much like madness.

A self-confessed sufferer from melancholy – a term and condition with an infinite variety of interpretation – he endured it with many Victorian contemporaries as the spirit of the age. Bridges was one who saw it as crucial to understanding his friend's life, although he fails to define its precise nature and working.[14] It could not truly describe loss of faith (which was Ruskin's analysis of the century's 'ennui') in Hopkins's case, although it must have been fed in his later life by the decline in fervour as he explained it while working at St Aloysius in Oxford:

Feeling, love in particular, is the great moving power and spring of verse and the only person that I am in love with seldom, especially now, stirs my heart sensibly.[15]

The struggle to Catholic faith in the 1860s, the misgivings about unregenerate man in the St Beuno's poems, his disgust with Liverpool, and instability of mood evinced at Stonyhurst might all be said to contribute to or be symptomatic of this melancholy. Self-depreciation is a strong feature of his behaviour and is indeed listed by Adolf Meyer, a turn-of-the-century American psychiatrist, as a prominent element of melancholy: the sufferer shows 'a susceptibility for the unpleasant and wearing aspect of things only, and a feeling of self-depreciation, of sinfulness. . . . The patient feels himself too bad to live.'

Other poets have suffered from it. Edward Thomas, whose complaints about his health have the same psychosomatic character, admitted that his 'self-criticism or rather . . . studied self-contempt is now nearly a disease' and at times we seem to be reading Hopkins's correspondence as we read Thomas.

Some time in 1885 came 'Spelt from Sibyl's Leaves', a cosmic utterance of melancholy, which opens at the moment when evening darkens into night, when 'earth her being has unbound; her dapple is at end'. Darkness destroys individuality. Death is humanity's final end and that will show, like life, that good and evil are the only final truths.

Despite the immense lines (of 16 to 18 syllables), the sonnet has a regular octet and sestet, but its verbal abundance suggests an orchestra of sound in which alliteration, repetition and rhyme combine with the richness of a Mahler symphony:

> part, pen, pack
> Now her all in two flocks, two folds – black, white; right, wrong;
> reckon but, reck but, mind
> But these two; ware of a world where but these two tell . . .

This sonnet, said Hopkins, 'essays effects almost musical' and like all his verse was 'made for performance . . . loud, leisurely, poetical . . . recitation . . . [and] shd. be almost sung'.[16] But it is a tragic symphony, without the comforting presence of God or Holy Ghost 'with warm breast', depicting a world governed by remorseless moral laws which make man's life a misery,

> Where, selfwrung, selfstrung, sheathe- and shelterless,
> thoughts against thoughts in groans grind.

Against this poem should be set from the same year two which are more optimistic in spirit (the chronology of many of the Irish poems cannot be certainly established, and there is no reason to assume that all the poems of a certain mood were written consecutively; human nature, particularly in the case of Hopkins, is liable to impulsive changes of feeling). 'To what serves mortal beauty' raises the perennial question of how much value is to be placed on material things, especially the beauty of the human body. The answer is that such beauty may lead the admirer to love of more important values, keep 'warm Men's wits to the things that are'; 'men's selves' are, by all the laws of God-given individuality, sacred: 'Self flashes off fame and face'. But caution is the watch-word, and the mind should be fixed on 'God's better beauty, grace'.

The poem proceeds by a dialectic common to Hopkins: the statement of a material, physical and worldly beauty with all its appeal, followed by a warning of the dangers of a dependence on such an ephemeral experiences of life. What marks this poem is the comparative optimism with which such a lesson is presented: the poem suggests the traps of earthly beauty, without wishing to destroy them; indeed, suggesting their value in the understanding of higher things. This is not the mood of the tragic Hopkins, and illustrates the presence of calmer moments in a year of much sombre verse.

Similarly, 'The Soldier' (as we know the title), composed while on retreat at Clongowes, the Jesuit boarding-school twenty miles away from Stephen's Green, stands outside the tragic mode, although much in Hopkins's experience explains its writing. Admiration for the ideals of duty and physical courage was deeply engrained in the conservative Victorian temperament, and Hopkins's interest in seamen, wrecks, concern for British arms abroad and his everyday awareness of the English presence in Ireland is naturally reflected in his poetry. 'Truly,' stated *The Tablet*, 'we are living in a time when war and rumours of war abound. From the snows of Canada to the burning sands of Ethiopia, from the plains of South Africa to the highlands of Afghanistan, the cry is the same. We seem to be standing face to face with a crisis in the national history.'[17]

One side of Hopkins would certainly have responded to the romantic patriotism implicit in such journalism, but the sonnet quickly establishes a realistic assessment of the normal soldier and sailor, 'frail clay . . . foul clay', before insisting that the 'manly' calling must bring out the best in them, while their admirers, like Hopkins, 'fain will find as sterling all as all is smart'. Christ is now cited as the ideal leader and soldier who blesses any man whom he sees 'do all that man can do'.

Elsewhere, in the Sermons, Christ is presented as one who 'led the way, went before his troops',[18] imagery which reminds us that the founder of Hopkins's order was at one time a soldier, as is reflected in some of the images of the *Spiritual Exercises*. A modern soldier martyr-figure, admired by Hopkins and his contemporaries, was General Gordon, slain early in 1885 at Khartoum and praised by *The Tablet* as a 'selfless and stainless hero'. A memorable endorsement of the heroic view of the ordinary fighting man is given by Ruskin in *Unto This Last* in terms with which Hopkins would have been in complete agreement:

> [The world] honours the soldier . . . because he holds his life at the service of the State. Reckless he may be – fond of pleasure or of adventure – all kinds of bye-motives and mean impulses may have determined the choice of his profession, and may affect . . . his daily conduct in it; but our estimate of him is based on this ultimate fact . . . that put him in a fortress breech with all the pleasures of the world behind him, and only death and his duty in front of him, he will keep his face to the front.[19]

Despite the positive tone of 'The Soldier', 1885 was marked by the set of what Bridges called the 'melancholy sonnets'.[20] In these, Hopkins's depression reached its nadir, the true 'darkness of the soul' described by St Ignatius as one of the fundamental experiences of the seeker after religious truth. In the First Week of the *Exercises*, which is concerned with the evocation of Hell, he speaks of this condition as

> a darkening of the soul, trouble of mind, movement to base and earthly things . . . loss of hope, loss of love; when the soul feels herself thoroughly apathetic, tepid, sad, and as it were separated from her Creator and Lord.[21]

Aspects of this experience are elaborated in 'Carrion Comfort' whose lines of up to fifteen syllables with their six heavy stresses give Hopkins's most dramatic, even melodramatic picture of despair. The opening four lines protest that it is still within the poet's power to defeat his despair, 'Can something, hope, wish day come, not choose not to be', but the lines, like this one, are so broken and disjointed that pain and hopelessness is suggested in the very effort of uttering them.

The next four lines recall the pursuit of the Hound of Heaven in Thompson's poem as the poet describes himself as 'frantic to avoid thee and flee', while the opening of the sestet offers as possible reason for his suffering that 'my chaff might fly; my grain lie, sheer and clear'. Abruptly the poet then turns his mind back to the experience which we recognise in the 'Wreck of the Deutschland', the time perhaps of his conversion, and realises that he has gained profoundly since that time when he 'lay wrestling with (my God!) my God'. The consolation, however, is not convincing and the poem's violence of ideas and sounds and the series of interrogations underline the general sense of distress.

The five, more orthodox sonnets that follow rehearse in various tones the poet's suffering and by so doing raise the issue of the propriety of its expression in verse, 'that immodesty', as John Keble's Victorian editor tendentiously describes it, 'which lays bare to the whole world the inmost secrets of the heart'.[22] In defence of Hopkins, if the modern reader thinks one necessary, he seems to have had no expectation of these poems being published; only Bridges appears to have seen them and his mother could only have known his unhappiness by the far more guarded comments of his letters.

At another level, these confessional sonnets might deserve the criticism which Newman makes of the dangers of self-contemplation:

> Surely it is our duty ever to look off ourselves, and to look unto Jesus; that is, to shun the contemplation of our own feelings, emotions, frame, and state of mind, as the main business of religion, and to leave these mainly to be secured in their fruits.[23]

But the introvert, perhaps, cannot help the contemplation of self, and it might be argued in Hopkins's case that the expression of his distress in verse helped in the purgation of it. Had he not written so, he might have had the breakdown or developed the insanity he feared, fates which befell some of his Jesuit contemporaries. One wonders if he could ever have brought himself to explain personally to a colleague, even in the confessional, the depth of his unhappiness.

In one of his unhappy poems, the twentieth-century melancholic Ivor Gurney wrote that 'The amazed heart cries angrily out on God',[24] a suitable epigraph for these five sonnets of Hopkins, and especially 'No worst, there is none' where the 'Comforter' and 'Mary' are in turn reproached for their failure to comfort. Hopkins finds only one major consolation and its minor daily equivalent: 'Life Death does end and each day dies with sleep.'

As the American critic, Yvor Winters, claimed, this sonnet does not say precisely what the grief is caused by: we learn it is forged on an 'age-old anvil' and that it is as profound as 'no-man-fathomed' depths, and it may be that Hopkins is dealing with a grief that verges on the pathological, a case of classic, inexplicable depression. Yet this is surely a recognisable state of mind to many people, that of absolute despair under the pressure of a sense of general hopelessness, and to attempt to make it more precise might interest the psychiatrist while depriving the experience of its universality.

Language and sentence-structure convey bitterness and violence. The abrupt opening is succeeded by a sentence hardly less abrupt, full of repetition and alliteration. The two questions that follow are short and unrespectful and the violence of tone continues in the next four lines, where the images are dramatic and immediate: 'herds-long', 'huddle in a main', 'age-old anvil'.

Typically, throughout the whole poem Hopkins deals freely with rhyme and line-endings: three rhymes are hyphenated words and in the sestet line after line ends in enjambment, consisting, in two cases, of adjectives that describe nouns which appear at the beginning of the following lines.

Although at first sight it is a monologue, there is a range of voices. The first two lines are a statement of the suffering. The next two are directed at God and Mary, followed by three of further commentary on the poet's state. Fury is given a speaking-role and, after another line and a half of reflection, general humanity is addressed, or its more sceptical elements, in 'Hold them cheap . . .'. In the last lines the dominant voice is that of the discerning sceptic addressing the poet with a message of sardonic comfort.

In this sonnet octet and sestet unite to suggest one despairing outflow of feeling. 'To seem the stranger' presents a fractionally more resigned state of mind; the despair has a melancholic, rather than passionate tone; the argument seems controlled and logical. Loneliness, whether felt or real, is the prime ingredient of depression and here the poet lives among strangers, exiled by faith and geography from family, from the country he loves and deprived by 'dark heaven's baffling ban' from, what one presumes to be, creative utterance (the complaint that Heaven frustrates him and that he wishes to write is a remarkable turnaround in attitude, but these lines are further treated below).

The first four lines are neatly (the word seems appropriate to the development of the whole poem) allocated to the division between him and his family. It is noticeable that in describing Christ as 'my peace / my parting, sword and strife' the negative outnumber the positive qualities by three to one.

In the next four lines, in which Hopkins's mastery of line-movement is again outstanding ('hear/Me' creates a heavy stress on both words), his patriotic feelings are depressed by his inability to do more than stand to one side at a time when England's military position is being challenged worldwide.[25] (One is reminded that, perhaps about this time, he also composed 'What shall I do for the land that bred me', a 'patriotic song for soldiers' that he found difficult to write without 'spoon or brag'.[26])

The first three lines of the sestet underline the gentler tone of this sonnet by admitting that in all his postings Hopkins 'can / Kind love both give and get', but this reflection is replaced by the crueller thought that for good or bad reason 'what word / Wisest my heart breeds' cannot be expressed. The sense of this is sufficiently imprecise to apply to religious or poetic expression: anyone in ignorance of Hopkins's background would find it still more 'baffling', but his mother, and presumably Bridges, would have had little doubt; as she wrote to Bridges soon after her son's death, returning him letters which he had let her see for the first time:

> true I see he suffered at times – and more especially that last year from great depression of mind, & it was a great deal from feeling that he could not fully use or develop [sic] the gifts he possessed.[27]

But the phrase 'heard unheeded' also implies that what has been written is unread or unappreciated, an appeal for audience which is part of the familiar picture of Hopkins caught between the demands of dedicated priest and ambitious poet. The poem is full of brilliant plays on meaning and sounds, from the England whom his heart 'woos, wife to my creating thought', through the clipped sounds of 'dark heaven's baffling ban / Bars', to end in the witty paradox of 'hoard unheard, / Heard unheeded'.

The calculated self-control of this poem is replaced in 'I wake and feel' by the disgust of self-pity. The symptom of sleeplessness is taken literally by Dorothy Rowe in *The Experience of Depression*[28] as typical of the depressive and it is a condition that allows Hopkins to luxuriate in the misery of those 'black hours'. But it is also a symbol for years of tragic experience, isolated in feeling from God, 'dearest him', and leading to the sense of the barrenness of self, 'my taste was me'. As Arnold wrote in 'Empedocles on Etna', 'We feel, day and night, / The burden of ourselves'.[29] In 'As kingfishers catch fire', self was the climax of being:

> *myself* it speaks and spells,
> Crying *What I do is me: for that I came.*

But in Ireland, the poet and priest experiences himself without the lightening strength of God, 'Selfyeast of spirit a dull dough sours', and he is almost nothing more than his material self . . . almost: 'The lost are like this . . . but worse'. They are worse, of course, because they *are* lost, while the poet still (perhaps only just) retains his faith.

The spirit of these three dreadful poems is also evident in a letter to Bridges written about this time, where the failure of poetic inspiration is given as a cause:

> With me, if I could but get on, if I could but produce work I should not mind its being buried, silence, and going no further;

but it kills me to be time's eunuch and never to beget . . . soon I am afraid I shall be ground down to a state like this last spring's and summer's, when my spirits were so crushed that madness seemed to be making approaches.[30]

Perhaps it was only patience that kept him going: the *Spiritual Exercises* declare: 'Let him who is in desolation labour to hold on in patience, such patience as makes against the visitations that harass him.'[31] He had spoken about it at Oxford as a student, and again as a priest at St Aloysius, the 'Patience exquisite, / That plumes to Peace thereafter'. In the next poem, it is 'Patience, hard thing', a virtue learnt through the hard experience of doing without and of obedience and especially, no doubt, through the duties of the common Jesuit life. The tone of resignation in this sonnet – despite the chilling harshness of 'We hear our hearts grate on themselves' – distinguishes it from others in the group, and at the same time, perhaps, makes it the least striking, for the resignation has to be argued for, rather than expressed in a spontaneous outpouring of feeling.

Although 'My own heart let me more have pity on' struggles to an optimistic conclusion, the octet is full of anger and despair, characteristic of the poet's most tragic moods. It is a monologue addressed to himself, to that part of him which will not, for whatever reason, let the whole man rest. Again, we are given a picture of a man driven back on himself, unable to escape his own sense of failure, and subjecting himself to an almost remorseless interrogation which finds no satisfaction. In the sestet the poet begs the 'jaded 'Jackself' to let God work in his own (unpredictable) way, bringing consolation to the troubled mind: the advice seems an anti-climax to the anguish of the first eight lines.

As far as one can tell, these sonnets preluded a silence of some two years in his poetry, although his correspondence with Bridges, Patmore, Dixon and others continued as vigorously as before. A series of letters to Alexander Baillie on Egyptology, to other correspondents about their poetry and many references to Irish politics show that his intellectual curiosity was as wide-ranging as ever, and his letter-writing even more necessary to him: 'It is a great help to me to have someone interested in something . . . and it supplies some sort of intellectual stimulus.'[32] He continued, too, to dabble with musical composition, although no piece was performed and the Professor of Music at Trinity was blunt, albeit friendly, in his criticisms.

The end to this barren period was signalled by a poem inspired by the contemporary scene. Throughout 1885–7, meetings of the unemployed, which developed into riots, had become almost commonplace in London and other centres, culminating in a serious outbreak of violence in Trafalgar Square and the surrounding area in November 1887. Hopkins's individual brand of conservatism was not unmoved by these events, and may well have been further tempered by the attitudes of Cardinal Manning and Bishop Vaughan of Salford who were actively sympathetic towards the poor. The theme of the 'dispossessed' had been touched on by Arnold in *Culture and Anarchy* where comments on the 'English rough' are in the radical tradition of Carlyle: 'The question of questions for him [the rough] is a wages question. . . . He has no visionary schemes of revolution and transformation. . . . Just as the rest of us . . . he has no idea of a State, of the nation in its collective and corporate character.'[33]

Such too is the view of Hopkins's poem 'Tom's Garland: upon the unemployed'. He wrote to Bridges in February 1888:

> This [anti-socialist criticism] is all very well for those who are in, however low in, the Commonwealth and share in any way the Common weal [he had told his Liverpool congregation they all did so]; but . . . the curse of our times is that many do not share it, that they are outcasts from it and have neither security nor splendour. . . . And this state of things, I say, is the origin of Loafers, Tramps, Cornerboys, Roughs, Socialists, and other pests of society.[34]

It is a poem that makes no concessions to popular taste, a mighty sonnet of two codas, 20 lines in all, recalling Milton's satirical 'On the new forcers of Conscience'. 'Declaimed,' wrote Hopkins, 'the strange constructions would be dramatic and effective,' but only, one feels, if the reader grasped the poem's meaning, as Bridges and Dixon did not, and for whom the author felt forced to provide a 'crib'.

The octet is relatively straightforward in its portrayal of the typical navvy who is quite content with his rough life, happily without all idealism provided he has his home comforts. The alliteration and sprung rhythm are forceful and uncompromising:

> . . . Tóm's fállowbóotféllow píles pick
> Bý him and ríps out róckfire hómeforth . . .

Hopkins's paraphrase of the whole poem is singularly unhelpful in its explication of detail in the final twelve lines, which include

> But no way sped,
> Nor mind nor main strength; gold go garlanded
> With, perilous, O no . . .

In writing of this cryptic nature each reader may perceive something different, and a private language seems to threaten. But the next poem, 'Harry Ploughman', if less original, is certainly more intelligible: the immediate picture offered seems to come from the hand of a painter:

> Hard as hurdle arms, with a broth of goldish flue
> Breathed round; the rack of ribs; the scooped flank; lank
> Rope-over thigh; knee-nave; and barrelled shank . . .

'I want,' said Hopkins, 'Harry Ploughman to be a vivid figure before the mind's eye,'[35] yet, in the end, this is perhaps the poem's shortcoming, for unlike 'Felix Randal', with its deep sense of emotional involvement, it is as a picture only that the later poem makes its effect. Moreover, it seems partly built on memories of previous verse by Hopkins: 'Soared or sank' recalls 'Swam or sank' ('Binsey Poplars'), 'What deed he each must do', 'What I do is me' ('Kingfishers catch fire'), and 'Hangs or hurls them', 'Half hurls earth for him off under his feet' ('Hurrahing in Harvest').

Ruskin gave as his vision of a new England: 'Agriculture . . . by the hand or by the plough drawn only by animals; and shepherds and pastoral husbandry, [these] are to be the chief schools of Englishmen.'[36] 'Harry Ploughman' belongs to the same nostalgic vision of the ideal nature of country life and in this respect, too, represents a looking-back by its author.

The poem has also attracted comment because of the alleged homo-erotic element that some readers have detected in its description of the male physique. This topic is always likely to be controversial and subject to personal impression: throughout the ages the human body has been admired, both in art and real life, without any necessary homosexual implication, and the appeal to Hopkins of femininity and marriage can equally well be demonstrated in his letters and poems. If images of the male sometimes played a larger part in his life than the female, this is hardly surprising in his vocation as a Catholic priest and in a culture dominated by masculine values.

There was no apparent diminution in the uncertainty and unhappiness of his personal life. He doubted whether his College could continue in the present unsettled political conditions, with the Irish bishops looking for a more nationalist stance and the Jesuits trying to preserve a neutral position. In a letter to Baillie in February 1887 he gave a long account of the troubled Irish scene and the difficulties of English rule in Ireland, concluding that in the end the best solution would be Home Rule:

> the mass of Irish people owe no allegiance to any existing law or government. And yet they are not a worthless people; they have many true and winning virtues. But their virtues do not promote civil order and it has become impossible to govern them . . . they must have Home Rule with all that it may cost both them and us.[37]

His attitude to his writing remained ambiguous. He had thoughts of a book on Greek metres and wrote in January 1887 that he had completed 'some part' of it, but nothing has survived, the same fate as a number of other scholarly projects that he mentions at different times in his letters. He insisted that 'what becomes of my verses I care little'[38] and a long gap ensued between 'Harry Ploughman' and 'That Nature is a Heraclitean Fire and of the comfort of the Resurrection' (July 1888).

The second half of the latter title perhaps reflects a revival in inspiration, for this massive 20-line sonnet is full of energy and confidence in its statement of belief in man's immortal being. It opens with an exciting, almost uproarious sense of the variety of Nature, the short phrases, assonance and alliteration suggesting pell-mell experience:

> Down roughcast, down dazzling whitewash, wherever an
>     elm arches,
> Shivelights and shadowtackle in long lashes lace, lance,
>     and pair.

Thus Nature, in one form or another, sustains herself, whereas Man, 'her clearest-selvèd spark', is finite, 'death blots black out', and we reach the middle of the fifteenth line before the heartening message of the 'Resurrection' begins. It is only 'flesh' and 'mortal trash' that 'fall to the residuary worm': the poet, like all men, shares both Christ's human suffering and his immortality, 'Is immortal diamond'.

The poem is a statement of faith, not the exploration of an argument, and it is in this mode that Hopkins is at his best. Different and similar sounds are played against each other, mingling alliteration, assonance and rhyme (or half-rhyme):

> Delightfully the bright wind boisterous ropes, wrestles, beats
>     earth bare
> Of yestertempest's creases.

Together with the sprung rhythm and the many exclamatory and short clauses, these effects create a poem in which sound and sense are appropriately related, never more so than in the long sentence which ends the poem in the triumphant realisation that man is 'immortal diamond'.

In October, to celebrate the Jesuit lay-brother, Alphonsus Rodriguez (died 1617), who had been canonised in January 1888, he composed a sonnet which he rather contemptuously labelled 'intelligible' – he was still smarting from Bridges's criticisms of earlier sonnets. Its plainness and traditional structure suit the purpose and audience (the Jesuit community in Majorca) for which it was intended and its subject, the patience of the Saint in question in his humdrum job as doorkeeper, had a personal significance for a nineteenth-century Jesuit condemned to the monotonous and 'killing work' of examining a 'nation'. Great deeds are known to the world,

> But be the war within, the brand we wield
> Unseen, the heroic breast not outward-steeled,
> Earth hears no hurtle then from fiercest fray.

At the beginning of January 1888 he had made a retreat at Tullabeg, Fr Delaney's old school in the depths of central Ireland. It resulted in a harrowing self-examination of his career since he had been in the country, perhaps the climax of his tragic self-searching and conscientious questioning. Of his work at the University he wrote, 'I do not feel . . . that outwardly I do much good,' and spoke of the 'loathing', 'helplessness' and 'fear of madness' that overcame him.

Such thoughts enter into the poems we have already considered and into 'Thou art indeed just, Lord' (words which he himself used to quieten his despair in his retreat notes), the sonnet that dates from spring 1889, and is one of the most tightly argued of the Dublin poems. Written in regular sonnet form, its direct address to God resembles Herbert:

> Thou are indeed just, Lord, if I contend
> With thee; but, sir, so what I plead is just.

But Herbert's poems end in submission; this one does not: 'O thou lord of life, send my roots rain', and the entire sonnet is a complaint about the poet's personal plight:

> . . . why must
> Disappointment all I endeavour end?

> Oh, the sots and thralls of lust
> Do in spare hours more thrive than I . . .

And the theme of sterility he makes so much of in his letters recurs again as he finally declares:

> . . . birds build – but not I build; no, but strain,
> Time's eunuch.

In a letter of January 1888 he had used the same image in a context where he was referring to both poetry and scholarly work: 'Nothing comes: I am a eunuch – but it is for the kingdom of heaven's sake.'[39] In the poem he complains to God that He is unfair to him, 'I that spend, / Sir, life upon thy Cause', and the overall tone of defeat and self-pity reveals Hopkins at his most human and least heroic.

In 'The Shepherd's Brow' the mood yet again develops into one of self-deprecation, although this is a masterly sonnet, written in sprung rhythm that at times achieves powerful effects. It opens by suggesting the dignity of the countryman's life confronting the terrors and glory of the heavens. Wonderful, too, are the exploits of God and the angels. But ordinary man is frail and temporary, his life determined by his material appetites: 'Hand to mouth he lives, and voids with shame.'

As in 'That Nature is a Heraclitean Fire', the contemptuous term 'Jack' is again used to describe the common man, but not, this time, to lead to a climax in which he is given final dignity by Christ, but as a statement about the low value of humanity, 'Man Jack the man is, just; his mate a hussy'. The poet realises that he is of the same nature, and all his despairing idealism is no more than a subject for derision: I, he writes,

> . . . in smooth spoons spy life's masque mirrored: tame
> My tempests there, my fire and fever fussy.

Bridges was disturbed by the 'cynical tone' of this poem and refused to place it with the other finished Irish poems in his edition of Hopkins. It is true it reaches neither their heroic heights nor tragic depths, but as an expression of the state of Hopkins's feelings it has as much claim as, for example, 'God's Grandeur', on the attention of those who wish to understand him.

A further drawback in Bridges's eyes must have been that it would also have had to be placed chronologically with Hopkins's last sonnet, which is dedicated to Bridges himself and is couched in dignified, not cynical terms. 'To R.B.', whose orthodox form would have pleased its dedicatee, apologises for the continued failure of the author's inspiration, explaining that the 'winter world' of Ireland and his own life is responsible for denying him 'that bliss'.

Stated with a fine dignity, this apology reflects Hopkins's growing skill at expressing a variety of moods in the sonnet form. The imagery of birth and gestation is immediately introduced in the opening line, 'The fine delight that fathers thought', and the description of inspiration as 'live and lancing like the blowpipe flame' recalls the passage in his devotional writings where he speaks of St Ignatius's image of the 'current of air in the blow-pipe' which throws a 'jet of flame this way or that'[40] – the reference here is to the 'instressed', or spiritually inspired soul.

The mind becomes the mother or womb of a poem, and may hold it unborn for many years, apparently a 'widow', yet shaping the inspiration. Hopkins declares that he seeks such 'sweet fire', but his 'winter world' offers him nothing. The resignation of the conclusion reflects the restrained atmosphere of the whole poem, underlined by the many 's' sounds: the poet perhaps has finally found the patience he so often desired.

It was, however, too late. He first mentions illness in a letter dated 1 May 1889; it was later identified as typhoid, for which the drains at the College seem to have been primarily responsible,[41] although the seriousness of his condition was not realised until the beginning of

June. His mother and father made their first visit to Dublin to see him, and his death came on Saturday 8 June.

## Notes

1. 'Psychotherapists or the Clergy', in Jung, *Collected Works* (London, 1969) XI, p. 331.
2. Quoted in Fr T. Morrissey, *Towards a National University* (Dublin, 1983) p. 67.
3. *Further Letters of Hopkins*, p. 164.
4. Quoted in Fr T. Morrissey, *Some Jesuit Contributions to Irish Education*, thesis, p. 511.
5. Morrissey, *Towards a National University*, p. 87.
6. *Further Letters of Hopkins*, p. 63.
7. *Letters of Hopkins to Bridges*, p. 190.
8. Ibid., p. 192.
9. Ibid., p. 193.
10. Ibid., p. 197.
11. According to Dr Molloy, Rector of the Catholic University, the emphasis on examinations tended to lower University professors 'to the condition of college grinders, and to extinguish all ardour for original research' (quoted in *Irish Ecclesiastical Record* (January 1884) p. 68).
12. *Further Letters of Hopkins*, p. 164.
13. Ibid., p. 254.
14. For an attempt to do so and sources of references used here, see G. Roberts, '"I know the sadness, but the cause know not": Reflections on Hopkins's Melancholy', in *The Hopkins Quarterly* (October 1991) pp. 97ff.
15. *Letters of Hopkins to Bridges*, p. 66.
16. Ibid., pp. 245–6.
17. *The Tablet* (28 March 1885) p. 486.
18. *Sermons of Hopkins*, p. 70.
19. *Unto This Last*, 1906 edn, pp. 25–6 (Section 17).
20. *Selected Letters of Bridges*, ed. Stanford, I, p. 192.
21. *Spiritual Exercises*, ed. Rickaby, p. 69.
22. Keble, *Miscellaneous Poems*, 2nd edn (London, 1869) p. xxii.
23. Newman, *Prose and Poetry*, ed. G. Tillotson, Reynard Library (London, 1957) p. 33.
24. 'Pain', in *Collected Poems of Gurney*, ed. Kavanagh (Oxford, 1984) p. 36.
25. See page 129 above.
26. *Letters of Hopkins to Bridges*, p. 283.
27. Bridges MSS, Bodleian Library, Letter no. 19.
28. D. Rowe, *The Experience of Depression* (Chichester, 1978).
29. *Empedocles on Etna*, ll. 127–8.
30. *Letters of Hopkins to Bridges*, p. 222.
31. *Spiritual Exercises*, ed. Rickaby, p. 70.
32. *Further Letters of Hopkins*, p. 263.
33. *Culture and Anarchy*, ed. J. D. Wilson (Cambridge, 1963) pp. 80–1.

34. *Letters of Hopkins to Bridges*, pp. 273–4.
35. Ibid., p. 265.
36. Ruskin, *The Crown of Wild Olive*, para. 157.
37. *Further Letters of Hopkins*, p. 283.
38. *Correspondence of Hopkins and R. W. Dixon*, p. 150.
39. *Letters of Hopkins to Bridges*, p. 270.
40. *Sermons of Hopkins*, p. 137.
41. N. White, 'Poetry as Biography and Letter', in *Hopkins and Dublin*, ed. R. Giles, *Hopkins Quarterly* Special Issue, April 1987–January 1988, pp. 91–2.

# 17
# Afterwards

*The serious problems in life . . . are never fully solved. . . . The
meaning and purpose of a problem seems to be not in its solution
but in our working at it incessantly.*

C. G. Jung, *The Stages of Life*[1]

However limited Hopkins's experience of life – he was only 44 when
he died and his last 20 years had been spent as a Jesuit – only that life
could have produced work of such marked character. 'Himself it
spoke and spelled': the Oxford seeker for religious certainty, the
St Beuno's enthusiast for God in Nature, the city priest oppressed by
urban England, the frustrated and disillusioned patriot in exile.

It is the relative narrowness of this career that helps to explain the
authenticity and absence of contemporary poetic affectation that
marks his work, for he had no motive to follow or adapt himself to
changing taste or literary fashion. He was used to shocking his small
public of Bridges and Patmore and his Jesuit editors, to argue over
their taste and defend his own, writing in the way he wished about
those subjects which seemed important to him.

This originality can be illustrated by comparing what he wrote
before he became a Catholic with his work afterwards, by comparing
the mixture of influences and styles pre-1868 with the newly emerging
self from 1875 onwards. Tennyson, Keats, Herbert, the ballad, the
dramatic fragment, the Browning monologue, the Miltonic sonnet,
pre-Raphaelitism, the Bible all jostle for place in his early years and
only hindsight recognises evidence of the mature Hopkins.

Even in relatively minor poems of his maturity, such as 'The
shepherd's brow' or 'To R.B.', the reader is struck by the personal
character of content and writing. Only out of his experience could
these sonnets have been written – the frustrated, embittered priest-
poet trapped in a way and vision of life which must now be patiently
accepted.

To know his (later) poetry is to know his life and a poet's response to life is also seen in his style. His preference for the compact and tensile form of the sonnet, for the energy of sprung rhythm, alliteration and rhyme, for abrupt syntactical forms, reflect an intellectually and emotionally dynamic personality. For Hopkins an image is not an occasion for a logically elaborated conceit or rich word-painting, but a brilliant flick of the artist's brush or sudden conceptual and linguistic insight; natural description is not static, but exciting, disturbing, and inevitably spiritual.

His re-organisation and re-invention of English syntax and vocabulary are to a great extent a consequence of his literary isolation: on the one hand he had no public to please, on the other, he gloried in being different by being 'himself'. This contrariness – as it seemed to Bridges – is reflected in the opposition within his style of colloquial and highly mannered elements: if at times his writing resembles a linguistic maze, the way through it is facilitated by stretches of informal English and rhythms familiar to common speech.

It was not surprising that Bridges approached the idea of an edition of his friend's poetry with great caution for some years after Hopkins's death. In the words of another writer, who was only starting his career at this time, had such poems appeared they would 'have been thought a deliberate outrage, and simply execrated'.[2] Yet, despite his critical scepticism, Bridges was determined on such an edition, and from 1889 onwards proceeded to collect and collate manuscript versions of the poems.

His intention was to introduce the poems gradually to the public, bearing in mind the difficulties, particularly obscurity, that they might present, and the first step in this direction was a small selection in a volume of Alfred Miles's important series, *Poets and Poetry of the Century* (1893). This was prefaced by an introduction giving an account of Hopkins's life and warning readers about his 'neglect of those canons of taste which seem common to all poetry'.[3]

As it happened, few reviewers noticed the poems, but Bridges was undaunted and in conjunction with Hopkins's family (and reluctant to cooperate with the Jesuits whom he distrusted) he continued to press on with preparations for a full edition. The turning-point in this slow process came with the appearance of more of the poetry in *The Spirit of Man*, the very popular patriotic anthology edited by Bridges and published in 1916. Auden, Ivor Gurney and F. R. Leavis all came across Hopkins in it for the first time. With a growing readership of Hopkins amongst the Jesuits and religious-minded readers, especially in the United States, and some discerning

English critics who were friendly with Bridges, his first English editor was finally encouraged to take the plunge.

In December 1918 *Poems of Gerard Manley Hopkins* appeared, with commentary by Bridges. Only 750 were printed, and at an expensive 12/6d apiece it was many years before the print was exhausted. Bridges's diffident memoir may well have been partly to blame, for it is a detailed (and somewhat depressing) list of the author's 'bad faults' which, we are told, have to be accepted alongside 'the very forcible and original effects of beauty'.[4]

Except to comment unfavourably on his anti-Catholic prejudices, critics were unanimous about the success of Bridges's editing, even if they seemed to take their tone from him in a generally mixed verdict on the poetry he had sponsored. Typical was the experienced reviewer in the *Times Literary Supplement* who spoke of the reader as involved but uncertain: 'You fight your way through the verses, yet they draw you on.'[5]

After the immediate response, critical silence more or less fell, but the seed had been planted. More comment by I. A. Richards and Robert Graves in the mid and later 1920s encouraged further readers, and when, after Bridges's death, the second edition by Charles Williams appeared in 1930, the reputation of Hopkins seemed finally established, although whether as a modern or Victorian poet was to be lengthily debated in the following decade.

### Notes

1.  Jung, *Collected Works* (London, 1969) vol. VIII, p. 394.
2.  Laurence Binyon, quoted in *Hopkins: The Critical Heritage*, ed. Roberts, p. 3.
3.  Quoted, ibid., p. 63.
4.  Quoted, ibid., p. 81.
5.  Quoted, ibid., p. 86.

# Further Reading

The most popular edition of Hopkins's *Poems* is still that edited by Norman MacKenzie and W. H. Gardner for Oxford University Press, 4th edition (1967) and frequently reprinted. More recent is the comprehensive (but very expensive) Oxford volume of 1990, also edited by MacKenzie and the Oxford University Press paperback edited by Katherine Phillips (1986), which also contains a selection of his prose.

Volumes published by OUP earlier in the century contain all Hopkins's prose (see Bibliography), but useful selections are to be found in the Phillips volume mentioned above, in her *Selected Letters* (Oxford, 1990), and in Gerald Roberts's edition published by OUP in 1980.

One of the standard selections of Hopkins's poetry and prose is the best-selling Penguin edition by W. H. Gardner (1953, but many times reprinted).

After a dearth of convincing biographies, a number have appeared over the last decade or so, the two most recent being R. B. Martin's *Gerard Manley Hopkins: A Very Private Man* (London, 1991) and, perhaps definitive, Norman White's *Hopkins: A Literary Biography* (Oxford, 1992). The sources for much of Hopkins's Jesuit life may be read in Fr A. Thomas's *Hopkins the Jesuit* (London, 1969).

A bibliography of Hopkins by Tom Dunne was published by Oxford in 1976. Since then, the periodical *The Hopkins Quarterly* has kept the record up to date: edited by R. F. Giles and published at Mohawk College, Ontario, it also prints current, often trans-atlantic work on Hopkins.

The most comprehensive critical work is still *Hopkins, a Study of Poetic Idiosyncrasy* (London, 1944 and 1948) by W. H. Gardner (in two volumes). Modern, as well as earlier critical essays have been reprinted in the Macmillan Casebook series edited by M. Bottrall (London, 1975) and in G. H. Hartman's selection in the Twentieth Century Views series (Englewood Cliffs, New Jersey, 1966).

Useful general critical surveys have been written by Graham

Storey, *A Preface to Hopkins* (London, 1981) and by Norman MacKenzie, *A Reader's Guide to Hopkins* (London, 1981) but a lucid modern one-volume critical account of Hopkins's poetry, taking into account current research and attitudes, would fulfil a growing need. A history of Hopkins criticism (up to 1940) is plotted in *Hopkins: The Critical Heritage*, edited G. Roberts (London, 1987) reflecting changes in the author's fortunes and reputation since 1889.

*The Language of Hopkins* by James Milroy (London, 1977) is a stimulating study of a crucial aspect of Hopkins's writing.

On the spiritual background, John Pick's *Hopkins, Priest and Poet* (London, 1942) is clear and enlightening. It is difficult to recommend modern studies in this area, where specialisation has taken over to an increasing, and often unliterary, extent.

# Bibliography

*Poems of Hopkins*, ed. W. H. Gardner and N. MacKenzie, 4th edn (London, 1970).

*Poems of Hopkins*, ed. N. MacKenzie (Oxford, 1990).

*Journals and Papers of Hopkins*, ed. H. House and G. Storey (London, 1966).

*Letters of Hopkins to Bridges*, ed. C. Abbott (London, 1970).

*Correspondence of Hopkins and R. W. Dixon*, ed. C. Abbott (London, 1970).

*Further Letters of Hopkins*, ed. C. Abbott, 2nd edn (London, 1970).

*Sermons and Devotional Writings of Hopkins*, ed. C. Devlin (London, 1959).

T. Dunne, *Hopkins: A Comprehensive Bibliography* (Oxford, 1976).

Fr A. Thomas, *Hopkins the Jesuit: The Years of Training* (London, 1969).

*Hopkins Quarterly* (Canada, since 1974).

*Letters and Notices* (London, since 1863) (internal periodical publication of the English Province of the Society of Jesus).

*Hopkins: The Critical Heritage*, ed. G. Roberts (London, 1987).

St Ignatius Loyola, *The Spiritual Exercises*, tr. and ed. J. Rickaby (London, 1915).

*The Tablet* (London, since 1840).

*Constitutions of the Society of Jesus*, tr. and ed. G. Ganss (St Louis, 1970).

J. Hunter, *Gerard Manley Hopkins* (London, 1966).

*Dictionary of National Biography*, ed. Leslie Stephen *et al.* (London, 1885).

# Index

# L'islam

**Direction éditoriale**
Thomas Dartige

**Édition**
Clotilde Oussiali

**Direction artistique**
Élisabeth Cohat

**Conception graphique**
Christine Régnier

**Maquette**
Maryline Gatepaille

**Coordination
iconographique**
Isabelle de Latour

**Iconographie**
Perrine Dragic

**Fabrication**
Christophe de Mullenheim

**Préparation**
Jean-Paul Harris

**Correction**
Lorène Bücher

**Index**
Isabelle Haffen


Les textes et documents
ainsi que les chiffres
et verbatim de la partie
Décrypter ont été
rassemblés à la
Documentation française
par Christine Fabre.

ISBN 978-2-07-061479-0
© Gallimard Jeunesse - La Documentation française 2008
Dépôt légal : février 2008
Numéro d'édition : 151942
Loi n° 49-956 du 16 juillet 1949
sur les publications destinées à la jeunesse
Photogravure : Scanplus
Imprimé par L.E.G.O. Spa en Italie

# L'islam

Élisabeth Combres

Illustrations : Diego Aranega
Carte : La Station Animation

Ville de **Joué** lès Tours

La **documentation** Française

GALLIMARD JEUNESSE

Mahomet est né à La Mecque en **570** et mort à Médine en **632**.

Le Coran est divisé en **114 sourates**, composées de **6 219 versets**.

**2 millions** de pèlerins se sont rendus à La Mecque en **2007**.

On compte **1,2 milliard** de musulmans dans le monde, soit à peu près **1/5e** de la population mondiale.

L'Indonésie est le **1er pays musulman** au monde avec **185,6 millions** de pratiquants.

Il y a **4 millions** de musulmans en France, **40 millions** de catholiques, **1,1 million** de protestants, **0,6 million** de juifs.

# L'islam

L'islam est une religion monothéiste apparue après
le judaïsme et le christianisme. Ces trois religions
ont des racines communes, mais ne donnent pas la même
interprétation du Dieu qu'elles vénèrent. L'islam est né
au VIIe siècle après Jésus-Christ : selon la tradition
musulmane, l'ultime et véritable parole de Dieu a été révélée
au prophète Mahomet, alors caravanier en Arabie.
Aujourd'hui, le monde musulman compte plus de un milliard
de personnes. Il est constitué de peuples, de sociétés, de
traditions et de pratiques religieuses d'une grande diversité.
D'abord centré sur le Maghreb et le Moyen-Orient, le monde
musulman s'est étendu vers l'Asie et l'Afrique subsaharienne.
Au cours du XXe siècle est né l'islamisme, un courant
politique qui veut soumettre la société aux règles de l'islam.
Certains islamistes respectent les principes démocratiques,
d'autres usent de la violence pour imposer leurs idées.
Depuis la série d'attentats commis dans les années 2000
par des islamistes extrémistes, les musulmans font l'objet
d'une méfiance et d'un rejet grandissants dans les pays
occidentaux. Pourtant, cette violence terroriste n'est pas
due à l'islam, mais à des extrémistes qui détournent
les textes religieux à leur profit.

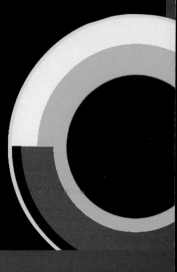

Les musulmans* mangent beaucoup de
pâtisseries pendant et à la fin du ramadan*.

# Décrypter
# les faits d'actualité

\* Les mots suivis d'un astérisque sont définis dans la partie
« Comprendre les mots de l'info » (p. 28).

# « Des caricatures de Mahomet* enflamment le monde musulman. »

En février 2006, des ambassades danoises ont été prises pour cibles dans plusieurs pays du monde musulman. Quatre mois auparavant, un journal danois avait publié une série de dessins caricaturant le prophète Mahomet*. L'un d'eux le représentait coiffé d'une bombe en guise de turban.

# Réactions en chaîne

**Fin septembre 2005, un quotidien danois publie douze caricatures de Mahomet\*, déclenchant des critiques au Danemark, mais pas de violence. Fin 2005, la tête des dessinateurs est mise à prix par des islamistes\* pakistanais. Puis des ministres de pays arabes réunis au Caire condamnent ces caricatures. Peu après, un magazine chrétien norvégien publie de nouveau ces dessins au nom de la liberté d'expression, suivi par d'autres journaux européens. Les réactions se multiplient alors, au Moyen-Orient, en Afrique, en Asie centrale. Dans ces régions, des ambassades scandinaves sont incendiées, des populations musulmanes et chrétiennes sont attaquées et des manifestations, réprimées, faisant plusieurs dizaines de morts.**

## L'œil critique

● *Caricature d'info*

De nombreux médias n'ont montré que les réactions violentes, donnant, à tort, l'impression qu'elles étaient le fait d'une majorité de musulmans. Or certaines de ces manifestations ont été encouragées par des groupes islamistes, voire par des pouvoirs en place, pour montrer l'Occident comme un agresseur. Cela permettait en effet aux extrémistes de diffuser leurs idées (qui ont gagné du terrain avec ces événements) et aux gouvernements de détourner l'attention des difficultés dans leur pays.

● *Le débat en spectacle*

Un des principes de la démocratie est de pouvoir s'exprimer librement, donc de pouvoir critiquer les religions. Aussi des journaux français ont-ils choisi de publier à leur tour les caricatures de Mahomet. La reprise de ces dessins a créé une vive polémique, dont les télévisions se sont emparées pour faire de l'audience. Elles ont mis en scène de virulentes joutes verbales opposant sans nuances les défenseurs du «on peut tout dire» à ceux du «il faut ménager les musulmans».

● *Occasion manquée*

En mettant l'accent sur les violences et la polémique, les médias ont raté l'occasion de proposer des explications sur l'islam\*, son histoire et sa place dans la vie des musulmans. Ainsi, ils auraient pu montrer comment les intégristes\* interprètent le Coran\* à leur avantage. Et ils auraient pu rappeler que l'islam, malgré des courants intolérants et des périodes d'extrême sévérité, a su, au cours de son histoire, ménager une place à la liberté de penser.

# Âge d'or islamique et modernité occidentale

Du VIII<sup>e</sup> au XIV<sup>e</sup> siècle, une civilisation d'une immense vitalité s'est développée autour de l'islam*. Aujourd'hui, des pays du monde musulman, très imprégnés de religion, s'adaptent mal à la modernité laïque définie par les pays occidentaux.

Le Coran* n'interdit pas les représentations de Mahomet*. Il en existe, à travers l'Histoire. Ainsi, ce manuscrit turc du XIV<sup>e</sup> siècle montre Mahomet et l'ange Gabriel. On trouve en revanche des interdits contre les images dans les hadith, ces recueils des actes et des paroles de Mahomet rapportés et interprétés par des experts en religion, parfois longtemps après sa mort.

## La naissance de l'islam

La religion musulmane est née au VII<sup>e</sup> siècle en Arabie, une région aride où des tribus arabes vénérant de multiples dieux et déesses côtoyaient des juifs et des chrétiens. Selon la tradition musulmane, un caravanier de La Mecque* du nom de Mahomet* reçoit la parole de Dieu à partir de l'an 610. Persécuté pour ses prédications, il fuit avec ses premiers fidèles vers Médine en 622. Mahomet est à la fois un chef religieux et politique. Il conquiert La Mecque en 630 et étend son pouvoir sur toute la péninsule Arabique. Mais après sa mort, en 632, ses proches se divisent autour de sa succession. Une guerre éclate qui, en 657, scinde l'islam en trois branches : le sunnisme* (majoritaire), le chiisme* et le kharijisme*.

## Dynasties islamiques

Divisée et multiple dès son origine, la civilisation islamique a compté de nombreuses dynasties, au sein desquelles le pouvoir politique et religieux s'est transmis par les liens du sang. La première de ces dynasties, celle des Omeyyades, est fondée en 661 et fait de Damas, en Syrie, la capitale du monde islamique. L'islam se répand très rapidement, par la conquête militaire, jusqu'en Espagne, en Chine, en Inde, en Afrique du Nord. En 750, les Omeyyades sont renversés par les Abbassides. Cette nouvelle dynastie choisit pour capitale de l'islam Bagdad, en

Irak. Dans le même temps, un Omeyyade survivant fonde une dynastie concurrente à Cordoue, en Espagne. Les Abbassides régneront jusqu'en 1258, année de la prise de Bagdad par les Mongols. Entre-temps, d'autres dynasties islamiques ont vu le jour, en Inde, en Iran, au Maghreb. Enfin, l'an 1299 marque le début de l'Empire ottoman, qui introduira durablement l'islam dans l'Europe des Balkans. Au début du XXᵉ siècle, cet empire disparaît, remplacé par une Turquie laïque.

## L'ère moderne

La civilisation islamique a fait preuve, au cours des siècles, d'une grande vitalité dans les domaines de la philosophie, des sciences et des arts. Dans ces sociétés musulmanes où religion et politique étaient étroitement liées, des penseurs ont su être critiques vis-à-vis de l'islam. Toutefois, ils sont restés attachés aux textes sacrés. En Occident, une séparation s'est opérée entre la morale religieuse et la pensée scientifique, artistique, politique… Ainsi, le XVIIIᵉ siècle européen, marqué par le courant philosophique des Lumières, a donné naissance au monde occidental actuel, fondé sur le progrès scientifique, les libertés individuelles et la vie matérielle. Aujourd'hui, dans des pays musulmans très religieux, ces principes n'ont pas la même valeur que dans les pays occidentaux. Cette différence est parfois à l'origine d'incompréhensions, alors utilisées par des extrémistes de tous bords, en Orient comme en Occident, pour monter les populations les unes contre les autres.

**CHRONOLOGIE SAVANTE ET ARTISTIQUE**

La civilisation islamique a brillé dans de nombreux domaines : architecture, mathématiques, médecine…
**690** Le Dôme du Rocher est érigé à Jérusalem.
**721-815** Les travaux de l'alchimiste Geber inspirent l'Europe médiévale.
**973** La mosquée* et université al-Azhar est construite au Caire.
**999-1003** Les chiffres arabes sont introduits en Europe par le pape Sylvestre II.
**IXᵉ-XIᵉ siècles** Les contes des *Mille et Une Nuits*, d'origine indienne, sont enrichis à Bagdad et en Égypte.
**980-1037** Avicenne, médecin et philosophe persan, met en relation les pensées de l'islam et celles des philosophes grecs Aristote et Platon.
**1122** L'Europe découvre la cartographie grâce aux musulmans.
**1126-1198** Averroès, médecin arabe, propose une lecture philosophique du Coran.
**XIIIᵉ siècle** La construction du palais de l'Alhambra débute à Grenade, en Espagne.
**1588-1629** L'art islamique connaît un âge d'or à Ispahan, en Perse.

**300** mots de la langue française proviennent de l'arabe (et seulement 100 du gaulois !) : abricot, alchimie, algèbre, amiral, azimuth, bougie, café, caramel, chiffre, gazelle, orange, roquette, sirop, tabouret, talc, zéro…

Mahomet ou Mohammed ? Mahomet est la forme latine du nom du prophète. Mohammed en est une transcription plus proche de l'arabe. Il signifie « celui qui est digne de louanges, le loué, le béni ».

Les **3** lieux sacrés de l'islam sont La Mecque et Médine, en Arabie saoudite, et Jérusalem.

# « L'École britannique autorisée à bannir le voile intégral »

En mars 2007, le gouvernement britannique a autorisé les directeurs des écoles du pays à interdire, au cas par cas, le port du *niqab*. Ce voile islamique* ne laisse apparaître que les yeux des femmes. Quelques mois auparavant, des propos du ministre Jack Straw contre ce voile avaient provoqué une vive polémique en Grande-Bretagne.

# L'islam dans l'espace européen

**Voile\*, jeûne du ramadan\*, alimentation halal\* : les débats sur le culte musulman se multiplient depuis quelques années en Europe. Dans les pays européens, majoritairement de tradition chrétienne, la religion est devenue une affaire privée. Le développement de l'islam\* relance aujourd'hui des questions sur la place des religions dans une société laïque. Le défi est de taille. L'Europe doit intégrer l'islam au nom de la liberté de culte, car une part importante de sa population est désormais de confession musulmane. Mais l'islam doit aussi s'adapter aux démocraties européennes, qui ont érigé la laïcité\* et l'égalité entre hommes et femmes en principes fondateurs.**

## L'œil critique

### ● *École et laïcité*

En France en 2004, la façon dont les médias ont relaté la polémique sur le port du voile a pu donner l'impression que l'École publique rejetait l'islam. Or, l'école s'est adaptée : les élèves musulmans\* ont la possibilité de ne pas manger de porc à la cantine ou de s'absenter pour une fête religieuse. Mais les médias se sont concentrés sur les quelques jeunes filles qui refusaient d'enlever leur voile. Ils ont mené peu d'enquêtes sur la vie des élèves musulmans pratiquants au sein de l'École publique.

### ● *Islam et identité*

L'esprit de polémique qui entoure la plupart des débats sur l'islam dans les médias européens laisse peu de place aux questions de fond. Or, derrière le développement du port du voile islamique se profile un mouvement plus large. En effet, de plus en plus d'adolescents européens issus de l'immigration se tournent vers l'islam pour affirmer leur identité. Confrontés au racisme et à la discrimination, ils rejettent à la fois leurs origines et leur pays, pour se déclarer musulmans avant tout.

### ● *Musulmans européens*

Dans de nombreux médias, la question de l'islam en Europe est traitée en opposition à la laïcité ou bien en lien avec l'islamisme\*. Or, l'islam peut s'intégrer dans une société laïque, comme les autres religions. De nombreux musulmans vivent en Europe depuis des décennies et ont adapté leur pratique religieuse. Mais cette dimension est peu visible dans les médias qui préfèrent montrer ceux qui ont choisi, au contraire, de vivre aux yeux de tous un islam des plus stricts.

# L'islam, le quotidien et les femmes

Hérités de l'Arabie du VII<sup>e</sup> siècle, les principes de l'islam* sont aujourd'hui suivis par des millions de personnes dans le monde. Les règles qui imposent la soumission des femmes aux hommes commencent à s'assouplir dans certains pays musulmans.

## LECTURES DU CORAN

De nombreux pays musulmans appliquent encore aujourd'hui un code de la famille fondé sur la lecture du Coran* et datant de l'Arabie médiévale. Des changements sont en cours, toutefois, comme en Égypte et au Maroc, où les femmes ont notamment obtenu le droit de divorcer. La lecture du Coran donne matière à des interprétations diverses, des plus sévères aux plus tolérantes. Depuis plusieurs années, quelques femmes ont entrepris de relire les textes de l'islam. Certaines sont désormais autorisées à prêcher, rôle jusqu'à présent réservé aux hommes. En s'imposant dans la hiérarchie religieuse, ces femmes souhaitent faire évoluer l'islam de l'intérieur, en s'emparant des textes pour en diffuser une interprétation plus égalitaire.

## Les cinq piliers de l'islam

Le culte musulman prescrit cinq obligations, observées par des croyants, quels que soient leur origine et le courant de l'islam auquel ils adhèrent. Le premier de ces piliers est la profession de foi (chahada, en arabe) consistant à dire sa croyance en un Dieu unique et en son prophète, Mahomet*. La prière (salat) est le deuxième pilier : cinq fois par jour, chez eux ou à la mosquée*, les croyants se prosternent en direction de La Mecque* pour prier. La troisième obligation est le jeûne (saoum) : durant le mois de ramadan*, il est interdit de manger, de boire, de fumer et d'avoir des relations sexuelles entre le lever et le coucher du soleil. Le quatrième pilier est l'aumône (zakat) aux plus pauvres. Enfin, le pèlerinage (haj) à La Mecque est le dernier pilier. Il réunit chaque année en Arabie saoudite quelque 2 millions de pèlerins du monde entier.

## Au quotidien

Les textes de l'islam réglementent la vie sociale. Ils interdisent la prostitution, la consommation d'alcool, les jeux de hasard, la spéculation… Une alimentation particulière (halal*) est prescrite : le porc est interdit et les animaux consommables doivent être abattus selon un rituel précis. Dans le domaine de la famille, l'adultère est réprimé, mais la polygamie* est autorisée (bien que désormais peu répandue), un mari a le droit de répudier sa femme comme il l'entend, l'homosexualité n'est pas tolérée. Les morts doivent être enterrés sans cercueil, la poitrine tournée vers La Mecque. Ces règles ne sont scrupuleusement appliquées que dans les pays où la loi est totalement soumise à l'islam, comme en Arabie saoudite ou en république islamique d'Iran. Dans les autres pays musulmans, certaines de ces règles se sont assouplies, notamment celles touchant aux droits des femmes.

### Le statut des femmes

Écrits au Moyen Âge, les textes de l'islam indiquent que la femme doit se soumettre à l'homme. Mais le statut des femmes musulmanes a été remis en question, à partir du XIX$^e$ siècle, par des hommes dans un premier temps. Puis, au cours du XX$^e$ siècle, des femmes ont refusé de se voiler et se sont battues pour avoir le droit de travailler, de voter, de s'engager en politique, en particulier en Tunisie, en Égypte, en Turquie. À l'inverse, dans les années 1970, la montée de l'islamisme* (un mouvement qui veut mettre l'islam au cœur de la politique) a poussé des femmes à se voiler. Certaines y ont été forcées, d'autres l'ont choisi pour montrer leur foi ou leur adhésion à l'islamisme. D'autres enfin l'ont fait pour circuler librement. Certaines de ces musulmanes, voilées mais modernes, sont ainsi parvenues à s'imposer dans la vie politique, sociale et religieuse de leur pays. Dans le monde musulman comme ailleurs, le statut des femmes ne dépend pas uniquement de la religion et s'améliore quand ce sont les femmes elles-mêmes qui se battent pour leurs droits.

Les femmes musulmanes d'Afrique de l'Ouest (ici au Sénégal) ne portent pas le voile*. Leur tenue traditionnelle est le boubou et les hommes sont coiffés d'une calotte. Dans de nombreuses régions d'Afrique, les principes de l'islam sont observés de façon moins sévère qu'au Maghreb et au Moyen-Orient.

**Chahada** (profession de foi musulmane) : « la ilaha ill Allah Muhammadun rasulu'Llah » (Il n'y a pas d'autre dieu que Dieu, et Mohammed est son prophète).

**70** « carrés » sont réservés aux musulmans dans différents cimetières en France.

En **1988**, au Pakistan, Benazir Bhutto devient la première femme à occuper un poste de Premier ministre dans un pays musulman.

# « Nouveau retard pour la mosquée* de Marseille »

En avril 2007, à la suite d'une plainte déposée par des élus d'extrême droite, la justice a fait annuler la location d'un terrain municipal sur lequel doit être construite une grande mosquée* à Marseille. La justice a considéré que le loyer accordé par la mairie était si faible que cela revenait à aider financièrement l'islam*. Or la loi de 1905 interdit le financement des religions par les pouvoirs publics.

# Le financement des mosquées

**Deuxième religion de France par le nombre d'adeptes, l'islam\* manque de lieux de culte. Les projets de mosquées\* sont nombreux, mais leur financement crée de vifs débats. Les mosquées françaises sont actuellement financées par (en ordre décroissant d'importance) des fonds venant des pays du golfe Persique et du Maghreb, des aides publiques de collectivités locales, le commerce de la viande halal\* et des dons. Les fonds étrangers proviennent en grande partie d'Arabie saoudite. Ils favorisent la diffusion d'un islam sévère en France où la plupart des croyants musulmans\*, originaires du Maghreb, pratiquent un islam modéré. Quant aux financements publics, ils butent contre la loi de 1905 sur la laïcité\*.**

## L'œil critique

**● *Rejet de l'islam ?***
En 2007, la justice a empêché des mairies de louer des terrains à bas prix à des associations qui souhaitaient construire une mosquée. Ces jugements ont été rendus au nom de la loi de 1905 qui impose la séparation des Églises et de l'État. Pourtant, beaucoup d'églises ont été construites après 1905 grâce à ce type d'arrangements. Ainsi, ce qui était accepté jusqu'à présent ne l'est plus pour l'islam. Cette situation, relevée par quelques médias, est rarement au centre des débats.

**● *Zoom sur la loi***
Le fait que la loi de 1905 interdise le financement public des lieux de culte est largement commenté dans les médias. Mais la loi dit aussi que chacun est libre de pratiquer le culte de son choix, sans entrave ni discrimination. Les médias parlent peu de cet aspect du texte. Ainsi, ils passent sous silence le fait que les collectivités locales ne sont pas forcément hors-la-loi si elles aident les musulmans à pratiquer leur religion dans de bonnes conditions, comme d'autres croyants.

**● *Pratiquants, croyants et athées***
La polémique sur le financement des mosquées diffuse l'idée que les musulmans sont tous pratiquants. Or, l'islam est comme les autres religions : il y a aussi des croyants non pratiquants et des personnes qui ne croient pas en Dieu dans les familles de confession musulmane. Dans les médias, dans les discours politiques, dans la vie courante, le mot «musulman» désigne souvent les personnes d'origine arabe. Comme si elles étaient toutes attachées à l'islam.

# L'islam en France

Devenue la deuxième religion de France, l'islam* n'a pas encore trouvé sa place dans le pays. Les influences étrangères sur l'organisation du culte sont aujourd'hui des freins à l'intégration de cette religion et de ses fidèles.

En 2005, la France comptait quelque 1 200 imams*, dont un tiers ne parlait pas le français. Deux instituts forment les imams en France, l'un est rattaché à la Grande Mosquée de Paris*, l'autre à l'Union des organisations islamiques de France (UOIF)*. Des voix s'élèvent depuis quelques années pour que l'État propose aux imams des cours sur les institutions et le droit français.

## Les musulmans

L'implantation de l'islam en France est liée aux vagues successives d'immigration du XXe siècle, pour la plupart encouragées par l'État. Ainsi, des soldats sont recrutés dans les colonies d'Afrique du Nord durant la Première et la Seconde Guerre mondiale. L'arrivée d'Algériens surtout, mais aussi de Marocains, se poursuit après 1945, car la France a besoin de main-d'œuvre pour se reconstruire. L'immigration s'accélère après la décolonisation de l'Algérie et du Maroc, puis de la Tunisie. Les années 1970 voient des immigrants arriver de Turquie, puis d'Afrique subsaharienne. Aujourd'hui, plus de 4 millions de personnes de culture musulmane vivraient en France, dont près de 3 millions venus du Maghreb, 300 000 de Turquie, 250 000 d'Afrique noire, 100 000 du Moyen-Orient. Un tiers d'entre elles sont françaises. Mais ces chiffres restent approximatifs, car la loi interdit les statistiques fondées sur l'appartenance religieuse.

## L'islam et l'État français

Les pouvoirs publics commencent à se soucier de l'islam à partir des années 1970. De nombreuses familles de confession musulmane ont alors choisi de s'installer en France et veulent pratiquer leur culte dans de bonnes conditions. En 1981, les associations musulmanes, françaises et étrangères, se multiplient grâce à un assouplissement de la loi concernant les associations présidées par des étrangers. Aujourd'hui, nombre d'entre elles sont regroupées au sein de fédérations nationales, dont la Grande Mosquée de Paris*, l'Union des organisations islamiques de France (UOIF)* et la Fédération nationale des musulmans de France (FNMF). En 2003, après une réflexion initiée en 1989, l'État français crée le Conseil français du culte musulman (CFCM)*. Voix officielle de l'islam auprès des pouvoirs publics, le CFCM réunit des élus des grandes fédérations musulmanes.

## Influences étrangères

L'islam français subit en partie l'influence d'États et d'organismes du monde musulman. Leur activisme depuis les années 1960 s'est en effet conjugué avec le manque d'intérêt de l'État français pour une religion longtemps considérée comme extérieure au pays. De nombreuses mosquées* ont ainsi été construites grâce à des fonds étrangers. Le culte y est souvent organisé par des associations liées à des pays du Maghreb ou par des organismes comme la Ligue islamique mondiale*, créée par l'Arabie saoudite et diffusant un islam sévère. L'islam en France ne se résume pas à ces influences étrangères, mais celles-ci ne facilitent pas l'intégration de cette religion ni de ses fidèles dans la société française. Aussi, en 2001, le Haut Conseil à l'intégration* recommandait-il aux pouvoirs publics d'aider au développement d'un islam français moderne, qui adapte la tradition musulmane à la culture laïque.

**DANS LES BANLIEUES**

On parle aujourd'hui d'une « islamisation » des banlieues populaires en France. Derrière ce terme se cache une réalité plus nuancée. Des études ne montrent qu'une légère augmentation des pratiques religieuses depuis vingt ans. Pourtant, il y a bien un retour vers l'islam* en tant que culture, de la part de jeunes gens issus de l'immigration. Mais il s'agit plus d'une recherche d'identité et d'une rébellion contre une société dont ils se sentent rejetés que d'une quête religieuse. C'est dans ce contexte que le salafisme* progresse aujourd'hui dans les banlieues françaises. Ce courant propose à ses adeptes de rompre avec la société et de pratiquer un islam strict. Une partie des salafistes, nommés jihadistes*, appellent à la violence pour atteindre leur but, mais ils restent minoritaires.

**1926** inauguration de la Mosquée de Paris construite pour commémorer le sacrifice des soldats musulmans pendant la Première Guerre mondiale.

« La République assure la liberté de conscience. Elle garantit le libre exercice des cultes ■ (art. 1 et 2 de la loi de séparation des églises et de l'État de 1905)

« La France respecte toutes les croyances ■ (art. 1 de la Constitution)

## « Bras de fer entre les Frères musulmans*
## et le pouvoir égyptien »

Au printemps 2007, à la veille des élections sénatoriales, les autorités égyptiennes ont arrêté plus de 800 membres du mouvement des Frères musulmans*. Dans les bureaux de vote, des candidats de ce groupe islamiste* très populaire dans le pays ont été interdits d'accès. Les élections, entachées d'autres fraudes, ont été remportées par le parti au pouvoir.

# Les Frères musulmans et l'islamisme

Fondé en Égypte en 1928, le mouvement des Frères musulmans*
a inspiré de nombreux groupes islamistes*. Son slogan pour les
élections sénatoriales égyptiennes de 2007 était « l'islam est la
solution ». Les membres de ce courant islamiste, le plus important
à ce jour, pensent que l'islam* doit organiser la vie des hommes
en société. Ils luttent pour établir des États islamiques, soumis
aux principes inscrits dans le Coran* et à la loi islamique (charia*).
En Égypte, en 1948, les Frères musulmans ont assassiné le Premier
ministre. Puis ils ont abandonné la violence dans les années 1970,
et ils se sont engagés en politique dans les années 1990,
comme beaucoup d'autres mouvements islamistes.

## L'œil critique

### ● Une origine politique

L'histoire de l'islamisme
est très rarement traitée
dans les médias. Or cela
permettrait de lutter
contre l'idée, fausse
mais très répandue,
que l'islamisme prend
de l'ampleur aujourd'hui
parce que l'islam est
une religion plus sévère
que les autres
et que l'ensemble
des musulmans* rejettent
les principes de la
démocratie. L'actuel
succès des partis
islamistes s'explique par
l'histoire politique des
pays du monde musulman
et non par leur religion.

### ● Violence islamiste

Quand on lance une
recherche sur le mot
« islamiste » dans
des sites web consacrés
à l'actualité, on trouve
surtout des informations
liées à des attentats
ou des arrestations. Cela
montre à quel point les
médias donnent la priorité
aux islamistes criminels. Ils
évoquent avec beaucoup
moins de régularité
les actions non violentes
des partis islamistes
(campagnes politiques,
manifestations...). Ils
donnent ainsi l'impression
qu'elles sont plus rares
que les attentats, ce qui
est faux aujourd'hui.

### ● Religion et pouvoir

Il est souvent question
dans les médias du fait
que de nombreux régimes
du monde musulman
mêlent étroitement
religion et politique.
Il est vrai que beaucoup
de ces pays sont dotés
de lois et d'institutions
très liées à l'islam.
À l'inverse, les pays
occidentaux ont, pour la
plupart, séparé les affaires
religieuses de celles de
l'État. Il serait toutefois
utile, pour bien saisir
les nuances, d'expliquer
les liens qui existent
aussi dans les démocraties
modernes entre la religion
et le pouvoir.

# L'islamisme, d'hier à aujourd'hui

Né à la fin des années 1920, l'islamisme* est un courant
qui veut mettre l'islam* au centre de la vie politique. Les islamistes
sont aujourd'hui partagés entre le recours à la violence
ou la participation aux élections pour accéder au pouvoir.

Le mouvement islamiste
palestinien Hamas* est
à la fois un parti politique,
une armée de combattants
prêts à la plus grande
violence et une organisation
d'aide aux plus démunis.
En 2006, le Hamas
a remporté les élections
législatives palestiniennes,
mais n'a pas pour autant
renoncé à la violence.

## Aux sources de l'islamisme

Au début du XXᵉ siècle, les pays
musulmans, pour la plupart coloni-
sés par les Européens, sont traversés
par un mouvement appelé le salafisme* réformiste. Les intellectuels
de ce courant placent l'islam au
cœur de la société, mais se consa-
crent à moderniser cette religion en
s'inspirant notamment du modèle
occidental. En 1928, un ancien disci-
ple de ces intellectuels réformistes,
l'Égyptien Hasan al-Banna, crée le mouvement des
Frères musulmans*. Cette date marque la naissance
de l'islamisme*. L'objectif des Frères musulmans
n'est plus d'adapter l'islam au monde moderne,
mais au contraire de soumettre les sociétés à l'islam
tel qu'il est défini dans le Coran*.

### Le choix de la violence

Au milieu du XXᵉ siècle, les pays du monde arabo-
musulman conquièrent leur indépendance.
Plusieurs d'entre eux sont alors dirigés par des régimes nationalistes autoritaires. Après l'humiliation
de la colonisation, ils rassemblent les populations
autour de la fierté d'être arabe et d'appartenir à une
nation forte. Ces régimes, dont certains sont laïcs,
partagent un même ressentiment envers les anciennes puissances coloniales (France, Grande-
Bretagne…), les États-Unis et Israël. Sur le plan
intérieur, ils répriment les partis islamistes et les

écartent du pouvoir, notamment en Égypte. En réaction, Sayyid Kotb, un penseur des Frères musulmans* (qui quittera le mouvement), met la violence au cœur du projet islamiste et appelle au combat contre les régimes en place dans le monde musulman.

### La lutte armée ou les urnes

Dans les années 1960 à 1980, des mouvements islamistes engagent une lutte violente contre le pouvoir dans leur pays. Ainsi, en 1979, les islamistes instaurent par la force une république islamique en Iran. En 1981, le président égyptien Anouar el-Sadate est assassiné par un groupe islamiste. Puis, en 1988, le Saoudien Oussama Ben Laden fonde le réseau terroriste al-Qaida, qui s'attaquera à la fois aux pays occidentaux et aux États du monde musulman. À partir des années 1990 toutefois, des islamistes choisissent de participer aux élections. Ces partis, qui viennent en aide aux plus démunis, remportent un succès grandissant auprès de ces populations délaissées par les régimes en place. En 2002, le Parti de la justice et du développement (AKP)* conquiert le pouvoir par les urnes en Turquie. En 2004, le Hezbollah* remporte les élections municipales au Liban. En 2005, les Frères musulmans font une percée historique aux élections législatives en Égypte. Mais participer aux élections ne signifie pas adhérer à la démocratie. La plupart des partis islamistes ne sont pas prêts à respecter des principes fondamentaux comme l'égalité entre les hommes et les femmes, la liberté d'expression ou le droit de choisir sa religion.

---

## LE POUVOIR DES RELIGIEUX EN IRAN

Depuis la prise du pouvoir par les islamistes en 1979, l'Iran s'appelle la république islamique d'Iran et ses institutions sont soumises à la charia*. Le pouvoir politique est détenu par le président de la République (Mahmoud Ahmadinejad), élu par les citoyens pour 4 ans. Mais il est contrôlé par le Guide suprême de la révolution (l'ayatollah* Ali Khamenei), nommé à vie par une assemblée de religieux. Le Guide suprême peut bloquer toute décision du gouvernement qui ne lui convient pas. Il intervient en particulier dans les affaires liées à la sécurité et à la politique étrangère. Par ailleurs, les lois votées par les députés doivent être approuvées par le Conseil des gardiens de la Constitution. Les religieux et les juristes qui composent ce Conseil peuvent demander l'annulation de lois jugées incompatibles avec les sourates du Coran*.

---

**«** L'ensemble des lois et règlements civils, pénaux, financiers, économiques, administratifs, culturels, militaires, politiques et autres doit être basé sur les préceptes islamiques **■** (4ᵉ principe de la constitution de la république islamique d'Iran, 1979)

**«** Nulle contrainte en religion **■** (Coran, sourate 2, verset 256)

### Juillet 2007
en Turquie, l'AKP (parti islamiste modéré) se maintient au pouvoir avec plus de 46 % des voix contre 2,3 % au parti islamiste pur et dur (le SP).

# L'islam dans le monde

Les personnes de confession musulmane sont aujourd'hui près de 1,2 milliard à travers le monde. Environ 20 % d'entre elles sont arabes, la majorité est asiatique. Le pays qui compte le plus de musulmans dans le monde est l'Indonésie.

**EUROPE**
**32** MILLIONS

*Océan Atlantique*

**TUNISIE**

**MAROC** **LIBYE**
**ALGÉRIE**

**MAURITANIE**

**AMÉRIQUES**
**6,5** MILLIONS

**MALI** **NIGER**

*Océan Pacifique*

1  3       9      10
2    5    8
4   6  7  **NIGERIA**
**CAMEROUN**

**AFRIQUE**
**320** MILLIONS

**PROPORTION DE MUSULMANS DANS LA POPULATION**

Plus de 74 %

De 50 à 74 %

De 20 à 49 %

Moins de 20 %

Nombre de musulmans

Régions du globe où les musulmans sont les plus nombreux

Principales villes saintes de l'islam

**TYPES DE RÉGIME**

État laïc

État appliquant la loi islamique (charia) dans certains domaines de la vie privée (droit de la famille, héritage...)

État où la loi islamique est appliquée dans certaines régions

État appliquant largement la loi islamique

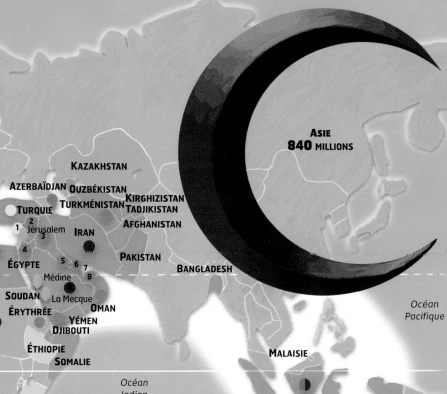

ASIE
**840** MILLIONS

KAZAKHSTAN

AZERBAÏDJAN OUZBÉKISTAN
TURQUIE TURKMÉNISTAN KIRGHIZISTAN
TADJIKISTAN
1 Jérusalem AFGHANISTAN
2
3 IRAN
4
ÉGYPTE 5 6 7 PAKISTAN
8 BANGLADESH
Médine
SOUDAN La Mecque
ÉRYTHRÉE OMAN
YÉMEN
DJIBOUTI
ÉTHIOPIE
SOMALIE MALAISIE

Océan
Indien INDONÉSIE
TANZANIE

MOZAMBIQUE

Océan
Pacifique

**AFRIQUE**
1 GAMBIE
2 GUINÉE-BISSAU  **ASIE**
3 SÉNÉGAL  1 LIBAN
4 SIERRA LEONE  2 SYRIE
5 GUINÉE  3 IRAK
6 LIBERIA  4 JORDANIE
7 CÔTE D'IVOIRE  5 KOWEÏT
8 GHANA  6 QATAR
9 BURKINA FASO  7 BAHREÏN
10 TCHAD  8 ÉMIRATS ARABES UNIS
9 ARABIE SAOUDITE

# Comprendre
# les mots de l'info

**A**choura • **A**ïd-el-Kébir • **A**llah • **A**yatollah •
**C**alendrier musulman • **C**alife • **C**haria • **C**hiisme •
**C**ommunautarisme • **C**onseil français du culte
musulman (CFCM) • **C**oran • **É**cole coranique • **F**atwa •
**F**ondamentalisme • **F**rères musulmans • **G**rande Mosquée
de Paris • **H**alal • **H**amas • **H**aut Conseil à l'intégration
(HCI) • **H**ezbollah • **I**mam • **I**ntégrisme • **I**slam • **I**slamisme
**I**slamophobie • **J**ihad • **J**ihadiste • **K**harijisme • **L**aïcité •
**L**igue islamique mondiale • **M**aghreb • **M**ahomet •
**M**arabout • **M**artyr • **M**ecque (La) • **M**ollah • **M**onothéiste •
**M**osquée • **M**oudjahid • **M**oyen-Orient • **M**ufti •
**M**usulman • **O**rganisation de la conférence
islamique (OCI) • **O**uléma • **O**umma • **P**arti de la justice
et du développement (AKP) • **P**olygamie • **P**roche-Orient •
**R**amadan • **S**alafisme • **S**oufisme • **S**unnisme •
**T**abligh • **T**aliban • **U**nion des organisations islamiques
de France (UOIF) • **V**oile islamique • **W**ahhabisme

## Achoura

**Fête musulmane, inspirée du jeûne juif de Yom Kippour.**

L'achoura a lieu le 10ᵉ jour du premier mois du calendrier musulman. Chez les sunnites, le jeûne est recommandé durant deux jours. Chez les chiites, l'achoura commémore aussi la mort de Hussein, petit-fils du prophète Mahomet, en 680. Un grand pèlerinage de l'achoura a lieu à Karbala, en Irak : des milliers de croyants s'y réunissent et certains se frappent violemment la poitrine et la tête pour exprimer collectivement la douleur du deuil.

## Aïd-el-Kébir

**Fête musulmane marquant la fin du pèlerinage à La Mecque.**

L'Aïd-el-Kébir, aussi appelée fête du Mouton, a lieu le 10ᵉ jour du dernier mois du calendrier musulman. Cette fête commémore un épisode commun aux religions juive, chrétienne et musulmane, durant lequel Abraham est prêt à sacrifier son fils à la demande de Dieu, lui prouvant ainsi sa soumission. Au dernier moment, un ange retient la main d'Abraham et un bélier est sacrifié à la place de l'enfant. Le jour de l'Aïd, chaque famille musulmane abat ou fait abattre un mouton selon un rituel strict. Au sein de l'Union européenne, l'animal doit être égorgé dans un abattoir.

## Allah

**Mot arabe signifiant « Dieu ».**

Le mot « Allah » est utilisé par les musulmans du monde entier pour désigner Dieu, ainsi que par des chrétiens et des juifs de langue arabe. Selon le Coran, le Livre de l'islam, Allah est unique, tout-puissant, créateur de toutes choses, et il s'agit du même dieu que celui vénéré par les juifs et les chrétiens.

## Ayatollah

**Religieux de haut rang dans l'islam chiite.**

En Iran, où les chiites ont installé un régime islamiste en 1979, les ayatollahs ont un pouvoir religieux et politique. Le premier d'entre eux, le « Guide suprême », est l'ayatollah Ali Khamenei. Il partage le pouvoir avec le président de la République, Mahmoud Ahmadinejad.

## Calendrier musulman (ou islamique)

**Calendrier religieux de l'islam.**

Le calendrier musulman débute le jour de l'hégire, c'est-à-dire de la fuite du prophète Mahomet de La Mecque vers Médine il y a près de quatorze siècles. L'an 1 du calendrier musulman correspond à l'an 622 du calendrier chrétien, qui compte les années à partir de la naissance du Christ. Une année du calendrier musulman compte 11 jours de moins qu'une année du calendrier chrétien, car le premier se base sur les phases de la Lune et le second sur la révolution de la Terre autour du Soleil. Ainsi, les fêtes musulmanes sont à des dates différentes chaque année sur le calendrier chrétien, qui est le calendrier officiel de la majorité des pays du monde.

**L'AÏD-EL-KEBIR ET LES ADOS**

« ...et pourquoi tu veux pas que j'y aille à cette fête? tous mes copains y vont... »

DIEGO ARANEGA

## Calife
**Nom donné aux successeurs du prophète Mahomet à la tête de la communauté des croyants.**
Dès les origines de l'islam, le calife détient un rôle à la fois religieux, politique et militaire. En 656, Ali, le gendre de Mahomet est élu quatrième calife, mais son pouvoir est contesté. Un conflit éclate alors, qui aboutit à la division de l'islam entre sunnites et chiites. Ces derniers ne reconnaissent plus l'autorité des califes choisis par les sunnites, mais celle des successeurs d'Ali, qu'ils appellent les imams. Des califes (parfois concurrents) se sont succédé dans le monde musulman jusqu'en 1924, année de l'abolition du califat par le président de la Turquie, Mustafa Kemal, attaché à la laïcité. Il n'existe plus de calife aujourd'hui dans le monde.

## Charia
**Loi divine autour de laquelle doit s'organiser la vie des musulmans. En Occident, on dit aussi loi islamique.**
La charia (mot arabe signifiant « la voie ») n'est pas constituée de règles précises, mais de principes établis à partir des textes du Coran et de la Sunna (qui réunit des actes et des paroles de Mahomet, rapportés après sa mort). Depuis des siècles, des théologiens, ou docteurs de la loi, interprètent ces textes de l'islam et enrichissent la charia de lois et de principes, parfois contradictoires. La charia peut s'appliquer au culte religieux comme aux différents aspects de la vie sociale des croyants : mariage, héritage, commerce, justice, etc. Des pays comme la république islamique d'Iran ou l'Arabie saoudite appliquent la charia de façon stricte dans tous les domaines de la vie publique et privée, parfois aux dépens des libertés individuelles et du respect des droits humains. Beaucoup de pays du monde musulman n'appliquent la charia que dans le domaine de la famille.

## ZOOM

### Le Coran appelle-t-il à la violence ?

Le Coran, tout comme la Bible, contient des passages violents. Ainsi, un verset appelle à tuer les païens, un autre à combattre les gens du Livre, c'est-à-dire les juifs et les chrétiens. Dans le même temps, de nombreux versets sont empreints de respect et de tolérance. L'un d'eux dit que la religion ne doit pas être imposée, un autre convie à la discussion avec les juifs et les chrétiens. Le Coran peut donc être interprété de différentes manières. Des intégristes brandissent ses versets violents pour justifier leurs crimes. Mais la majorité des musulmans lisent le Coran comme un message de paix. Certains d'entre eux appellent surtout l'islam à intégrer, comme les autres religions, les principes des démocraties modernes et à évoluer en leur sein.

## Chiisme
**Une des trois branches de l'islam, avec le sunnisme et le kharijisme.**
Le chiisme est né d'une division de l'islam, au VIIe siècle, sur la question de la succession du prophète Mahomet. Pour les chiites, les premiers successeurs de Mahomet devaient être Ali, l'époux de sa fille Fatima, et leur fils Hussein, tous les deux assassinés lors des conflits qui ont divisé l'islam. Les chiites considèrent que seuls leurs imams, les successeurs d'Ali, détiennent les vérités du Coran. Le chiisme s'est longtemps opposé au sunnisme, il a été persécuté et s'est développé dans la clandestinité, avant de devenir, au XVIe siècle, la religion officielle en Iran. Les chiites représentent aujourd'hui 10 % des musulmans dans le monde, mais sont majoritaires en Iran, en Irak ou au Liban. Les villes irakiennes, Nadjaf et Karbala, sont des lieux saints chiites.

## Communautarisme
**Fait de donner la priorité aux règles de sa communauté,** notamment religieuse, parfois aux dépens des lois de la République.
Le communautarisme est aussi une pensée qui veut que les membres d'un même groupe aient tous le même comportement et les mêmes idées. Utilisé depuis les années 1980, le mot communautarisme porte en général un sens négatif, synonyme de repli sur soi. Il est aujourd'hui fréquemment utilisé, dans les médias notamment, à propos des musulmans.

## Conseil français du culte musulman (CFCM)
**Organisation qui représente les musulmans auprès de l'État français.**
Le CFCM a été créé en 2003, après de longues discussions entamées dès 1989. Il réunit plusieurs courants de l'islam en France. Les principaux sont représentés par la Grande Mosquée de Paris (proche de l'Algérie), la Fédération nationale des musulmans de France (FNMF, proche du Maroc) et l'Union des organisations islamiques de France (UOIF, proche

de l'Arabie saoudite et inspirée des idées de l'organisation islamiste des Frères musulmans). Le CFCM est présidé par Dalil Boubakeur, le recteur de la Grande Mosquée de Paris. Les membres dirigeants du CFCM sont élus par des représentants des mosquées françaises. Le CFCM et ses 25 conseils régionaux du culte musulman (CRCM) traitent de questions comme la construction des mosquées, l'organisation des fêtes religieuses, la formation des imams et des aumôniers pour les prisons et les hôpitaux...

## Coran

**Livre de l'islam, du mot arabe al-Qur'an, qui signifie «la récitation».** Pour les adeptes de l'islam, le Coran est la dernière parole de Dieu aux humains, révélée au prophète Mahomet par l'ange Gabriel au VIIe siècle. Le Coran compte 114 sourates (chapitres) organisées en versets (paragraphes), au nombre de 6 219.

## École coranique

**École où les enfants apprennent le Coran, le Livre de l'islam.**

Les écoles coraniques, ou madrasa, accueillent en général les enfants à partir de 5 ou 6 ans. Dans de nombreux pays musulmans, ces enfants suivent aussi une scolarité non religieuse, mais une partie d'entre eux n'a pas d'autre formation. Dans certains pays, les écoles coraniques forment des religieux destinés à de hautes fonctions.

# F

## Fatwa

**Avis énoncé par un spécialiste interprétant le Coran et la loi islamique.** Le mot «fatwa» est apparu dans les pays occidentaux en 1989. Cette année-là, l'ayatollah Khomeyni appela les musulmans à tuer l'écrivain britannique d'origine indienne Salman Rushdie, pour avoir publié un roman intitulé *Les Versets sataniques*. Le chef religieux iranien considérait que cette œuvre littéraire insultait l'islam. Cette fatwa condamnant à mort l'écrivain souleva une immense indignation à travers le monde. Depuis, le mot «fatwa» est souvent associé, à tort, à l'idée de condamnation. La fatwa peut porter sur des domaines très divers : alimentation, pratiques rituelles, règles fiscales...

## Fondamentalisme

**Pensée religieuse extrémiste, du nom d'un courant du protestantisme américain qui défend une lecture stricte de la Bible.** Selon les fondamentalistes, les textes sacrés doivent se comprendre à la lettre, sans aucune interprétation, même dictée par les autorités religieuses. Ainsi, les fondamentalistes chrétiens rejettent les théories scientifiques de l'évolution, sous prétexte qu'il est écrit dans la Bible que Dieu créa le monde en six jours. Le mot «fondamentalisme» s'applique aujourd'hui à d'autres religions, notamment à l'islam. Certains fondamentalistes ont recours à la violence pour imposer leurs idées.

## Frères musulmans
**Organisation internationale luttant pour l'établissement d'États islamiques.**
Le mouvement des Frères musulmans a été créé en 1928 en Égypte, par Hasan al-Banna, un musulman sunnite. Responsable de l'assassinat du Premier ministre égyptien en 1948, le mouvement fut dissous en 1954, puis interdit par le président Nasser. Harcelés par le pouvoir égyptien durant plusieurs décennies, les Frères musulmans ont pourtant conservé leur influence, notamment grâce à leurs œuvres sociales. Ils ont renoncé à la violence dans les années 1970, puis se sont engagés en politique. Depuis sa création, le mouvement s'est étendu à tout le monde arabe, à travers des organisations autonomes en Syrie, au Liban, en Irak, au Maroc... mais aussi en Occident. Les Frères musulmans ont combattu auprès des Palestiniens dès les années 1930 et créé le Hamas en 1987. Leurs idées inspirent de nombreux mouvements ou partis islamistes. Certains sont modérés comme l'AKP, au pouvoir en Turquie, d'autres radicaux et violents comme le réseau terroriste al-Qaida.

## Grande Mosquée de Paris
**Lieu de culte musulman et institution dédiée au rayonnement de la culture islamique.**
Située dans le V<sup>e</sup> arrondissement de la capitale, la Grande Mosquée de Paris a été construite dans les années 1920 par l'État français. Elle est aujourd'hui essentiellement financée par l'Algérie. La Grande Mosquée forme des religieux musulmans (imams et aumôniers) et rassemble des associations qu'elle représente au sein du Conseil français du culte musulman (CFCM). Le recteur de la Grande Mosquée de Paris est Dalil Boubakeur, qui est aussi le président du CFCM.

# H

## Halal
**Se dit de l'alimentation autorisée par la religion musulmane.**
Halal signifie «permis» en arabe. Seule la viande obtenue en tuant des animaux selon un rituel strict est dite «halal» : ils doivent être égorgés au nom de Dieu. Ainsi, un animal mort accidentellement ne peut pas être consommé par un musulman pratiquant. De même, le porc n'est pas une viande halal : le Coran en interdit la consommation, quelle que soit la manière dont l'animal est tué.

## Hamas
**Parti islamiste palestinien.**
Le Hamas (Mouvement de la résistance islamique), dont le nom signifie «zèle» en arabe, est né lors du premier soulèvement palestinien (Intifada), en 1987. Ce parti a été créé par l'organisation islamiste des Frères musulmans. Soutenu et financé par l'Iran, le Hamas est le seul parti palestinien qui ne fait pas partie de l'Organisation de libération de la Palestine (OLP). Il s'oppose au parti nationaliste Fatah, du président de l'Autorité palestinienne, Mahmoud Abbas. Les dirigeants du Hamas, réputés honnêtes, sont très populaires auprès des Palestiniens, surtout dans la bande de Gaza. Le Hamas persiste à refuser l'existence d'Israël et l'attaque à travers sa branche armée, les brigades al-Qassam, par des attentats suicides notamment.
En janvier 2006, le Hamas a remporté les élections législatives palestiniennes et exercé le pouvoir jusqu'en juin 2007. Puis il a pris le contrôle de la bande de Gaza par les armes.

## Haut Conseil à l'intégration (HCI)
**Institution publique française chargée de faire des propositions au gouvernement pour favoriser l'intégration dans la société des personnes immigrées et issues de l'immigration.**
Créé en 1989, le HCI est présidé depuis 2002 par la philosophe Blandine Kriegel.

## Hezbollah
**Mouvement islamiste libanais.**
Le Hezbollah, dont le nom signifie «parti de Dieu» en arabe, a été créé en 1982. Son objectif est de faire du Liban un État gouverné par les lois de l'islam chiite, comme l'Iran. Le Hezbollah voit en Israël son principal ennemi : il a combattu les troupes israéliennes au Sud-Liban et organisé de nombreux attentats suicides et prises d'otage contre des Israéliens. Depuis 2001, ce mouvement est classé sur la liste des organisations terroristes par l'administration américaine. Financé et armé par la Syrie et l'Iran, le Hezbollah entretient d'étroites relations avec l'Organisation de libération de la Palestine (OLP). Dans le Sud-Liban, il s'est rendu populaire par des actions d'aide sociale, comme la reconstruction d'habitations détruites par l'armée israélienne. En 2004, il a remporté pour la première fois les

## Divisions politiques et religieuses

Une des particularités de l'islam est d'avoir mêlé, dès sa naissance au VII$^e$ siècle, le spirituel (la foi, la relation à Dieu) et le temporel (la réalité du temps présent, la politique). Ainsi, les successeurs de Mahomet furent à la fois les guides spirituels de la communauté des croyants et les chefs qui menèrent les guerres de conquête. C'est à cette époque que l'islam s'est divisé sur la question politique de la succession de Mahomet. De cette opposition sont nés le sunnisme, le chiisme et le kharijisme. Ces trois branches de l'islam proposent des interprétations du Coran et des organisations du pouvoir différentes. Elles sont aujourd'hui divisées en nombreux courants, des plus ouverts aux plus intolérants.

élections municipales libanaises et contrôle plus d'une centaine de villes. En 2006, une guerre a éclaté entre le Hezbollah et Israël, qui a fait de nombreuses victimes libanaises et des dégâts considérables au Liban.

## I

### Imam
**Religieux musulman.**
Dans l'islam sunnite, l'imam est celui qui dirige les prières à la mosquée. Dans l'islam chiite, les imams sont les successeurs du prophète Mahomet (que les sunnites appellent les califes).

### Intégrisme
**Courant de pensée qui veut appliquer une religion ou un système politique dans sa plus stricte tradition, sans accepter aucune évolution.**
Le mot « intégriste » est apparu en France, dans le monde catholique. Au début du XX$^e$ siècle, les intégristes s'opposaient

à ceux qui souhaitaient faire évoluer la pratique de la religion catholique pour l'adapter au monde moderne. Aujourd'hui, le mot « intégriste » s'applique à des fidèles ultraconservateurs de toutes les religions. Il est souvent utilisé dans le sens de « fanatique », c'est-à-dire excessif, zélé et intolérant en matière de religion, et pour désigner les islamistes radicaux usant du terrorisme.

### Islam
**Religion monothéiste fondée sur la croyance que la dernière parole de Dieu aux humains a été révélée au prophète Mahomet au VII$^e$ siècle.**
Les musulmans croient en un Dieu unique (Allah), en sa parole écrite dans le Coran, à la vie après la mort. La pratique de l'islam est basée sur cinq principes (piliers) : la profession de foi, les cinq prières quotidiennes, le jeûne du ramadan, l'aumône et le pèlerinage à La Mecque. Peu après la mort de Mahomet, l'islam s'est divisé en trois courants (sunnisme, chiisme et kharijisme) et s'est répandu très rapidement. Il a d'abord

rayonné au Moyen-Orient, au Maghreb, en Asie centrale et dans l'actuelle Espagne. Puis il a atteint l'Afrique subsaharienne, le sud-est de l'Europe, l'Inde et l'Extrême-Orient.

## Islamisme
**Mouvement politique qui veut soumettre la société et les institutions à l'islam.**
L'islamisme a pris de l'ampleur durant les années 1970. Son but est d'établir des États islamiques, comme c'est le cas en Iran notamment depuis 1979. Dans un État islamique, les institutions, le droit, le gouvernement doivent se conformer aux règles de l'islam. Certains courants islamistes pensent atteindre cet objectif par le prêche ou par l'action politique, d'autres veulent l'imposer par la force et le terrorisme.

## Islamophobie
**Rejet de l'islam et de tout ce qui s'y rapporte.**
Le terme « islamophobie » est apparu en Grande-Bretagne en 1997 et en France au lendemain des attentats du 11 septembre 2001. Ce terme, dont la définition est large, est souvent détourné de son véritable sens. Ainsi, il est parfois utilisé pour désigner un rejet des populations arabes, là où il serait plus juste de parler de racisme. De même, certains extrémistes n'hésitent pas à traiter d'islamophobe toute personne qui émet une critique sur l'islam, même modérée et argumentée. Ils tentent ainsi d'empêcher les discussions sur cette religion.

## Jihad
**Lutte, effort que doit faire tout musulman dans sa vie de croyant.**
Dans l'islam, le mot « jihad » désigne deux sortes de luttes : le combat intérieur que doit mener chaque fidèle contre ses propres faiblesses et la guerre de conquête destinée à propager l'islam. Le combat intérieur est

**NE PAS CONFONDRE**

**Islamique et islamiste**

La ressemblance entre les mots « islamique » et « islamiste » est source de confusion. L'adjectif « islamique » désigne ce qui se rapporte à l'islam. Le mot « islamiste », quant à lui, est utilisé pour désigner les partisans de l'islamisme et tout ce qui renvoie à ce courant religieux et politique parfois violent. Ainsi, une librairie « islamique » vend des livres sur l'islam et le monde musulman. Une librairie « islamiste », quant à elle, vendrait surtout des ouvrages favorables à l'islamisme, afin de propager ce mouvement.

appelé le grand jihad, et la guerre le petit jihad. Ce dernier renvoie aux origines de l'islam, au VIIe siècle. Il n'a de sens aujourd'hui que pour les islamistes extrémistes usant du terrorisme.

## Jihadiste
**Se dit des personnes ou des mouvements islamistes qui veulent**

imposer leurs idées par le combat et la violence.

Le mot «jihadiste» renvoie souvent aux adeptes les plus extrémistes du salafisme, un courant très conservateur de l'islam sunnite.

extrémistes pour justifier leurs attaques contre des musulmans. Les kharijites sont très minoritaires au sein de l'islam. On en trouve de petits groupes en Algérie, en Tunisie et dans le sultanat d'Oman.

# K

## Kharijisme
**Une des trois branches de l'islam, avec le sunnisme et le chiisme.**
Le kharijisme est né peu après le chiisme, lors de la guerre qui a éclaté à propos de la succession du prophète Mahomet, en 657. Les kharijites étaient d'abord chiites, avant de créer un nouveau courant, exigeant une pratique très sévère de l'islam. Ils ont ainsi inventé la notion de *takfir* : le rejet (l'excommunication) des «mauvais musulmans», c'est-à-dire de ceux qui n'acceptaient pas leur vision puritaine de l'islam. Cette notion est aujourd'hui reprise par des islamistes

# L

## Laïcité
**Séparation des Églises et de l'État.**
Dans un régime laïc, les autorités religieuses ne s'occupent pas des affaires politiques et chaque citoyen est libre de choisir sa religion. En France, la laïcité est inscrite dans la Constitution. Les citoyens sont égaux devant la loi et ont tous droit à un lieu de culte. La laïcité s'applique en particulier à l'enseignement : les Églises n'ont pas de pouvoir sur les écoles publiques. Mais des écoles privées religieuses (essentiellement catholiques) existent en France et certaines reçoivent des aides de l'État.

## Ligue islamique mondiale
**Organisation islamique internationale créée par l'Arabie saoudite.**
Fondée en 1962, la Ligue islamique mondiale diffuse à travers le monde un islam strict, inspiré du wahhabisme saoudien. Cette organisation possède des bureaux dans le monde entier, finance des mosquées et des centres islamiques, forme des imams, traduit et diffuse des textes religieux. Le siège de la Ligue islamique mondiale se trouve à La Mecque, en Arabie saoudite. Beaucoup de ses membres actifs à travers le monde sont des islamistes.

# M

## Maghreb
**Région qui couvre le nord-ouest de l'Afrique : Maroc, Algérie, Tunisie.**
Le Grand Maghreb inclut, en plus de ces trois pays, la Mauritanie et la Libye.

# LAÏCITÉ PRATIQUANTE

Bonjour, je suis athée et je recherche une bible laïque ...

Z'auriez ça ?...

DIEGO ARANEGA

## Mahomet
**Prophète fondateur de l'islam.**
Mahomet était un caravanier arabe. Il est né à La Mecque vers 570 et mort à Médine en 632. Son nom arabe est Mohammed Ibn Abdallah. Selon la tradition musulmane, Mahomet a fondé l'islam à partir de 610, année où il a reçu de l'ange Gabriel les premières révélations du message de Dieu.

## Marabout
**1. Religieux musulman, en Afrique subsaharienne.**
Dans certaines régions d'Afrique noire, la pratique de l'islam a évolué en se mêlant à des croyances traditionnelles plus anciennes. Le marabout est souvent à la fois un religieux musulman et le détenteur de savoirs considérés comme magiques.
**2. Saint homme de l'islam, dont le tombeau est vénéré, au Maghreb en particulier.**

## Martyr
**Personne morte au nom de sa foi.**
Le mot « martyr » vient, à l'origine, de la religion chrétienne : les martyrs étaient les croyants persécutés et tués car ils refusaient de renoncer à leur foi. Selon le Coran, le Livre de l'islam, le martyr (*chahid* en arabe) est celui qui meurt en propageant l'islam par le combat (le *jihad*). Aujourd'hui, l'expression « martyr » est utilisée par les islamistes extrémistes pour désigner ceux d'entre eux qui commettent des attentats suicides.

## Mecque (La)
**Première ville sainte de l'islam.**
Située en Arabie saoudite, La Mecque est la ville où est né le prophète Mahomet. C'est aujourd'hui le lieu d'un pèlerinage, le *haj*, que tout musulman est appelé à faire une fois dans sa vie s'il en a les moyens et s'il est en bonne santé. Quelque 2 millions de pèlerins se rassemblent chaque année à La Mecque. La deuxième ville sainte de l'islam est Médine, la ville d'Arabie saoudite où est mort Mahomet. La troisième ville sainte de l'islam est Jérusalem, actuellement partagée entre l'État d'Israël et les territoires palestiniens.

## Mollah
**Nom donné aux spécialistes des textes sacrés de l'islam, notamment en Turquie,**

## Islam, christianisme et judaïsme

Les trois religions monothéistes ont des racines communes. La plus ancienne, le judaïsme, est apparue il y a environ 4 000 ans, son livre est la Bible hébraïque. À sa création au Ier siècle, le christianisme a conservé les textes de la Bible hébraïque, mais les a réunis sous le nom d'Ancien Testament et complétés par le Nouveau Testament. De même, l'islam reconnaît la Bible hébraïque et le Nouveau Testament, mais il considère son propre livre, le Coran, comme la véritable et ultime parole de Dieu. Ainsi, Mahomet aurait reçu la révélation de Dieu à partir de l'an 610, car les deux autres religions se seraient, au fil des siècles, détournées de la vraie foi. Mahomet, dernier des prophètes après Moïse et Jésus, aurait ainsi le rôle de transmettre l'ultime message de Dieu aux « gens du Livre », c'est-à-dire les juifs et les chrétiens.

en Iran, au Pakistan et en Inde.
Les mollahs sont aussi appelés les docteurs de la Loi. Ils enseignent le Coran et le droit musulman, font appliquer la loi islamique (charia) et peuvent exercer de hautes fonctions religieuses ou politiques. Le premier chef religieux des talibans, au pouvoir en Afghanistan de 1996 à 2001, était le mollah Omar. Il avait été formé dans une école coranique au Pakistan avant de prendre la tête de ce régime islamiste.

## Monothéiste
**Se dit d'une religion fondée sur la croyance en un Dieu unique.**
Le judaïsme, le christianisme et l'islam sont les trois principales religions monothéistes.

## Mosquée
**Lieu de culte de l'islam.**
Une mosquée est aussi un lieu d'échanges et d'apprentissage. Ainsi, l'édifice religieux est parfois accompagné d'une école coranique, d'un centre de formation, voire d'une université. Les hommes et les femmes prient séparément. On compte

environ 1 300 mosquées en France, pour plus de 4 millions de musulmans.

## Moudjahid
**« Combattant » en arabe. Personne combattant au nom de l'islam.**
On trouve des groupes de moudjahidin en Afghanistan, en Iran, au Liban, en Palestine, en Irak... Les moudjahidin luttent pour installer un régime islamiste dans leur pays ou pour le libérer d'une occupation étrangère ou d'une dictature. En Afghanistan, durant les années 1990, les moudjahidin de l'Alliance du Nord ont été les adversaires les plus acharnés des talibans.

## Moyen-Orient
**Région comprise entre la Méditerranée et l'Asie centrale.**
Le Moyen-Orient englobe la Turquie, la Syrie, le Liban, Israël, la Jordanie, l'Égypte, l'Arabie saoudite, l'Irak, l'Iran, le Koweït, Bahreïn, le Qatar, les Émirats arabes unis, Oman, le Yémen. Selon certaines définitions, le Moyen-Orient ne comprend ni l'Iran ni la Turquie, selon d'autres, il englobe l'Afghanistan, le Pakistan et la Libye.

**Mufti**
Savant musulman
qui interprète la loi
islamique et émet des
fatwas, des avis sur des
situations particulières.

**Musulman**
Adepte de l'islam.
On compte aujourd'hui
1,2 milliard de musulmans
dans le monde,
d'une grande diversité
ethnique. L'islam est né
dans le monde arabe,
où il demeure la religion
dominante : les
musulmans y sont très
nombreux, comme dans
l'ensemble du Moyen-
Orient. Toutefois, la
majorité des musulmans
sont désormais
asiatiques : 400 millions
vivent en Inde,
au Pakistan et au
Bangladesh, 240 millions
entre Indonésie et
Malaisie et 15 millions
en Chine. Les musulmans
sont également
nombreux en Afrique
subsaharienne, où l'islam
est en expansion. Enfin,
l'Europe possède une
population musulmane
d'origine européenne,
forte d'environ 12 millions
de personnes, dans les
Balkans essentiellement,
et une population
de musulmans issus
de l'immigration, plus
dispersée. Ces derniers

seraient entre 14 et
17 millions en Europe,
dont un peu plus de
4 millions en France.

**Organisation
de la conférence
islamique (OCI)**
Organisation
intergouvernementale
de coopération entre
des pays du monde
musulman.
Créée en 1969, l'OCI
compte 57 pays
membres et siège
à Djedda, en Arabie
saoudite. Les objectifs
de l'OCI sont religieux
et politiques : assurer
la sauvegarde des lieux
saints de l'islam,
développer les échanges
entre pays musulmans,
soutenir la cause
palestinienne, etc. En
1990, l'OCI a adopté la
« Déclaration des droits
de l'homme en islam ».
Ce texte est inspiré de la
Déclaration universelle
des droits de l'homme,
mais il est fondé sur
la charia (loi islamique).
Une première version
de ce texte reconnaissait

l'égalité des droits des hommes et des femmes. Mais ce n'est plus le cas dans la version finalement adoptée.

## Ouléma
**Nom donné aux spécialistes des textes de l'islam.**
Les oulémas sont aussi appelés les docteurs de la Loi. Dans certains pays, on leur donne le nom de mollah.

## Oumma
**Communauté des croyants musulmans.**
Selon la tradition islamique, tout musulman fait partie de la oumma, indépendamment de sa nationalité, de sa langue, de son origine ethnique ou sociale.

## Parti de la justice et du développement (AKP)
**Parti islamiste au pouvoir en Turquie depuis novembre 2002.**
L'AKP (Parti de la justice et du développement) s'affirme respectueux de la démocratie, de la laïcité et se montre favorable à l'entrée de son pays dans l'Union européenne. Mais le gouvernement AKP a commis plusieurs entorses aux droits de l'homme en Turquie.

## Polygamie
**Fait d'être marié(e) à plusieurs personnes.**
La polygynie désigne le mariage d'un homme avec plusieurs femmes, la polyandrie le mariage d'une femme avec plusieurs hommes. Le mot « polygamie » est en général utilisé à la place du mot « polygynie ». L'islam permet aux hommes d'avoir plusieurs épouses, mais la polygamie existait avant l'islam. Le Coran indique qu'un homme peut avoir jusqu'à quatre femmes simultanément, à condition d'être équitable envers chacune. En France, la polygamie est interdite par la loi, mais elle est toutefois tolérée. Selon la Commission nationale consultative des droits de l'homme (CNCDH), il y aurait entre 16 000 et 20 000 familles polygames en France.

EXCLU SALON DU DESIGN : LA COUSCOUSSIÈRE POUR BOULIMIQUE EN PÉRIODE DE RAMADAN

## Proche-Orient
**Région qui comprend les pays de l'est de la Méditerranée : Turquie, Syrie, Liban, Israël, Jordanie, Égypte.**
Selon certaines définitions, le Proche-Orient ne comprend ni la Jordanie ni la Turquie. Selon d'autres, il englobe les pays du golfe Persique.

## Ramadan
**Neuvième mois du calendrier musulman, durant lequel le Coran aurait été révélé à Mahomet.**
Le ramadan est un mois de jeûne pour les musulmans : ils ne doivent ni manger ni boire du lever au coucher du soleil. En France, on appelle en général ramadan le jeûne lui-même. Le ramadan est aussi, selon l'islam, une période de recueillement et de compassion envers les plus pauvres. Le jeûne est rompu le dernier jour du mois de ramadan, lors de la fête de l'Aïd-el-Séghir (ou Aïd-el-Fitr). Ce jour-là, les musulmans versent une aumône et participent à une grande prière à la mosquée. Le ramadan n'est pas imposé aux personnes malades, aux vieillards, aux enfants avant leur puberté, aux femmes enceintes ou qui allaitent.

## Salafisme
**Mouvement fondamentaliste de l'islam sunnite, qui appelle au retour à la pratique des anciens (salaf).**
Le salafisme est apparu au XIXe siècle au sein du monde musulman. Il s'agissait alors d'un mouvement visant à réformer l'islam, notamment à la lumière des sciences occidentales. Aujourd'hui, les chefs religieux salafistes défendent une pratique très stricte de l'islam, inspirée du wahhabisme. Ils proposent aux musulmans de se retrouver dans une communauté de croyants qu'ils placent au-dessus des nations. Le salafisme se développe depuis quelques années dans les pays d'Europe, en France notamment. Ce courant se partage en deux tendances : les « cheikistes » diffusent leurs idées par le prêche, les « jihadistes » par la violence. Les groupes terroristes se réclamant d'al-Qaida s'inspirent du salafisme jihadiste.

## Soufisme
**Courant de l'islam fondé sur la méditation et la relation individuelle à Dieu.**
Le soufisme, ou mystique musulmane, est né en Perse (actuel Iran) au VIIIe siècle. Ce courant inspiré par la philosophie grecque et les religions indiennes s'est développé en marge du sunnisme, du chiisme et du kharijisme, les trois branches de l'islam. Les adeptes du soufisme sont regroupés en différentes confréries religieuses dirigées par des cheikhs (guides).

## Sunnisme
**Une des trois branches de l'islam, avec le chiisme et le kharijisme.**
Le terme «sunnisme» vient du mot «sunna» qui signifie tradition. La sunna est l'ensemble des récits, ou hadith, rapportant les actes et les paroles du prophète Mahomet. Le sunnisme est fondé sur le strict respect de la parole de Dieu écrite dans le Coran et interprétée par les oulémas, les spécialistes des textes sacrés. Le sunnisme est partagé en courants différents, certains très ouverts, d'autres très conservateurs. Près de 90 % des musulmans dans le monde sont sunnites.

# T

## Tabligh
**Courant puritain de l'islam, qui cherche à convertir de nouveaux fidèles.**
Le Tabligh a été créé en 1926 en Inde, par un maître du soufisme. Ses premiers missionnaires sont apparus en France dans les années 1960, puis le mouvement a pris le nom de «Foi et Pratique» à partir de 1972. Vêtus de longues tuniques blanches, les prédicateurs du Tabligh sont très présents dans les banlieues, où ils ont souvent permis l'ouverture de lieux de prière pour les musulmans.

## Taliban
**Partisan du régime islamiste au pouvoir en Afghanistan de 1996 à 2001.**
Les talibans ou «élèves en religion» ont été formés dans des écoles pakistanaises à une lecture extrémiste du Coran. En 1996, ils ont conquis l'Afghanistan et imposé un régime islamiste autoritaire, par la violence et la répression. Les Afghanes ont été particulièrement persécutées par les talibans, qui leur interdisaient d'aller à l'école, de travailler et même de se faire soigner. À la suite des attentats du 11 septembre 2001, les talibans ont été accusés par les États-Unis de soutenir et de cacher Oussama Ben Laden et son réseau, al-Qaida. Le régime taliban a été abattu par une coalition militaire internationale en novembre 2001. Mais ses partisans, repliés dans les régions frontalières avec le Pakistan, poursuivent aujourd'hui leur activisme politique, religieux et militaire.

## Union des organisations islamiques de France (UOIF)
**Fédération d'associations défendant une vision stricte de l'islam et la soumission de la politique à la loi islamique.**
L'UOIF fait partie de l'Union des organisations islamiques d'Europe (UOIE), dont le siège est à Londres et dont les financements proviennent en grande partie d'Arabie saoudite. L'UOIF a des représentants au sein du Conseil français du culte

musulman (CFCM), dont il est le courant le plus intégriste. L'UOIF possède des mosquées et forme des imams. Sa vision de l'islam est inspirée des idées des Frères musulmans, une organisation internationale luttant pour l'installation d'États islamiques.

## V

### Voile (ou foulard) islamique
**Tissu couvrant, porté par des femmes de religion musulmane.**
Le port du voile par les femmes n'est pas prescrit dans le Coran. Aujourd'hui, certaines musulmanes pratiquantes ne le portent pas. Toutefois une majorité d'entre elles sont voilées. *Hijab* est le nom le plus courant du foulard islamique. Il couvre les cheveux, le cou, la nuque et les épaules. Le *niqab* est un voile porté par les femmes du golfe Persique, il cache toute la tête

sauf les yeux. Souvent, ces femmes cachent aussi leurs mains dans de longs gants noirs. Le *tchador* est un tissu, noir en général, qui recouvre tout le corps des femmes, sauf le visage, les mains et les pieds. Ces femmes maintiennent souvent leur tchador d'une main, car elles ne doivent pas non plus montrer leur menton. Le tchador est surtout porté par les musulmanes chiites, en Iran notamment. Enfin, la *burqa* recouvre tout le corps, sa seule ouverture est une grille tissée à hauteur des yeux. Elle était surtout portée en Afghanistan, sous la dictature islamiste des talibans, mais des Afghanes doivent la porter encore aujourd'hui.

## W

### Wahhabisme
**Courant très conservateur de l'islam sunnite.**
Le wahhabisme a été fondé au XVIIIᵉ siècle par Mohammed Ibn Abd el-Wahhab. Il s'est développé parmi les tribus bédouines de l'actuelle Arabie saoudite, dont est issue la dynastie des Saoud. Aujourd'hui, la vie et les institutions de ce pays sont dominées par ce courant puritain et intransigeant qui applique la loi islamique (charia) de la façon la plus stricte.

ATELIER DE HAUTE COUTURE AFGHAN

« Il n'y a d'autre dieu que Dieu et Mohammed est son prophète », dit cette calligraphie arabe.

# Chercher
# textes et documents

* Les mots suivis d'un astérisque sont définis dans la partie
«Comprendre les mots de l'info» (p. 28).

## Pèlerinage

La Kaaba («bâtiment carré», en arabe) est un édifice de 15 mètres de haut recouvert de soie noire, situé dans la cour de la grande mosquée de La Mecque*, capitale de l'Arabie saoudite et première ville sainte de l'islam. Durant le *haj*, le pèlerinage annuel, les musulmans effectuent le *tawaf*, ou circumambulation, ils tournent sept fois autour de la Kaaba en se recueillant, puis effectuent les autres rites du pèlerinage. Le *haj* réunit chaque année à La Mecque environ deux millions de pèlerins venus du monde entier. À cette occasion, les autorités saoudiennes mettent en place un important dispositif de sécurité, pour éviter les perturbations et secourir les pèlerins en cas d'accident.

# L'âge d'or d'Al-Andalous

La mosquée de Cordoue,
joyau de l'art islamique,
a été construite entre
le VIIIᵉ et le Xᵉ siècle par
les Arabes de la dynastie
des Omeyyades. La moitié
sud de l'Espagne s'appelle
alors Al-Andalous.
Les musulmans y tolèrent
les juifs et les chrétiens
et développent une brillante
civilisation qui rayonne
dans le domaine
de l'architecture, des sciences,
de la littérature... À partir
du Xᵉ siècle, Cordoue,
devenue capitale d'un califat
de 7 millions d'habitants,
attire savants et lettrés
de l'ensemble du monde
musulman. L'année 1126
voit la naissance à Cordoue
d'Ibn-Rushd, dit Averroès,
un médecin arabe dont
les travaux, sur le philosophe
grec Aristote notamment,
ont durablement marqué
l'Occident.

## À l'école du Coran*

Des enfants musulmans*
étudient dans une madrasa,
dans l'Est de l'Inde. Le mot
madrasa, ou medersa,
signifie école en arabe.
En Occident, ce mot désigne
les écoles coraniques*,
qui enseignent les textes
du Coran à des enfants
à partir de 5 ou 6 ans.
Une partie des élèves de ces
établissements suit, en même
temps, une scolarité non
religieuse, d'autres non.
Les madrasas accueillent
également des étudiants,
plus âgés. Dans certains pays,
comme l'Iran, elles forment
des religieux destinés à de
hautes fonctions. Au Pakistan,
une partie des madrasas
est entre les mains
d'islamistes* extrémistes
qui les utilisent pour faire
de la propagande et recruter
des volontaires pour leurs
actions violentes.

# Les cinq piliers de l'islam

L'islam* est fondé sur cinq devoirs principaux (les cinq piliers de l'islam) : le témoignage qu'il n'est de dieu que Dieu (Allah*) et que Mohammed* est le messager de Dieu, l'accomplissement de la prière, l'acquittement de la zakat (aumône), le jeûne de ramadan* et, pour ceux qui le peuvent, le pèlerinage à La Mecque*.

## La profession de foi

« Dis (ô Mohammed) : « Ô hommes ! Je suis pour vous tous le Messager d'Allah, à qui appartient la royauté des cieux et de la terre. Pas de divinité à part lui. Il donne la vie et il donne la mort. Croyez donc en Allah, en son messager, le Prophète illettré qui croit en Allah et en ses paroles. Et suivez-le afin que vous soyez bien guidés. »

Sourate 7, verset 158

## La prière cinq fois par jour

« Heureux sont les croyants [...] qui observent strictement les heures de la prière. »

Sourate 23, versets 1 et 9

« Ô croyants ! Quand vous vous disposez à faire la prière, lavez-vous le visage et les mains jusqu'aux coudes ; essuyez-vous la tête et les pieds jusqu'aux chevilles. »

Sourate 5, verset 6

## L'aumône aux pauvres

Le Coran contient plus de 80 versets qui renferment l'ordre de s'acquitter de la zakat.

« Ô croyants ! Faites l'aumône des meilleurs choses que vous avez acquises [...]. Ceux qui feront l'aumône en recevront la récompense de Dieu. La crainte ne descendra point sur eux, et ils ne seront pas affligés. »

Sourate 2, versets 267 et 274

« Soyez assidus à la prière, faites l'aumône, vous retrouverez auprès d'Allah le bien que vous aurez acquis à l'avance, pour vous-même. »

Sourate 2, verset 110

## Le jeûne durant le mois de ramadan

« La lune du ramadan durant laquelle le Coran* est descendu d'en haut pour servir de direction aux hommes est le temps destiné au jeûne. [...] Il vous est permis de manger et de boire jusqu'au moment où vous pourrez distinguer le fil blanc du fil noir. À partir de ce moment, observez strictement le jeûne jusqu'à la nuit.»

Sourate 2, versets 185 et 187

### Le pèlerinage à La Mecque

«Il incombe aux hommes, à celui qui en possède les moyens, d'aller, pour Allah, en pèlerinage à la Maison.»

Sourate 3, verset 97

### La piété selon le Coran*

«La piété ne consiste point en ce que vous tourniez vos visages vers le Levant ou le Couchant. Vertueux sont ceux qui croient en Dieu et au jour dernier, aux Anges, au Livre et aux prophètes, qui donnent pour l'amour de Dieu des secours à leurs proches, aux orphelins, aux nécessiteux, aux voyageurs indigents et à ceux qui demandent l'aide, et pour délier les jougs, qui observent la prière, qui font l'aumône. Et ceux qui remplissent les engagements qu'ils contractent, se montrent patients dans l'adversité, dans les temps durs et dans les temps de violences. Ceux-là sont justes et craignent le Seigneur.»

Sourate 2, verset 177

# La Constitution saoudienne

**Le «Statut fondamental du gouvernement» (Constitution) du royaume d'Arabie saoudite, adopté en 1992, montre comment le caractère islamique de l'État peut être au cœur de toute son organisation.**

**Article 1:** Le Royaume d'Arabie saoudite est un État arabe islamique jouissant d'une souveraineté entière. Sa religion est l'islam*. Sa Constitution est le Livre de Dieu et la sunna de son Prophète, que Dieu le bénisse et le salue. Sa langue officielle est la langue arabe et sa capitale est Riyad.

**Article 2:** Les deux fêtes nationales sont Aïd-el-Fitr et Aïd-el-Adha.

**Article 3:** le drapeau de l'État est le suivant:

**a.** la couleur est verte.

[...]

**c.** Au milieu figure la phrase suivante: «Il n'y a que Dieu et Mohammed est son Prophète.» [...]

**Article 7 :** Le Gouvernement du Royaume d'Arabie puise son autorité du Livre de Dieu et de la sunna du Prophète, que Dieu le bénisse et le salue.

Ces deux sources régissent le présent Statut fondamental et tous les statuts et règlements de l'État. [...]

**Article 23 :** L'État protège le dogme de l'islam. Il applique sa charia*, ordonne le bien et interdit le mal et assume le devoir d'appeler les gens vers Dieu. [...]

**Article 45 :** La source des fatwa* au Royaume d'Arabie saoudite est le Livre de Dieu et la sunna de son Prophète, que Dieu le bénisse et le salue. [...]

**Article 48 :** Les tribunaux appliquent, aux affaires qui leur sont soumises, les dispositions de la charia islamique conformément à ce qui est indiqué dans le Livre et la sunna et aux règlements pris par le Souverain qui ne sont pas incompatibles avec le Livre et la sunna.

## Le credo des Frères musulmans

**Créé en 1928, en Égypte, par Hasan al-Banna, le mouvement des Frères musulmans* marque la naissance de l'islamisme* qui a pour objectif de soumettre les sociétés à l'islam tel qu'il est défini dans le Coran*.**

**1.** Je crois que tout est sous l'ordre de Dieu ; que Mohammed est le sceau de toute prophétie adressée à tous les hommes, que la rétribution [éternelle] est une réalité, que le Coran est le Livre de Dieu, que l'islam est une Loi complète pour diriger cette vie et l'autre. Et je promets de réciter [chaque jour] pour moi-même une section du Coran, de m'en tenir à la Tradition authentique, d'étudier la vie du Prophète et l'histoire des compagnons. [...]

**2.** Je crois que l'action droite, la vertu et la connaissance sont parmi les piliers de l'islam. [...]

**3.** Je crois que le musulman est responsable de sa famille, qu'il a le devoir de la conserver en bonne santé, dans la foi, dans les bonnes mœurs. Et je promets de faire mon possible en ce sens et d'insuffler les enseignements de l'islam aux membres de ma famille. Je ne ferai pas entrer mes fils dans une école qui ne préserverait pas leurs croyances, leurs bonnes mœurs. Je leur supprimerai tous les journaux, livres, publications qui nient les enseignements de l'islam, et pareillement les organisations, les groupes, les clubs de cette sorte.

**4.** Je crois que le musulman a le devoir de faire revivre l'islam par la renaissance de ses différents peuples, par le retour de sa législation propre, et que la bannière de l'islam doit couvrir le genre humain et que chaque musulman a pour mission d'éduquer le monde selon les principes de l'islam. Et je promets de combattre pour accomplir cette mission tant que je vivrai et de sacrifier pour cela tout ce que je possède.»

Extraits du credo
des Frères musulmans, 1935

## L'islam doit marcher avec son siècle

**Une réforme de l'islam\* est possible et nécessaire pour lui éviter une marginalisation dans le monde moderne : c'est la conviction que Soheib Bencheikh expose dans une interview donnée en 2001, alors qu'il était grand mufti\* de la mosquée\* de Marseille. Soheib Bencheikh est l'un des musulmans progressistes les plus connus en France.**

«En islam, le fidèle est libre de son interprétation. L'islam est une religion libérale — tentons le mot — et individuelle. Elle n'a pas de clergé. Sa seule autorité, c'est son texte. L'islam ne possède qu'un Coran, mais une multitude d'interprétations, variables selon les lieux, les conditions de vie, les classes, le degré de civilisation. C'est ce qui fait, je crois, sa richesse, sa souplesse, son éternelle jeunesse.

Mais la contrepartie est qu'aucune interprétation ne doit s'imposer par la force, par un quelconque moyen d'intimidation, au risque de la dérive. Or, aujourd'hui, nous sommes en pleine dérive avec des groupes qui veulent imposer une interprétation unique, littérale et obscurantiste des textes.

Je fais allusion aux groupes dits wahhabites* ou salafistes* qui veulent imiter, au millimètre près, l'exemple du prophète Mahomet* ! [...] Or ce type d'imitation servile est une source de marginalisation pour l'islam dans le monde moderne. Le prophète n'a jamais demandé au musulman de vivre comme un marginal dans son siècle. Suivre la sunna, c'est-à-dire la tradition, ce n'est pas revenir au premier siècle de l'Hégire, mais suivre un chemin pour le siècle d'aujourd'hui. [...]

– Pourquoi est-il si difficile de réformer l'islam [...] ?

– Un texte sacré ne s'exprime jamais tout seul. Il passe à travers une compréhension, intelligente ou pas, littérale ou pas, rationnelle ou pas. Prenons l'exemple des talibans : ils n'appliquent pas le Coran, ou plutôt, s'ils en appliquent quelques bribes, c'est toujours à travers l'interprétation la plus archaïque et la plus anachronique. Ils appliquent un droit musulman qui est le fruit d'une œuvre humaine, non divine comme ils le prétendent, élaboré du IXe au XIIe siècle qui, ensuite, a été sacralisé. Et ils osent appeler cela charia ! La charia est un mot mystique, c'est la voie qui mène à Dieu. [...]

Faire d'un droit musulman issu des sociétés patriarcales une sorte de droit universel, valide en tout temps, c'est ce que j'appelle la « bédouinisation » de l'islam, une autolimitation de l'évolution des sociétés musulmanes. La justice d'un siècle devient injustice dans un autre siècle. Par exemple, en Algérie s'applique encore le *fiqh* (droit) malékite, véritable gestionnaire de la vie privée et de la vie familiale. Si je divorce de ma femme, c'est elle qui doit quitter l'appartement avec ses enfants. Pourquoi ? Parce que dans le *fiqh* malékite, à une époque où la vie s'organisait autour des clans – et non des HLM –, la femme divorcée devait quitter le clan de son mari pour réintégrer celui de son père. Rien n'a changé, même si les structures de la vie sociale ont été bouleversées.

Toute tentative de réformer l'islam – et le droit musulman en particulier – passe donc par un travail de désacralisation, par une relecture des textes à la lumière de l'intelligence moderne, par la recherche d'une orientation, d'une courbe comme on dirait en mathématiques, pour permettre au musulman de bien vivre son islam aujourd'hui. [...] Ou [l'islam] marche avec son siècle, ou il reste à la marge de la société moderne.

Je reste optimiste. Je crois que la barbarie commise au nom de l'islam – les tueries en Algérie, la réduction d'un peuple en esclavage dans l'Afghanistan des talibans, le terrorisme qui a dramatiquement frappé les États-Unis – a définitivement éveillé la conscience internationale. Il est désormais clair que l'islam ne peut plus être la propriété d'un groupe de musulmans ou d'États musulmans qui veulent en monopoliser l'interprétation. L'islam a vocation à l'universel, c'est-à-dire qu'il doit être soumis à la critique, accepter certaines valeurs qui relèvent d'un droit universel, en refuser d'autres.»

Entretien avec Soheib Bencheikh, © Le Monde, 19 novembre 2001, propos recueillis par Henri Tincq (extraits)

## Législation française et abattage rituel

**La loi prévoit que, dans les abattoirs, les bêtes destinées à la consommation soient étourdies, par exemple par un choc électrique, avant d'être tuées. Mais, dans les rituels d'abattage juif et musulman, la bête est traditionnellement saignée, alors qu'elle est consciente. L'abattage rituel est cependant autorisé, afin de ne pas entraver la pratique religieuse. Un décret de 1997 régit les conditions de l'abattage rituel.**

**Article 8.** L'étourdissement des animaux est obligatoire avant l'abattage ou la mise à mort, à l'exception des cas suivants : a) Abattage rituel ; (...)

**Art. 11.** Il est interdit à toute personne de procéder ou de faire procéder à un abattage rituel en dehors d'un abattoir. La mise à disposition de locaux, terrains, installations, matériel ou équipement en vue de procéder à un abattage rituel en dehors d'un abattoir est interdite.

**Art. 12.** Avant l'abattage rituel, l'immobilisation par un procédé mécanique des animaux des espèces bovine, ovine et caprine est obligatoire. L'immobilisation doit être maintenue pendant la saignée.

**Art. 13.** Sous réserve des dispositions du troisième alinéa du présent article, l'abattage rituel ne peut être effectué que par des sacrificateurs habilités par les organismes religieux agréés, sur proposition du ministre de l'Intérieur, par le ministre chargé de l'agriculture. Les organismes agréés mentionnés à l'alinéa précédent doivent faire connaître au ministre chargé de l'agriculture le nom des personnes habilitées et de celles auxquelles l'habilitation a été retirée.

Si aucun organisme religieux n'a été agréé, le préfet du département dans lequel est situé l'abattoir utilisé pour l'abattage rituel peut accorder des autorisations individuelles sur demande motivée des intéressés. [...]

Décret n° 97-903
du 1er octobre 1997 relatif
à la protection des animaux
au moment de leur abattage
ou de leur mise à mort (extraits)
**www.legifrance.fr**

# Sites Internet

**L'islam**
France 5 et l'Institut du monde arabe proposent un site pour découvrir, à l'aide de vidéos et de jeux, l'islam et la civilisation arabo-musulmane.
**education.france5.fr/islam/**

**Le Coran**
Le site du ministère des Affaires islamiques d'Arabie saoudite propose sur son site une division thématique du Coran et des hadith.
**www.al-islam.com**

**Le monde arabe**
Le site de l'Institut du monde arabe présente l'histoire du monde arabe et des musulmans.
**www.imarabe.com**

**L'islam**
Histoire de l'islam, pratique, droit.
**www.portail-religion.com/FR/dossier/islam/**

**Le chiisme**
Pour découvrir le chiisme.
**www.cliosoft.fr/05_03/chiisme_index.htm**

**Le soufisme**
Une page sur le soufisme ou l'humanisme en islam.
**www.archipress.org/batin/soufisme.htm**

**Les musulmans en France**
**www.oumma.com**

## L'art islamique

Pour découvrir l'art et la culture
islamiques en Méditerranée.
**www.discoverislamicart.org/
exhibitions/ISL/**

## La laïcité en France

Un dossier proposé
par la Documentation française
sur la laïcité en France aujourd'hui.
**www.ladocumentationfrancaise.fr
/dossiers/laicite/index.shtml**

### INSTITUTIONS MUSULMANES

## Grande Mosquée de Paris

Le site de la Grande Mosquée
présente brièvement l'islam et le Coran
que l'on peut écouter en ligne, ainsi
que les activités de l'institution.
**mosquee-de-paris.org/**

## Union des organisations islamiques de France

Le site officiel de l'Union des
organisations islamiques de France
présente cette institution, ses objectifs,
ses activités. Le site propose des
brochures informatives sur la prière,
le ramadan, l'aumône, la notion de
Dieu en islam, ainsi qu'une traduction
du Coran et une sélection de hadith.
**www.uoif-online.com/**

## Organisation de la conférence islamique

Le site de l'Organisation de la
conférence islamique présente
cette institution, ses États-membres,
l'actualité de l'organisation.
**www.oic-oci.org/**

### INFORMATIONS GÉNÉRALES

## Agence France Presse

**www.afp.com/francais**

## Actualités sur Google

Pour rechercher dans tous les organes
de presse francophones.
**news.google.fr**

## Le dessous des cartes

Pour comprendre le monde :
textes courts et cartes claires.
**www.arte-tv.com/fr/histoire-
societe/le-dessous-des-
cartes/392.html**

## Clemi

Des fiches pédagogiques pour
décrypter les médias et une liste des
sites des principaux médias français.
**www.clemi.org**

## France 5

Site pour apprendre à décrypter
les médias et l'actualité.
**www.france5.fr/education/actu/**

## CNN et LCI

Les sites des chaînes de télévision
d'information en continu américaine
et française.
**www.cnn.com, www.lci.fr**

## Radio France

**www.radiofrance.fr**

## Courrier international

L'actualité mondiale à travers la presse
internationale.
**www.courrierint.com**

# Index

# Table des illustrations et crédits photographiques

**4-5** Musulmanes pakistanaises priant le premier jour de l'Aïd-el-Fitr à la mosquée Badshahi à Lahore, le 26 octobre 2006. © Arif Ali/Getty Images/AFP
**8** Tunisien préparant des pâtisseries dans une boutique de Tunis, 22 septembre 2007, durant le mois de ramadan. © Fethi Belaid/AFP
**10** Violentes manifestations contre les caricatures du prophète Mahomet devant le consulat du Danemark à Beyrouth, 5 février 2006. © Ramzi Haidar/AFP
**12** Le prophète Mahomet et l'ange Gabriel, gouache et papier, école turque du XVIe siècle, palais Topkapi, Istanbul, Turquie. © Bildarchiv Steffens/ The Bridgeman Art Library
**14** Une femme musulmane vêtue d'un hijab traditionnel fait des courses à Londres, 6 octobre 2006. © Bruno Vincent/Getty Images/AFP
**17** Femmes vendant de la bière de millet sur le marché Nombori, région de la tribu Dogon au Mali. © David Sutherland/Corbis
**18** Des musulmans se photographient le 29 octobre 2004 à Strasbourg devant le panneau du projet

de construction de la grande mosquée de Strasbourg à l'issue de la cérémonie de la pose de la première pierre. © Thomas Wirth/AFP
**20** L'imam Tarek Oubrou prêche à la mosquée de Bordeaux avant les prières du vendredi. © Philippe Lissac/ Godong/Corbis
**22** Un policier égyptien contrôle le premier tour du vote des élections parlementaires au Caire, le 15 novembre 2005. © Khaled Desouki/AFP
**24** Membres du Hamas masqués dans la ville de Gaza, Palestine, avril 2006. © Abid Katib/ Getty Images/AFP
**46** Écriture coranique et tuiles décorées, État du Penjab, Pakistan. © Photos12.com - World Religions Photo Library
**48-49** Pèlerins musulmans devant la Kaaba à La Mecque, Arabie saoudite. © Kazuyoshi Nomachi/Corbis
**50-51** La salle des prières de la Mezquita (mosquée- cathédrale), Cordoue, Espagne. © Wysocki Pawel/hemis.fr
**52-53** Un jeune musulman étudie dans la *madrasa* de l'Institut islamique de Motinagar en Inde, avril 2007. © Parthajit Datta/AFP

**Couverture**
h : haut, b : bas, d : droite, g : gauche, m : milieu

**1er plat**
Un jeune musulman étudie dans la *madrasa* de l'Institut islamique de Motinagar en Inde, avril 2007. © Parthajit Datta/AFP
**hg** La Mecque, Arabie saoudite. © Kazuyoshi Nomachi/Corbis
**hmg** Écriture coranique, Pakistan. © Photos12.com - World Religions Photo Library
**hm** Le prophète Mahomet et l'ange Gabriel, gouache et papier, école turque du XVIe siècle, palais Topkapi, Istanbul, Turquie. © Bildarchiv Steffens/ The Bridgeman Art Library
**hd** Marché au Mali. © David Sutherland/Corbis

**2e plat**
**hg** Tunis durant le mois de ramadan, septembre 2007. © Fethi Belaid/AFP
**hm** Membres du Hamas, Gaza, Palestine, avril 2006. © Abid Katib/Getty Images/AFP
**hmd** Mezquita, Cordoue, Espagne. © Wysocki Pawel/hemis.fr
**hd** Musulmanes pakistanaises priant à la mosquée Badshahi à Lahore, le 26 octobre 2006. © Arif Ali/Getty Images/AFP